Palgrave Macmillan Studies in Family and Intimate Life

Series Editors
Lynn Jamieson
University of Edinburgh
Edinburgh, UK

Jacqui Gabb
Faculty of Arts & Social Sciences
Open University
Milton Keynes, UK

Sara Eldén
Lund University
Lund, Sweden

Chiara Bertone
University of Eastern Piedmont
Alessandria, Italy

Vida Česnuitytė
Mykolas Romeris University
Vilnius, Lithuania

'The Palgrave Macmillan Studies in Family and Intimate Life series is impressive and contemporary in its themes and approaches'

– Professor Deborah Chambers, Newcastle University, UK, and author of *New Social Ties.*

The remit of the Palgrave Macmillan Studies in Family and Intimate Life series is to publish major texts, monographs and edited collections focusing broadly on the sociological exploration of intimate relationships and family life. The series encourages robust theoretical and methodologically diverse approaches. Publications cover a wide range of topics, spanning micro, meso and macro analyses, to investigate the ways that people live, love and care in diverse contexts. The series includes works by early career scholars and leading internationally acknowledged figures in the field while featuring influential and prize-winning research.

This series was originally edited by David H.J. Morgan and Graham Allan.

Kahryn Hughes • Anna Tarrant

Men, Families, and Poverty

Tracing the Intergenerational Trajectories of Place-Based Hardship

Kahryn Hughes
University of Leeds
Leeds, UK

Anna Tarrant
University of Lincoln
Lincoln, UK

ISSN 2731-6440   ISSN 2731-6459   (electronic)
Palgrave Macmillan Studies in Family and Intimate Life
ISBN 978-3-031-24921-1   ISBN 978-3-031-24922-8   (eBook)
https://doi.org/10.1007/978-3-031-24922-8

This Palgrave Macmillan imprint is published by the registered company Springer Nature Switzerland AG.
The registered company address is: Gewerbestrasse 11, 6330 Cham, Switzerland

Kahryn: I would like to dedicate this first full-length book to my parents, Allan and Elisabeth Hughes. Thank you for your precious and unique take on the world. This is all your fault. Love you x
Anna: For my Mama and Pops B, my lovely parents. I love you x

ACKNOWLEDGEMENTS

Enormous thanks to our Editor at Macmillan Palgrave, Linda Braus. This book was written through interesting times including a pregnancy and birth and, less pleasantly, COVID-19. Deadlines didn't just slip, they crashed. Our sincere gratitude to Linda for sticking with it and helping us get this book over the finishing line.

We owe a tremendous intellectual debt to the original research teams of the studies on whose data we draw, especially Professor Nick Emmel, University of Leeds, Professor Joanne Greenhalgh, University of Leeds, Professor Bren Neale, University of Leeds, and Professor Carmen Lau-Clayton, Leeds Trinity University. Generous with their ideas and support in the early stages of Anna's Leverhulme Fellowship, their comments and insights provoked questions that were integral to our early shared work. We would also like to thank Adam Sales, Dr Lou Hemmerman, Dr Esmee Hanna, Dr Laura Davies, and Dr Linzi Ladlow who were fieldworkers on the Accessing Socially Excluded, Midlife Grandparents and Following Young Fathers studies respectively. They too were integral to the formative development of these research projects, recruiting and researching with participants, developing new analyses and providing significant insights as findings developed. The work and intellectual contribution of you all in developing and delivering the studies discussed in this book, as well as the diverse and important range of outputs from these, has contributed to the formulation of so many of the arguments taken forward here.

Thank you too, to the anonymous reviewers of the book proposal, and first full draft of the manuscript. Your generous engagement and insightful reviews helped us craft a much clearer set of arguments than we would have done otherwise.

Finally, our most heartfelt thanks to the many and varied participants of the four studies we analyse. They have shown tremendous generosity, not only once but often repeatedly over many years, sharing some of the most important details of their lives during such difficult times. Foundational to their participation is a degree of trust: that their life stories will be treated respectfully and with care. We hope we have achieved that here.

CONTENTS

About the Authors

Kahryn Hughes is Associate Professor of Sociology at the University of Leeds. She is Director of the Timescapes Archive, Editor-in-Chief of *Sociological Research Online*, and Senior Fellow of the National Centre for Research Methods. She is internationally recognised for innovation in methods of Qualitative Secondary Analysis and lead editor of *Qualitative Secondary Analysis* with Sage. Her substantive interests include intergenerational poverty, and addiction.

Anna Tarrant is Professor of Sociology at the University of Lincoln and a UK Research & Innovation Future Leaders Fellow, leading a study called 'Following Young Fathers Further'. Her work examines men's family participation in low-income families. She is the author of *Fathering and Poverty* (2021) with Policy Press, co-editor of *Qualitative Secondary Analysis* with Sage, and *Men and Welfare* with Routledge.

ABBREVIATIONS

CAFCASS	Child and Family Court Advisory and Support Service
CPAG	Child Poverty Action Group
CSA	Child Support Agency
ESRC	Economic and Social Research Council
GBH	Grievous Bodily Harm
UC	Universal Credit

CHAPTER 1

Tracing Men's Longitudinal Trajectories in Low-income Families

INTRODUCTION: POVERTY AND PARTIAL ACCOUNTS OF MEN

Interviewer: Yeah…well, yeah that's relevant to my next question really is that when people start to get to your stage of life, they often have parents who are ageing, who rely on them, but neither of you have an older generation relying on you.

Bob: Well, well apart from our Anne [*Bob's older sister*]. An' 'er [*his wife, Dianne's*] father. I go down there cos, 'specially with the way 'er [*Dianne's*] heart's going now, an' her breathing when she's going up hills, her dad's is on opposite side of the estate. I mean my legs and my breathing it takes me all me time when I'm walkin' up that hill. You know what I mean? I mean I used to go down everyday, dinner Monday t'…Sunday, but that hill now I don't what it is (inaudible) seems how they're getting longer or steeper, you know what I mean? An' me legs by time I get in, in here it aches like hell, you know in back n' that? So, I go down about three, four times a week now. I mean he don't like it, because I think he expects me t' go down every day but he's got to realise that I've got a life n'all, n' so's Dianne, you know what I mean?…I mean I was

© The Author(s), under exclusive license to Springer Nature Switzerland AG 2023
K. Hughes, A. Tarrant, *Men, Families, and Poverty*, Palgrave Macmillan Studies in Family and Intimate Life,
https://doi.org/10.1007/978-3-031-24922-8_1

	supposed to go down yesterday but I 'ad all me bedrooms to do yesterday, an't I?
Dianne:	Yeah.
Interviewer:	So you do a lot of stuff around the house?
Bob:	Yeah, well we do it between us. I mean, I do the tidying up cos I like cleaning up, Dianne does the washing, n' the cooking, the shopping, or I'll help, you know what I mean, it's like shared. I mean Dianne's brought five bairns up so it's about time I did a bit. I'm up ten to six on a morning, half past five, ten to six. By' time she gets up, it's all tidied up, innit love?
Dianne:	Yeah. *Bob (mid-fifties) and Dianne (mid-fifties), Round One, Midlife Grandparents Study*

We rarely read or hear accounts like Bob's, or of older men living in low-income localities. This excerpt from a research interview with Bob introduces experiences that are often only partially foregrounded in scholarship on families in poverty, namely men's changing participation in and across families and low-income localities over time. Here, Bob and Dianne, a married couple living in a low-income estate in a city in Northern England, are discussing their responsibilities for older family members who live nearby. In this excerpt, Bob not only describes what it is he does and for whom, but indicates a shifting pattern of responsibilities towards different family members over the shared lifetimes of their family. We learn that Bob's deteriorating health is limiting his mobility, *'the hills are growing steeper'*, and he vividly expresses a changing experience of his neighbourhood as he ages. Notably, Bob is only in his mid-fifties but is experiencing the early onset of health problems. In an excerpt that ostensibly focuses on how his family participation is shaped by the geographical features of his locality, his account becomes a qualitative description of the acceleration of health inequalities for people in low-income localities. Bob's narrative links to broader evidence concerning the relationship between midlife morbidity and longitudinal processes of disadvantage and hardship in low-income areas, and Bob himself is not unaware of this. Across his interviews, he associates his ill health with the increasing precariousness of employment and economic decline in his locality over several decades, a view which is supported in broader sociological debate (McDowell, 2000; Cummins et al., 2007; Emmel & Hughes, 2010; Beatty et al., 2021). Locality-driven change and decline have consequences not only for his health but also for his intergenerational relationships and responsibilities.

Our treatment of this snippet from one of Bob's interviews illustrates the approach taken more generally throughout this book, whereby we interrogate the interconnectedness of poverty, family, and place, with explicit attention to the trajectories of men through and across low-income families. Working across four linked qualitative datasets from research with low-income families over a 20-year period, we aim to capture and explain the intergenerational and longitudinal dynamics of men's family participation in relation to their trajectories through hardship living in low-income localities. While an empirical focus on men in low-income families may seem narrow, we argue there is much to be gained from foregrounding accounts of, and by, men. In particular, this focus has supported greater theoretical sophistication in how we account for the dynamic and place-based character of poverty, its implications for families, and the experiences of the individuals that comprise them.

Throughout the book we pursue three central concerns that combined, establish a compelling case for advancing a new sociology of family poverty. The first is to identify and explore how men navigate experiences of multidimensional disadvantage and hardship over time in low-income families. We conceptualise these as the longitudinal dynamics of poverty. Our second, connected, concern is to trace men's trajectories through poverty across their lifecourse, considering the consequences of these for men's intergenerational family participation by examining what they do in and for their families through multiple generational identities (e.g. as father, son, brother, cousin, and so on). Third, and in relation to these trajectories, we interrogate how and why enduring poverty shapes opportunities and limits for family participation for men. Attention to these also means interrogating how the broader formal and informal policy involvements and dependencies *characteristic* of longitudinal poverty may both shape the everyday experiences of family members and family configurations—namely the dynamic relational networks people comprise—intergenerationally. While not our main focus, this approach additionally mobilises our feminist ethical agenda by affording greater insights into how enduring poverty shapes opportunities and limits for family participation for women.

The Longitudinal Dynamics of Poverty and Family

Situating our analyses within a literature that treats poverty as a dynamic, rather than static process, our work provides a timely and pertinent contribution to debates concerned with accelerating rates of 'deep poverty' (Edmiston et al., 2022) that now define the UK following successive socio-economic crises and policy and welfare changes and interventions over the 20-year period of our fieldwork and beyond (see also, Stewart, et al., 2021; Garthwaite et al., 2022; Tarrant et al., 2023). Associated with these changes, poverty[1] in the UK has increased over the last decade to the extent that one in four people are estimated to live in hardship. This deepening of poverty has been driven by an 'austerity agenda' that can be understood as a programme of continuing welfare cuts (Beatty et al., 2021). These have resulted in an uptick of poverty for those in work (Beatty & Fothergill, 2016), with the bottom two deciles of the income distribution becoming 10% worse off than pre-recession levels (Portes & Reed, 2018). The consequences of increasing poverty are most starkly expressed through data demonstrating a widening of inequality in life expectancy, where since 2010–2012 life expectancy has worsened in more deprived areas of England relative to wealthier areas, especially for women (Public Health England, 2018). Rather than the experience of a marginalised minority, roughly a quarter of the nation's population are now living in poverty (Joseph Rowntree Foundation, 2022), a trend that is expected to rise (CPAG, 2021). Poverty, and the consequences of such for people in relation to their health, their longevity, their education and employment opportunities, the welfare of their children, the very family arrangements comprising their everyday lives, can be considered as endemic to, and *characterising*, social relations in the UK. As Financial Times commentator Burn-Murdock (2022) noted: 'Britain (and the US) are poor societies with some very rich people'.

The dynamic and uneven patterning of poverty and changing wealth inequalities are best apprehended through the longitudinal capture and analysis of changing disadvantage and hardship (Bradbury et al., 2001; Aassve et al., 2007). Attention to the sequencing of periods in poverty for people across their lifecourse enables insight into how and through what

---

[1] We are using the language of poverty in relation to households. Low-income households in the UK are defined here, in relative terms, as households whose disposable income, after deducting housing costs, is at or below 60% of the average (median) income (Daly & Kelly, 2015, p. 15).

circumstances they may enter, or indeed exit hardship. Longitudinal analyses are also important in establishing how and why poverty may become enduring and thereby provide insight into the distinctive features and consequences of persistent poverty for people's everyday lives (Layte & Whelan, 2003; Whelan et al., 2003; Whelan & Maitre, 2006; Mendola et al., 2011; Bennett & Daly, 2014; Edmiston, 2021). Accordingly, within the social sciences, there has been a steady and widespread engagement interrogating poverty processes through qualitative longitudinal research engagement (Davidson et al., 2018; Emmel & Hughes, 2010; Millar, 2007; Morrow, 2013), namely through research orientated towards the fine-grained interrogation of lived experiences of continuity and social change (Neale, 2020; Millar, 2021). Evidence demonstrates how the uneven impacts of these social changes mean those with dependents experience greater poverty risk (Stewart et al., 2021), indicating family circumstances and arrangements are important domains through which to consider changing poverty dynamics. Qualitative longitudinal research enables insight into precisely *how* such dynamics may be variously experienced and understood, and the implications for these in affecting or producing different family arrangements (Leisering & Walker, 1998; Millar & Ridge, 2009; Ridge & Millar, 2008; Bastos et al., 2009; Shildrick et al., 2012; McKenzie, 2015; Daly & Kelly, 2015; Erhard, 2020; Millar, 2021) through broader socio-historical and economic processes (Edwards & Irwin, 2010). Qualitative longitudinal approaches are important in countering political rhetoric and social policy orientation that tend towards blaming those in poverty, particularly via welfare, health, and social care interventions designed to address a perceived inadequacy or failure in those struggling with hardship (see also Lister, 2005; Dorey, 2010; Dwyer & Wright, 2014; Jensen, 2014; Neale, 2016; McArthur & Reeves, 2019).

Theorising Longitudinal Family Poverty and QSA

While we situate our own research within and alongside this existing corpus, there are several distinctive features of our work worth noting. First, where qualitative longitudinal (QL) research is an established methodological approach in developing explanations of the longitudinal dynamics of poverty, the reuse of existing qualitative research data for this purpose is less developed. We contribute a novel methodological approach, namely using Qualitative Secondary Analysis of data from QL studies with families living in poverty, discussed in Chap. 3, to generate new findings. Second, our participant samples are also distinctive, in that they comprise a specific socio-economic population of people living in absolute or deep poverty (see Edminston, 2021). Third, the cumulative timeframes of the various research studies, themselves longitudinal, span a period of 20 years, which enables us to build extended longitudinal analyses of intergenerational experiences of poverty. For example, the majority of the participants have been born into families in low-income contexts, whose economic fortunes—linked with those of their locality—have experienced a persistent decline, over time and relative to the broader UK population. Consequently, both they, their parent generation, and their children's and grandchildren's generations live in circumstances of poverty and have done so for decades. Experiences of 'stubborn', intergenerational poverty, often problematically framed as a culture of poverty by policy makers and social commentators, are perhaps best articulated by Bob (above) who says, '*Recession, it's all the same to us son*' (Emmel & Hughes, 2010). Finally, two research studies on which we paid explicit attention to the fortunes of the broader city and region, encouraged participants to describe their localities in terms of the people that lived there, and their perceptions of others living there. In this way, we have been able to capture the changing character and experiences of living in these localities through the cumulative data of successive studies in these areas through participants' deliberations and theories of such changes. For example, across his interviews, Bob attributes his experiences of hardship to policies destabilising manufacturing in the UK, introduced by Margaret Thatcher some 15 years prior to his interview. These had a catastrophic impact on Bob's local labour market, which had been dominated by clothing manufacturing. The decline and retreat of these businesses resulted in the economic decline and collapse of the estates that had been built to supply them with labour (Emmel & Hughes, 2010), reflecting the spatial concentration of unemployment. In explaining the profound, persistent poverty of the area, he acknowledges that the broader succession of socio-economic and policy crises in the past three decades prior to his interview means that the 2008 global economic crash that occurred at the time of interview had had limited observable consequences for his neighbourhood.

In taking account of these broader socio-economic processes in the localities of the research participants, our analyses seek to understand the intergenerational sedimentation of stubborn poverty in these localities without recourse to an over individualisation and responsibilisation of the people living there. In particular, our empirical engagement disrupts the persistent emphasis on paid work as the route out of poverty (Daguerre & Etherington, 2014; Stewart et al., 2021) in political rhetoric blaming inhabitants for the dearth of resources in their localities.

To interrogate men's longitudinal participation in families through circumstances of poverty as we observe these across the datasets, we draw on contemporary literature that combines attention to poverty with attention to family in producing an account of both (Lister, 2005; MacDonald et al., 2005; Ridge, 2009; Daly & Kelly, 2015; Erhard, 2020). Our approach supports examination of the intersections of broad economic and social trends and personal biographies (Gillies & Edwards, 2005; Edwards & Gillies, 2012; Edwards & Irwin, 2010; Gray et al., 2016; Barg & Baker, 2021). Qualitative Secondary Analysis of these longitudinal datasets leant itself well to an investigation of individuals' lifecourse trajectories within and as part of larger family networks, as well as for tracking the trajectories of families, through tracing intergenerational relationships in and across place.

The complementarity of QL and lifecourse approaches supports theorising which contends that:

1. contemporary individual and family biographies and lifecourses are characteristically complex and diverse;
2. lives remain linked and interdependent over the lifecourse, regardless of socio-economic status; and,
3. social and policy contexts matter, especially when families are vulnerable or are at risk of vulnerability. (Tarrant, 2021, p. 57, drawing on Mills, 1959; Elder, 1994; Gray et al., 2016)

In using the language of lifecourse, we draw on Daly's (1996) assertion that a lifecourse view facilitates understanding of the broad diversity of people's lifespan, including aspects which vary over time and space, rather than presuming a life cycle associated with age hierarchies that link to fixed or discrete life stages. The lifecourse approach consequently allows us to refer to 'families' and 'generations' in their most general sense a point elaborated further in Chap. 3, where we develop our own distinctive theoretical lifecourse framework.

The family lifecourse framework we develop in this book is essential for understanding how normatively prescribed meanings of generation and family in low-income contexts, such as through health and social care interventions and engagements, impinge upon and even shape family arrangements, where those families are simultaneously experiencing persistent disruption and crises caused by hardship. For example, in previous work, we observed that where services focus on a particular individual, *in a particular generational position*, this not only serves to obscure the many other possible 'generational positions' they could take, but also the various 'generational positions' being taken by other members of the family (Emmel & Hughes, 2014; Tarrant & Hughes, 2019). The premise of this framework is that working from one specific generational position disguises broader family experiences in the round, and the diversity of men's (and women's) participation in and across families. However, to foreground family forms is also analytically limiting, because this ignores how families are produced through a complex of shifting multigenerational relationships where individuals themselves have multigenerational identities. This theoretical framework therefore addresses both *the experience of family life* that is, the complex situating of individuals within families, their transitions in and through different family contexts and generational positions and their interdependencies over time, and *the lives of families*, namely the shifting, complex of longitudinal family networks shaped through, and shaping, peoples' involvements, transitions, and trajectories.

Our language of family, then, refers to people sharing and living across households regardless of generational position; in partner relationships, whether married or not; and/or related biologically or through adoptive (kinship) relations and arrangements. Through this broad capture, we have endeavoured to illustrate the continued importance of 'family' to the people who participated in these studies, and a key dimension of the relationships they lived in, with and for others (see also Edwards et al., 2012). A lifecourse approach has salience both for understanding the longitudinal dynamics of poverty for families, and accommodates a flexible conceptualisation of family to examine the broadest spectrum of meanings, behaviours, practices, and responsibilities encompassing the *doing* of family (Morgan, 1996, 2011), 'kinship' (Comas d'Argemir & Soronellas, 2019), and relating, themes developed across the chapters.

In focusing on families, and family poverty, there is a risk of restricting analytic attention to the interiority of families, especially the definitions, qualities, organisation and socio-affective meanings of their family identities and relationships. To counterbalance this possibility, and to develop empirically driven explanations of men's family participation and their 'doing' of families through poverty, we focus on *families in place*. Here, we attend to people's descriptions and histories of their localities; how and where they go; where they do not go and why; the relationships they establish and sustain; their histories of ill health and how these coincide with changing employment; and their relationships and partnerships, as parents, associates, and friends, including the responsibilities they may have for others or others have for them. We specifically address men's histories and trajectories in, through, and out of families, work, friendships, and so on, and compare these across the four datasets on which we draw to identify commonalities, continuities, and differences for men sharing these localities.

In building a *placed-based* account of families, we bring these qualitative accounts into dialogue with quantitative evidence on place-based health inequalities in these localities. Such an approach is a necessity for an understanding of families in low-income localities because these families are so fundamentally shaped by place-based poverty. Place-based explanations of how and why poverty shapes families additionally enable us to avoid 'poverty of culture' accounts which assume families remain impoverished because of the moral failings of their members across generations (e.g. Dennis & Erdos, 1992). Finally, a place-based approach allows us to conceive of and interrogate the longitudinal intermeshing of the broader complex of relationships that both comprise and have consequences for poverty processes.

WHY AN EMPIRICAL FOCUS ON MEN IN LOW-INCOME FAMILIES?

It is a truism in academic writing that we often start with our conclusions, and this was certainly the case for this text. We grappled for some considerable time with how to manage the ordering of our discussion: should we start first with the data, or with the literature and existing debate? When we tried to develop a cogent account of men's family participation in the round that captured all complexity, we were confounded by a tendency in existing literature to deal with men in generational silos (as partners/husbands, as fathers, and as grandfathers). While there is a burgeoning scholarship using qualitative longitudinal approaches to the study of men's generational identities (e.g. Henwood et al., 2012; Neale et al., 2015), there is nevertheless a limited empirical focus on men in low-income families and localities more generally (Tarrant, 2021). This is underscored by a discursive context that accepts, and indeed promotes, the 'absence' of low-income men as fathers. Perhaps inadvertently, this tendency is buttressed by limited empirical engagement with the experiences of these men in and across low-income families (ibid., 2021). In a case of 'smoke and mirrors' elaborated in Chap. 2, we were able to see these men in existing data from different empirical vantages but lacked the analytic frameworks to explain the wider tenor and diversity of their family participation through longitudinal poverty. Men, in the ways we were seeking to apprehend them, were either absent from the data or described as absent. Our first task, therefore, became to understand these different absences.

Multiple and different forms of male *absence* and *presence* in low-income contexts are currently unaccounted for in scholarship on families and poverty. In seeking to develop a multilayered explanation of men's trajectories in and through a variety of institutional contexts and across the lifecourse and through poverty, that include family and locality, we have been repeatedly constrained by existing explanatory frameworks and analytical foci. In particular, in the field of family sociology, while men have a presence in sociological accounts of poverty and of family life (predominantly in fatherhood research, for example Dermott & Miller, 2015; Tarrant, 2021), detailed qualitative research about men's experiences of the dynamics of low-income family life from their own perspectives in the UK context is underdeveloped (although we note some important contributions from the US, including but not limited to Roy, 2014; Roy & Jones, 2014; Abdill, 2018; Stack, 1974; Mincy et al., 2015).

Limited empirical engagement with men sits in a context where the normative constitution and discursive framing of families in circumstances of poverty in scholarship, and through various forms of policy engagement, produce particular claims of *male* absence from these families (Tarrant, 2021). These manifest predominantly as 'absent' and 'feckless' fathers, often blamed by social commentators and policy makers for the criminal and antisocial behaviours of young and teenage boys in low-income families (see De Benedictis, 2012; Neale, 2016; Tarrant, 2021). This, sometimes unintentional, and multiple absenting of low-income men, positions and represents them as 'men in the margins' (Abdill, 2018; Elliott, 2020), with consequences for how and even whether men are included or 'seen' in empirical research on families in poverty contexts. Additionally, when we sought to understand the longitudinal dynamics of men's absences from families that *were* observable in our data (beyond 'absent fathers'), there was again limited engagement with these in sociology of family and poverty literature. Existing debate thus serves to formulate the questions we develop in our work, yet has limitations in answering these. Somewhat paradoxically, we therefore carve out our rationale and a research agenda for exploring men's accounts of low-income family life directly *from* the very debates that serve to obscure them, a discussion elaborated further in Chap. 2.

This book explicitly addresses the question of how and why men have come to be described, and treated, as either 'absent' or 'missing' from their families. Through the following chapters we demonstrate how various competing analytic foci may be foregrounded, perhaps at the expense of others, in ways which serve to render men 'missing' (O'laughlin, 2008; McKenzie, 2015).[2] For example, where men are considered in sociological research in relation to experiences of poverty, their working or breadwinning roles are predominantly foregrounded. Where men are considered in family relations and configurations, a primary and almost overwhelming emphasis is placed on their father roles (e.g. Nelson, 2004). A conflation of these interests—on men in poverty, on men as fathers in families—has not resulted in any consistent elaboration of the microdynamics of men's family experiences from multiple generational positions and across the lifecourse.

To address the existing evidentiary gaps identified, we pose three key questions that underpin our analyses:

1. How and why have men come to be described, and treated, as either 'absent' or 'missing' from their families?
2. How do enduring and intergenerational experiences of poverty shape and constrain men's intra- and intergenerational family participation across the lifecourse and in place? How might we observe these?
3. How and in which ways are the interactions of policy and place implicated in men's trajectories through poverty and what are the consequences for their family participation?

In answering these questions, we develop a new theoretical family lifecourse framework and address the following key aims:

---

[2] Notable examples of research where the language of 'absent' *fathers* in relation to low-income men has been challenged include Stack, 1974, Sullivan, 1989; and Hamer, 2001, in the US, and Bradshaw et al., 1999, and to some extent Busby and Weldon-Johns 2019, in the UK.

to develop a sociological account of the longitudinal dynamics of men's family participation through poverty, by 'recovering' men's experiences of family life from different generational positions;

to interrogate whether, how, and with whom men engage in the strategic resourcing of families to address basic needs through multiple disadvantages, and consider the consequences of this for men's visibility in changing family configurations (such as through repartnering) over time;

to consider the usefulness of the concept of 'participation' in understanding what men (and family members living in poverty) do in the sustaining and provision of families;

to consider how the distinctive challenges of enduring poverty may shape the intra- and intergenerational character of men's longitudinal family participation, through the 'ordering' of family relationships, arrangements, and experiences via formal health and social care policy and intervention;

to synthesise men's accounts with locality-based evidence identifying the effects of multiple disadvantages on their health, housing, and employment trajectories, and the consequences of these for the possibilities or limits of families for men.

Before addressing our questions and aims in the remainder of the book, we outline how our shared research history, the datasets, and our distinctive expertise and interests aligned and culminated in a shared exploration of how we might capture and understand men's accounts of family poverty in new and novel ways. We conclude with a brief overview of the book's contents and a case for the academic gains made through the work we present here.

OUR WORK: A BRIEF HISTORY

This book is a culmination of nine years of careful, collaborative work. Beginning in Prague, at a three-day workshop that interrogated questions of intergenerational exchange, we established a distinct set of shared interests in the longitudinal and intergenerational dynamics of low-income life, linked to empirical research around the role of grandparents in families. Following the workshop, Anna approached Kahryn to support her in applying for a Leverhulme Trust Early Career Fellowship, for the Men, Poverty and Care study, described with the other three research studies below. Men, Poverty and Care examined the care responsibilities of men in different generational positions in low-income families and contexts. This substantive focus was driven by Anna's own personal research history and interests in the gender transformative potential of men's positive involvements in family life, either as fathers or grandfathers (see Tarrant, 2014; 2015, 2016; Tarrant et al., 2017). It also built on research conducted as part of a postdoctoral position where her work evolved to explore the role of grandparents in low-income and child protection contexts (e.g. Tarrant et al., 2017), alongside critical consideration of male role model discourses and their influence in policy and practice (Tarrant et al., 2015). Anna was also raising new questions of gender that were underexplored in research about poverty and family life. At this time, questions of the absence of men's voices and accounts were beginning to take root. As project mentor, Kahryn identified an opportunity for methodological innovation, including exploration of the potential value of reusing existing Qualitative Longitudinal (QL) data for the purposes of methodological and substantive advancement.

In the early years, Kahryn mentored Anna drawing on her expertise of researching low-income life, but this relationship migrated to one of mutual exchange and endeavour. As the study progressed, what began as a mentoring relationship flourished into a collaborative one and via this work, we have taken forward numerous ideas, some of which were originally developed in previous research (Hughes & Emmel, 2012; Emmel & Hughes, 2010, 2014). These include:

- questions of time and temporality and how such questions make possible conceptual engagement concerning enduring social processes;
- intergenerational exchanges of resources in their broadest sense within and across families in low-income contexts, including how older family members try to intervene in the lives of younger family members and what might mitigate against those efforts;
- place-based socio-economic and policy change including declining industry, employment and welfare investment and provision, and their longitudinal implications for their family life;
- how families knit together in particular ways, across intergenerational relationships through shared and ongoing circumstances of hardship and disadvantage;
- the value of qualitative longitudinal (or QL) methodologies, the potentials of archived qualitative data, and the usefulness of existing data resources.

Kahryn's interest in these themes, analytic orientations, and empirical directions have been shaped through and supported by the longitudinal research designs and concerns of the two studies in which she was involved; Accessing Socially Excluded People (Emmel & Hughes, 2003–2005), and Intergenerational Exchange: Midlife Grandparents (Hughes & Emmel, 2007–2010). Her particular interests include temporally oriented analyses of the microdynamics of inequality with specific reference here to place-based poverty and gender. Relatedly, this research supports an interrogation of how intergenerational and lifecourse approaches mobilise more comprehensive research engagement with the broadest constituency of family members across the lifecourse.

It was through the early phase of research in Men, Poverty and Care, Anna observed a two-fold 'absenting' of men in research and policy (Tarrant, 2016). First, through the analytic foci of social sciences literature on low-income families, and second through methodological assumptions that 'men don't talk', apparently manifested as refusals to be interviewed, and especially about 'feminised' topics (arguments critiqued by Cunningham-Burley, 1984; Butera, 2006; Tarrant, 2014). While men's family participation was being captured through their roles as grandfathers and male kinship carers in some of our prior research (Hughes & Emmel, 2012; Tarrant et al., 2017) and elsewhere (e.g. Cunningham-Burley, 1984; Mann et al., 2016, on grandfathers), we were aware that the longitudinal and configurational 'in/out' character of men moving through, moving out, and creating new and different families and familial networks was overlooked. Indeed, Anna's analyses of the datasets on which we draw here, foregrounded the intellectual rationale for a new phase of fieldwork in the Men, Poverty and Care study, which sought systematically to develop an empirical case that captured the longitudinal dynamics of men's family participation in and through low-income contexts (see also Tarrant, 2021). The key questions underpinning this book were refined through our shared discussions as they were linked to these research endeavours. Accordingly, our history as researchers and collaborators is integral to the thesis of this book.

THE DATA AND METHODOLOGICAL INNOVATION: QUALITATIVE SECONDARY ANALYSIS

Reflecting the methodological engagement that characterises our work, somewhat uniquely this book is entirely based on qualitative secondary analysis (or QSA, Hughes & Tarrant, 2020) showcasing the possibilities of drawing on longitudinal datasets gathered over a 20-year period to address contemporary concerns and debates. Our arguments are based entirely on existing and, to an extent, completed research, and methodological advances we have made in QSA (e.g. Tarrant, 2016; Hughes & Tarrant, 2020, Tarrant & Hughes, 2020; Hughes et al., 2020, 2021; Tarrant & Hughes, 2021). Nevertheless, the ideas, approaches, and questions we outline above build out of shared programmes of work with a broader network of colleagues, wherein both the substantive and methodological strands of this work have their roots. Our evolving expertise and corpus of methodological work, for example, are directly informed by earlier methodological advances contributing to, or fostered through, the *Timescapes Changing Lives and Times* programme of research (Neale & Holland, 2007–2012), the largest qualitative longitudinal study funded in the UK at that time. The *Timescapes Programme* comprised three strands of work over five years. First, seven qualitative longitudinal empirical studies that cohered around the themes of the family, lifecourse, generation, intergenerationality and identities. All followed on from heritage studies. Second, a secondary analysis strand that explored the possibilities of working across these datasets, which linked to a third strand of work, the creation of what is now known as the Timescapes Archive.[3] Innovation in methods of qualitative secondary analysis were pioneered by many of our colleagues under *Timescapes* (e.g. Irwin & Winterton, 2011a, b; Irwin et al., 2012; Irwin, 2013; Bishop, 2007, 2009; Bornat & Bytheway, 2012; Edwards et al., 2020), developments taken forward in our own work.

A second connection to *Timescapes* involves the origins of the four datasets which we use for our analyses here, outlined in Box 1.1 below. In brief, and in chronological order, these are: (1) the Accessing Socially Excluded People study, (2) the Midlife Grandparents study, (3) the Following Young Fathers Study, and (4) the Men, Poverty and Care study. The first, Accessing Socially Excluded People, was the precursor and 'heritage study' for the Midlife Grandparents study, one of the seven original *Timescapes* studies. Following Young Fathers Built Out of Young Lives and Times, a different study under *Timescapes*, and the questions and some of the sample of Men, Poverty and Care connected to all three earlier studies via an early phase of QSA (Tarrant, 2017; Tarrant & Hughes, 2020). Collectively, these studies shared the unifying framework

---

[3] https://timescapes-archive.leeds.ac.uk/, *Link to website, also a short description.* The Timescapes Archive is a specialist resource of Qualitative Longitudinal (QL) Research data built for the purposes of data sharing and re-use.

underpinning *Timescapes*, especially thematic orientations to questions of personal lives and relationships across the lifecourse, and to questions of time (historical, biographical, generational).

As the descriptions in Box 1.1 demonstrate, these four studies are linked across other important dimensions including geographical and socio-economic (Tarrant & Hughes, 2019). All four studies share similar localities which, as we observe with Bob, support our interrogation of longitudinal experiences of place-based poverty for low-income families. Socio-economically, these localities are estimated to be among the 10% most deprived areas in the UK using the Index of Multiple Deprivation calculated by the Office for National Statistics (ONS) (Emmel & Hughes, 2010). These localities are described in more detail throughout the chapters. Establishing these connections was an essential part of earlier

---

Box 1.1   The Datasets: A Brief Introduction

1. The 'Developing methodological strategies to recruit and research socially excluded groups, examining health inequalities' (referred to as 'Accessing Socially Excluded') (Emmel et al. 2002–2005). This study was primarily methodological, aimed at identifying, developing, and refining methods of access to people living in marginalised localities and circumstances, who are typically experienced as harder to reach for research purposes, and interviewed about their longitudinal experiences of hardship (Emmel et al., 2007; Emmel & Hughes, 2009). Through this research we accessed 16 people in 12 households, and the life history interviews often included contributions from partners and children, who came and went during the interviews. The life history interviews explored their experiences of deprivation and living in their locality. As part of the access process, 34 in-depth interviews were gathered with a wide spectrum of formal and informal service providers across a range of public and third-sector service provision, and the interviews explored the nature of their work, their relationships with socially excluded individuals and groups, and their understanding of social exclusion policy. As well, during this study, a Drugs Outreach Service was also accessed, and interviews were conducted with those delivering the service. These people lived in

(*continued*)

(continued)

the locality of the service centre and had grown up there, and the iterative methodological strategy underpinning this study meant that researchers in tandem with the participants themselves developed methods, strategies, and ethical practices for ongoing recruitment. A core of ten people from this centre were interviewed repeatedly, including by telephone, singly in in-depth interview, group in-depth interviews, general group interviews, and individual life history interviews. Topics ranged from their own family and drug-using history to the history of the locality, and experiences of stigma for those who lived there when trying to engage, such as getting work, in the wider city. Preliminary findings in this study provided the empirical case for the central questions of the Midlife Grandparents study, which was the next to be conducted. Because both questions, participants and the locality were shared with the Midlife Grandparents study, below, the Accessing Socially Excluded study dataset became a 'heritage' dataset for the Midlife Grandparents study under the Timescapes programme of research, and was consequently archived as such in the Timescapes Archive.

2. The 'Mid-Life Grandparenting: charting trajectories of inter-generational poverty and health' (referred to as 'Midlife Grandparents') (Hughes & Emmel, 2007–2012).

   This study was part of the *Timescapes Programme* of research (see below) and was a Qualitative Longitudinal study that investigated how midlife (35–55 years) grandparents in low-income areas, in circumstances of poverty, describe what they do for their grandchildren to improve their grandchildren's life chances. The criteria for selection included being grandparents between the age of 35 and 55 years, and either they or their families were considered by service providers to be vulnerable, as understood within current policy and practice discourse (see for instance Department for Work and Pensions, 2011). The sample comprises 12 grandparents from eight families. Two of the grandparents (a couple and an estranged and now widowed grandmother) have been tracked since 2003. Using a visual family tree, 319 immediate family members were tracked over the four rounds of in-depth life history interviews, where participants discussed the changing

(continued)

(continued)
circumstances of their wider family members. This participatory exercise was conducted in the first of four rounds of in-depth life history interviews carried out at six-monthly intervals throughout the study. The family tree was a prompt used in later interviews in which relations with many of the family members identified through this method were discussed. The first interview also focused attention on life's ups and downs, what participants felt their lives were like, and by what routes they became the person they are today. We enquired about everyday routines, how life is now, and how it might change or stay the same. In the second interview a key focus was on the people and agencies who help and the experiences of being a grandparent. In the third interview our thematic focus was place, where grandparenting happens and cannot happen for example. The fourth and final interview paid particular attention to pressures within and beyond the family, crisis, and the life-course of their grandchildren. We asked participants to imagine their grandchildren's futures (Emmel & Hughes, 2014). Each of the interviews also included a catch-up on changes since we last met. This dataset has been archived in the Timescapes Archive, as part of the original Timescapes programme of research.
3. 'Following Young Fathers' (referred to as 'Young Fathers') (Neale & Lau-Clayton, 2012–2015).
This was also a qualitative longitudinal study that tracked a cohort of 31 young men through their fatherhood journeys over a period of approximately four years in the same city in the North of England as both the Accessing Socially Excluded and Midlife Grandparents study, sharing some specific localities. The study addressed the lived experiences and support needs of young fathers to explore how and why young men become fathers at an early age, how young fatherhood is constituted and practised in varied socio-economic and familial contexts, and what impact policy interventions or other kinds of support may have on these processes. Young Fathers had a baseline study, Young Lives and Times, conducted under Timescapes, which tracked a cohort of young people, including a subsidiary sample of young fathers, sharing participants and questions with this earlier research phase. Nineteen of the thirty-one fathers who participated in Young Fathers are identified as living in low-income families, ten are identified as highly disadvantaged,

(continued)

(continued)

and eight report some form of involvement with external agencies such as social services, Criminal Justice Agencies or CAFCASS (the Child and Family Court Advisory and Support Service, Neale et al., 2015). These subsets of young fathers were living in the same city and low-income localities in which the Midlife Grandparents Study had been conducted, and two participated in Anna's Men, Poverty and Care study. The data from FYF has also been archived in the Timescapes Archive.

4. Men, Poverty and Lifetimes of Care (referred to as Men, Poverty and Care) (Tarrant, 2014–2018, Leverhulme Trust Early Career Fellowship, ECF-2014–228).

This study involved a phase of secondary analysis of data from the Midlife Grandparents and Young Fathers studies, and shared questions and concerns with all three earlier studies, some of which are detailed below in our description of the antecedents of this book and published elsewhere (e.g. Tarrant, 2017; Tarrant & Hughes, 2019). The Men, Poverty and Care study examined men's care responsibilities, support needs, and patterns of care across the life-course in low-income families. As part of a new phase of fieldwork in similar localities, including with some of the participants from the Young Fathers study, a multigenerational sample of men were interviewed, including 7 young fathers (aged 25 and under), 12 midlife fathers (aged 26 and 45) with primary care responsibilities for their children, and 6 male kinship carers (aged 38–73).

epistemological work to determine the complementarity of the data (Tarrant & Hughes, 2020), and was the groundwork for refining our questions and developing our methodologies, particularly in Qualitative Secondary Analysis (QSA). More detailed discussion of the particularities of these connections can be found in Chap. 3.

We describe the methods of QSA used in this book as a form of 'data ethnography', involving synthesising across a range of data sources to support theoretical development of questions concerning the dynamic, processual character of specific dimensions of social life. While traditional ethnographies involve long immersion in place, producing research data through a range of different forms of engagement (e.g. photographs, interviews, observations) (Hughes, et al., 2016, (see also Whitaker &

Atkinson, 2022; Atkinson, 2017)), our immersive data ethnography involves the two-fold process of understanding the content and context of these data and their formative contexts. We elsewhere discuss these activities as the (re)contextualisation and (re)connection of data, to understand how these data reflect the context of their becoming, and make sense of how they can be used to speak beyond those contexts (Hughes et al., 2022).

Accordingly, we foreground the life history and in-depth interviews comprising the datasets and consider how these both capture and describe longitudinal histories of place as they unfold over time. We bring these into synthetic dialogue with outputs and associated materials from the originating studies, as well as analyses of workshop discussions with original research team members (Tarrant & Hughes, 2020; Hughes et al., 2021) to understand the sociological formulation of these studies and samples. Finally, we situate the two decades of research covered by the four datasets alongside other existing data, for example, trend data for these localities over this period of time, and other evidence in the form of broader scholarship. Our data ethnographies therefore involve methods of casing (Emmel & Hughes, 2009) from across multiple datasets for the careful building of narrative trajectories about people and place, that in turn are situated within and informed by additional forms of evidence and scholarship. In this respect, we have sought to establish multidirectional analyses to simultaneously trace the trajectories of individuals through families, the longitudinal trajectories of changing family configurations over time, and the interrelationship of these various trajectories through poverty and disadvantage.

Substantive and Theoretical Contributions

Contemporary social sciences literature on UK family life in low-income contexts is less expansive than research on more resourced families. Where it does report on low-income families, attention is often divided between focus on parenting and poverty (Dermott, 2012; LaPlaca & Corlyon, 2015; Rose & McAuley, 2019), the impacts of long-term poverty on children and families (Millar & Ridge, 2009; Millar, 2019; Treanor, 2020), or the dynamics of low-income families (Daly & Kelly, 2015; Gray et al., 2016; Cooper, 2021). Given that women are at most risk of living in poverty (e.g. Chant, 2006; Bastos et al., 2009; Bullock, 2013; Bennett & Daly, 2014; Dermott & Pantazis, 2014; Women's Budget Group, 2018; Joseph Rowntree Foundation, 2022) and most closely associated with family life as a substantive theme in research, qualitative accounts of their lived experiences of family life have logically informed much research about family poverty (Ridge, 2009). Furthermore, women and poverty and women and families are often conflated, where it has been argued that for women, poverty not only provokes an intensification of caring role responsibility (MacDonald, 1997; Fodor, 2006), but there has been a 'feminisation' of experiences of poverty (Pearce, 1978; McLanahan & Kelly, 2006). Here women are more likely to be trapped in serving and providing for families. This is evidenced through a rise in female-headed families from which men are 'absent' (Lichtenwalter, 2005; Hübgen, 2018; Women's Budget Group, 2018). Finally, in the history of policy development addressing families in low-income contexts, and in family policy more generally, there has been a conflation between the mother and child/ren dyad with the language of families (Neale & Patrick, 2016; Tarrant & Neale, forthcoming), thereby marginalising or sidelining men in policies addressing family needs. Sidelining men is problematic for a feminist orientation to understanding longitudinal social processes integral to the gendering of experiences and relationships of people in poverty.

In response to the limitations of binary conceptualisations of men as either absent or present/involved, Tarrant (2021) uses instead the language of family *participation* in her work on low-income fathers. The language of participation supports the capture of the complexities and dynamics of low-income family life in the round, as well as the broader dynamics of family change, encompassing diverse patterning, responsibilities, and interdependencies that change over time. Where men have been central to policy, there has been a persistent overfocus on specific and often single, generational identities—namely men as fathers (ibid.). Such overfocus has, first, confirmed men as 'absent' from particular family configurations and, second, contributed to the obscuring of men's diverse family participation from multiple generational positions, across the lifecourse, through policy interventions, legal systems, and their involvement in broader institutional processes (e.g. work, education, third sector, healthcare). A key advance we make here involves interrogating how family members, their relationships and arrangements, and changing family configurations over time, are shaped or 'ordered' through these processes and involvements.

Attention in men's accounts of their family participation in relation to how they managed and navigated poverty on behalf of themselves and others in their everyday lives, unexpectedly facilitated new theorisations of how what they did and with whom could be understood as entailing processes of 'civic' and interpersonal *ordering* of family life. Our use of the language of ordering more generally draws in part on Wacquant's work on how marginalised populations are seen as socially disruptive and rendered invisible through certain forms of civic ordering. This may, for example, involve incarceration in prisons for low-income men (Wacquant, 2004), as we explore in Chap. 7. Our theorisation here serves to address questions of how qualitative analyses of families in low-income circumstances may reveal the microdynamics of such social ordering processes, and thereby support explanation of how and why particular social trends emerge (e.g. higher rates of low-income men in prison).

We use the language of 'civic' ordering to conceptualise how collective forms of intervention may serve to produce particular configurations of family in low-income circumstances. We focus specifically on health and social care interventions, legal adjudications, and other formalised (such as employment) and institutional involvements. Chapter 6, for example, discusses how families in poverty are more likely to involve kinship care arrangements, shaped by explicit interventions from social services and legal systems. *Becoming* a grandparent kinship carer involves a 'rewriting' of people's normative expectations of grandparenting and patterns of family participation across the lifecourse, producing a *reordering* of family identities, relationships, and responsibilities. In both seeking for, and securing, the resources required to sustain grandparent kinship care, a new language of 'family' must be learned and deployed by the grandparent kinship carers, new institutional relationships must be forged and navigated, and new ways of 'doing' family must be learned and, furthermore, 'displayed' (Finch, 2007).

Interpersonal forms of ordering refers, in contrast, to how people in their family relationships may organise or reorder them, such as through violence, or indeed as Chap. 7 demonstrates, limit the possibilities of family for men where families cease to be safe spaces for them. Violence is endemic to the interview narratives across all four studies. As Ray (2018, p. 7) points out, 'since violence is intimately interconnected with the body, pain and vulnerability, its discussion evokes fundamental issues of security, embodiment, culture and power'. In building on Ray's work, we interrogate multimodal forms of violence that are both individual and collective, with a specific focus on how violence manifests in interpersonal forms of ordering of and through family and other relationships. Here, violent 'ordering' refers to behaviours involving the subjugation and dominance of others, such as is traditionally reported in relation to drug-using and crime (Houborg et al., 2022). However, violent 'ordering' may also involve the protections of some family members by others. This includes parents of themselves and their children, perhaps against other parents but also other relatives; men against other men in protection of their families, and as a means of boundarying localities, especially between groups of young men from different estates; disciplining and managing younger relatives, and boundarying families themselves, such as through excluding problematic or violent relatives, whether partners, parents, or children. Themes of violence are especially prevalent in Chap. 7, where we seek to develop a cogent account of men's lifecourse trajectories through poverty and consider their locality-based relationships. In our conclusion, we provide a fuller account of our theoretical treatment of violence and the challenges involved in accounting for its complexities in our data.

We also make distinct contributions to a small, but burgeoning academic literature that examines the lived experiences of marginalised men in urban contexts (Edin & Nelson 2013; Neale et al., 2015; Tarrant, 2021). Our analyses have sought to understand how longitudinal, perhaps intergenerational, experiences of enduring poverty characterise family lives, the possibilities for certain 'modes of relating' (Bucholc, 2013) within and across families, localities, and institutional networks, and thereby move away from situating social explanation solely *within* accounts of individual family members or specific families. In this endeavour, we present a uniquely sociological view of place-based interdependencies in low-income families, drawing on a diverse range of interdisciplinary scholarship to explore much longer-term family trajectories and longitudinal experiences of poverty which 'recover' and foreground accounts of men. We provide detailed insights into the lived experience of family poverty both for men and women via a range of familial identities and family configurations and do so through critical attention to the formal, institutional networks and arrangements in which these occur.

OVERVIEW OF THE BOOK

While this first chapter introduces the history and rationale for our work, Chap. 2 discusses our engagement with existing literature and how men might, often inadvertently, be rendered 'missing' through existing research in its focus, namely the discursive and theoretical framing of men in low-income families. Chapter 3, details our methodological developments and approaches, specifically in methods of QSA, and the development and implementation of our theoretical family lifecourse framework.

The empirical Chaps. 4, 5, 6, and 7, introduce cases of participants drawn from across the four linked studies to support and illustrate our analyses of the broader datasets. Chapter 4 explores how QSA enables us to observe and recover men's longitudinal engagement, participation, and otherwise in families through women's accounts in research on low-income families. We develop four longitudinal cases of women drawn from across the datasets, exploring representations of men (e.g. as villains and saviours), and accounts of how and when men are considered 'absent'. Through these cases we take a multigenerational approach to identify how men work to sustain families longitudinally and 'do kinship' in a diverse set of familial positions.

Chapter 5 develops two longitudinal cases of men drawn from across the datasets, foregrounding older men's accounts of their experiences and perceptions of low-income family life. Using our theoretical family lifecourse framework, we interrogate how and when men may be described as 'absent' from families and offer a counter perspective in which we recover their family participation in different generational roles and positions across the lifecourse. In dialogue with these two cases, we demonstrate the need to shift from the language of bread-winning to provisioning, to capture more fully the complex resource terrains men in low-income families navigate, through changing family configurations. We can also observe what formal and informal services landscapes these men are navigating, their support needs and struggles, and the choices that they must make. Significant dimensions of these relationships include support and help, such as with young children, service demands and regulations, especially those around parental obligations and responsibilities towards children, sanctions including the withdrawal of resources or access to children, and prohibition including the refusal for some relatives to look after children in preference to others, that emerge as ongoing entanglements and involvements that, longitudinally, can be seen to shape family organisations and people's very modes of relating to each other *as* family. Critically, although these interventions often focus on one family member or set of relationships, formal health and social care interventions usually have intergenerational implications and consequences, and in this respect constitute forms of 'civic ordering'. Here, we also begin to establish a picture of the sorts of distinctive relationships that men have with other men in the locality, and the implications of the localities for these relationships, a theme we further develop across the chapters.

Chapter 6 provides an overview of definitions of kinship care and kinship care arrangements, reviewing existing academic literatures that evidence the relationship between low-income family life and interventions into parenting both by the state and other family members (Farmer & Moyers, 2008; Hunt et al., 2008; Tarrant et al., 2017; Smethers, 2015; Hunt, 2018). Few studies have adopted a gendered lens or explored kinship care from the perspectives of men (although see Sullivan, 1989; Tarrant, 2021) and we use two longitudinal cases of men to address these lacunae. The motivations, gendered meanings, lived experiences, and relational dynamics of the lives of male kinship carers are examined here, alongside a broader consideration of the economic hardships that kinship care may produce. In Chap. 6, we demonstrate how our theoretical family lifecourse framework provides for an investigation into long-term formal kinship care arrangements of the two men we examine. We demonstrate its utility for recovering an account of the diversity of men's care responsibilities in low-income families. These men's experiences again demonstrate the importance and centrality of long-term relationships with formal and informal health and social care service providers, not only to sustain and resource the everyday lives of low-income families (see also Emmel et al., 2007; Neale & Lau Clayton, Neale & Lau Clayton, 2014) but also to create new opportunities to *be* families through gaining formalised recognition of certain forms of 'relating' and kinship (see also Tarrant & Hughes, 2019).

In Chap. 7, we discuss the distinctive challenges for men's family participation in low-income families and localities and consider the limitations of family for men. We address how longitudinal and intergenerational hardship shapes men's lifecourse trajectories in distinctive ways, such as through insecure labour market conditions, and ill health as related to poverty. Here, we also consider how both helpful (Parton, 2012) and punitive health and social care involvements and interventions in relation to men's family lives may be. We also consider the extent to which these reorder their family participation, and their ripple effect across the broader, intergenerational complex of family relationships.

In this chapter we consider how violence may be considered as part of the ongoing *interpersonal* ordering of relationships within these localities. While we do not elaborate on this in great depth, it is precisely this interpersonal ordering, sometimes manifesting as violence (Houborg et al., 2022), that is treated as characterising these localities by formal services including policing, such that the residents become treated as a form of threat to the wider localities. We revisit our attention to experiences of violence in these localities and families through the data, for and by these men, and consider the value of understanding how these experiences may articulate the many violences of poverty (Harding, 2009; Hearn, 2004). Here, violence reemerges *as threat* (Stanko, 2001), but so do people's experiences of hardship as symbolic disorder. In this way those that live in these localities become infused with multiple forms of stigma that constrain their ability to seek work elsewhere, or are treated with suspicion and hostility by the wider city (Hughes, 2007). Moreover, these residents become subject to certain forms of disciplinary regulation, such as through additional police surveillance and suspicion, in response to such perceived threat (see also Arendt, 1970). Violence intrinsic to collective modes of 'civic ordering' by surveillance and regulatory agencies, such as the police, thus produces distinctive experiences of marginalisation and exclusion for people in these localities. In effect, by interrogating collective forms of violence we become better able to situate and understand interpersonal forms of violence as contextualised experiences of poverty. Finally, we reflect on how our theoretical family lifecourse framework enables analytic capture of men's longitudinal involvement in, and exclusion from, specific family configurations and forms of family participation in low-income localities, and discuss how our analyses have addressed the key aims set out above.

Chapter 8 concludes the book by considering how, combined, these chapters provide a cogent account of the dynamics of men's family participation through circumstances of poverty, built on a novel longitudinal data ethnography. Our work contributes to a growing tranche of research unpicking the multiple intersections of family, governmental, policy, health and social care, and judicial services. We discuss how these may be understood as integral to the shaping and ongoing formation of families and—to some degree—the 'life-worlds' of poverty in these localities (Erhard, 2020). We therefore contribute to existing sociological evidence on families and poverty, with explicit focus on men, and evidence for professionals and practitioners, through detailed insights into how low-income families experience and navigate broader socio-economic, social policy, and welfare terrains. By detailing the impact these encounters and interventions have on the everyday lives of these families in these localities, we provide insights into how they shape peoples' longitudinal experiences, arrangements, and understandings of family which may be of use for professionals working with people in such circumstances of hardship. On the basis of our analyses and conclusions, we make a case for a new sociology of family poverty.

Through a range of empirical, theoretical, methodological, and substantive approaches, the remainder of this book involves the empirical 'telling' of the longitudinal stories of families through poverty and place.

References

Aassve, A., Davia, M., Iacovou, M., & Mazzuco, S. (2007). Does Leaving Home Make You Poor?: Evidence from 13 European Countries. *European Journal of Population, 23*, 315–338.

Abdill, A. (2018). *Fathering from the Margins: An Intimate Examination of Black Fatherhood*. Columbia University Press.

Arendt, H. (1970). *On Violence*. Allen Lane.

Atkinson, P. (2017). *Thinking Ethnographically*. Sage.

Barg, K., & Baker, W. (2021). Better Than Average? Parental Competence Beliefs and Socioeconomic Background, *Families, Relationships and Societies* (published online ahead of print 2021). Retrieved July 3, 2022, from https://bristoluniversitypressdigital.com/view/journals/frs/aop/article-10.1332-204674321X163169379497373/article-10.1332-204674321X16316937949373.xml

Bastos, A., Casaca, S. F., Nunes, F., & Pereirinha, J. (2009). Women and Poverty: A Gender-Sensitive Approach. *The Journal of Socio-Economics, 38*(5), 764–778.

Beatty, C., Bennett, C., & Hawkins, A. (2021). Managing Precarity: Food Bank Use by Low-Income Women Workers in a Changing Welfare Regime. *Social Policy Administration, 55*, 981–1000.

Beatty, C., & Fothergill, S (2016). *The Uneven Impact of Welfare Reform: The Financial Losses to Places and People*. Project Report. Sheffield, Sheffield Hallam University. http://shura.shu.ac.uk/15883/

Bennett, F., & Daly, M. (2014). *Poverty Through a Gender Lens: Evidence and Policy Review on Gender and Poverty*. Joseph Rowntree Foundation Report.

Bishop, L. (2007). A Reflexive Account of Reusing Qualitative Data: Beyond Primary/Secondary Dualism. *Sociological Research Online, 12*(2). http://www.socresonline.org.uk/12/3/2.html

Bishop, L. (2009). Ethical Sharing and Reuse of Qualitative Data. *Australian Journal of Social Issues, 44*(3), 255–272.

Bornat, J., & Bytheway, B. (2012). Working with Different Temporalities: Archived Life History Interviews and Diaries. *International Journal of Social Research Methodology, 15*(4), 291–299.

Bradbury, B., Jenkins, S., & Micklewright, J. (2001). *The Dynamics of Child Poverty in Industrialised Countries*. Cambridge University Press.

Bradshaw, J., Stimson, C., Skinner, C., & Williams, J. (1999). *Absent Fathers?* Routledge.

Bucholc, M. (2013). Outside the Moral Circle: Polish Political Refugees in Norway: Between the Established and the Outsiders. *Everyday Practices and Long Term Processes: Overcoming Dichotomies with the Work of Norbert Elias, 2*(3).

Bullock, H. (2013). *Women and Poverty: Psychology, Public Policy, and Social Justice*. Wiley Blackwell.

Burn-Murdock, J. (2022). *Britain and the US Are Poor Societies with Some Very Rich People*, The Financial Times. Retrieved October 18, 2022, from https://www.ft.com/content/ef265420-45e8-497b-b308-c951baa68945

Busby, N., & Weldon-Johns, M. (2019). Fathers as Carers in UK Law and Policy: Dominant Ideologies and Lived Experience. *Journal of Social Welfare and Family Law, 41*(3), 280–301.

Butera, K. (2006). Manhunt: The Challenge of Enticing Men to Participate in a Study on Friendship. *Qualitative Inquiry, 12*(6), 1262–1282.

Chant, S. (2006). Re-thinking the "Feminization of Poverty" in Relation to Aggregate Gender Indices. *Journal of Human Development, 7*(2), 201–220.

Comas-d'Argemir, D., & Soronellas, M. (2019). Men as Carers in Long-Term Caring: Doing Gender and Doing Kinship. *Journal of Family Issues, 40*(3), 315–339.

Cooper, K. (2021). Are Poor Parents *Poor* Parents? The Relationship between Poverty and Parenting among Mothers in the UK. *Sociology, 55*(2), 349–383.

CPAG (2021). *200,000 More Children Pushed into Poverty the Year Before the Pandemic - Dismal Data Warning.* https://cpag.org.uk/news-blogs/news-listings/200000-more-children-pushed-poverty-year-pandemic-dismal-data-warning

Cummins, S., Curtis, S. V., Diez-Roux, A., & Macintyre, S. (2007). Understanding and Representing 'Place' in Health Research: A Relational Approach. *Social Science & Medicine, 65*(9), 1825–1838.

Cunningham-Burley, S. (1984). 'We Don't Talk About it…': Issues of Gender and Method in the Portrayal of Grandfatherhood. *Sociology, 18*(3), 325–338.

Daguerre, A., & Etherington, D. (2014). *Workfare in 21st Century Britain: The Erosion of Rights to Social Assistance.* Middlesex University.

Daly, K. J. (1996). Spending Time with the Kids: Meanings of Family Time for Fathers. *Family Relations, 45*(4), 466–476.

Daly, M., & Kelly, G. (2015). *Families and Poverty: Everyday Life on a Low-Income.* Policy Press.

Davidson, E., Edwards, R., Jamieson, J., & Weller, S. (2018). Big Data, Qualitative Style: A Breadth-and-Depth Method for Working with Large Amounts of Secondary Qualitative Data. *Quality & Quantity, 53*, 363–376.

De Benedictis, S. (2012). Feral Parents: Austerity Parenting Under Neoliberalism. *Studies in the Maternal, 4*(2).

Dennis, N., & Erdos, G. (1992) *Families without Fatherhood.* Wiltshire: The Cromwell Press.

Dermott, E. (2012). 'Poverty' versus 'Parenting': An Emergent Dichotomy. *Studies in the Maternal, 4*(2), www.mamsie.bbk.ac.uk.

Dermott, E., & Miller, T. (2015). More Than the Sum of its Parts? Contemporary Fatherhood Policy, Practice and Discourse. *Families, Relationships and Societies, 4*(2), 183–195.

Dermott, E., & Pantazis, C. (2014). Gender and Poverty in Britain: Changes and Continuities Between 1999 and 2012. *Journal of Poverty and Social Justice, 22*(3), 253–269.

Dorey, P. (2010). A Poverty of Imagination: Blaming the Poor for Inequality. *The Political Quarterly, 81*(3), 333–343.

Dwyer, P., & Wright, S. (2014). Universal Credit, Ubiquitous Conditionality and its Implications for Social Citizenship. *Journal of Poverty and Social Justice, 22*(1), 27–35.

Edin, K., & Nelson, T. J. (2013). *Doing the Best I Can: Fatherhood in the Inner City.* University of California Press.

Edminston, D. (2021). Plumbing the Depths: The Changing (Socio-Demographic) Profile of UK Poverty. *Journal of Social Policy* [online first].

Edmiston, D., Begum, S., & Kataria, M. (2022). *Falling Faster Amidst a Cost-of-living Crisis: Poverty, Inequality and Ethnicity in the UK.* London: Runnymede Trust.

Edwards, R., & Gillies, V. (2012). Farewell to Family? Notes on an Argument for Retaining the Concept. *Families, Relationships and Societies, 1*(1), 63–69.

Edwards, R., & Irwin, S. (2010). Lived Experience Through Economic Downturn in Britain – Perspectives Across Time and Across the Life-course. *Twenty-First Century Society, 5*(2), 119–124.

Edwards, R., McCarthy, J., & Gillies, V. (2012). The Politics of Concepts: Family and Its (Putative) Replacements. *The British Journal of Sociology, 63*(4), 730–746.

Edwards, R., Davidson, E., Jamieson, L., & Weller, S. (2020). Theory and the Breadth-and-Depth Method of Analysing Large Amounts of Qualitative Data. *Quality and Quantity, 55*, 1275–1280.

Elder, G. (1994). Time, Human Agency, and Social Change: Perspectives on the Life Course. *Social Psychology Quarterly, 57*(1), 4–15.

Elliott, K. (2020). Bringing in Margin and Centre: 'Open' and 'Closed' as Concepts for Considering Men and Masculinities. *Gender, Place & Culture, 27*(12), 1723–1744. https://doi.org/10.1080/0966369X.2020.1715348

Emmel, N., & Hughes, K. (2010). 'Recession, It's All the Same to Us Son': The Longitudinal Experience (1999-2010) of Deprivation. *Twenty-First Century Society, 5*(2), 171–181.

Emmel, N., & Hughes, K. (2014). Vulnerability, Intergenerational Exchange and the Conscience of Generations. In R. Edwards & J. Holland (Eds.), *Understanding Families Over Time: Research and Policy*. Palgrave Macmillan.

Emmel, N., Hughes, K., Greenhalgh, J., & Sales, A. (2007). Accessing Socially Excluded People—Trust and the Gatekeeper in the Researcher-Participant Relationship. *Sociological Research Online, 12*(2), 43–55.

Emmel, N., & Hughes, K. (2009). Small-N Access Cases to Refine Theories of Social Exclusion and Access to Socially Excluded Individuals and Groups. In D. Byrne & C. Ragin (Eds.), *The SAGE Handbook of Case-Centered Methods*. SAGE.

Erhard, F. (2020). The Struggle to Provide: How Poverty Is Experienced in the Context of Family Care. *Journal of Poverty and Social Justice, 28*(1), 119–134.

Farmer, E., & Moyers, S. (2008). *Sociology*, 14 (1): 65–81.

Finch, J. (2007). Displaying Families. *Sociology, 14*(1), 65–81.

Fodor, E. (2006). A Different Type of Gender Gap: How Women and Men Experience Poverty. *East European Politics and Societies, 20*(1), 14–39.

Garthwaite, K., Patrick, R., Power, M., Tarrant, A., & Warnock, R. (2022). *Covid Collaborations: Researching Poverty and Low-Income Family Life During the Pandemic*. Policy Press.

Gillies, V., & Edwards, R. (2005). Secondary Analysis in Exploring Family and Social Change: Addressing the Issue of Context. *FORUM: Qualitative Social Research, 6*(1). https://doi.org/10.17169/fqs-6.1.500

Gray, J., Geraghty, R., & Ralph, D. (2016). *Family Rhythms: The Changing Textures of Family Life in Ireland*. Manchester University Press.

Hamer, J. (2001). *What it Means to Be Daddy: Fatherhood for Black Men Living Away from Their Children.* Columbia University Press.

Harding, D. J. (2009). Violence, Older Peers, and the Socialization of Adolescent Boys in Disadvantaged Neighborhoods. *American Sociological Review, 1, 74, 3*, 445–464. https://doi.org/10.1177/000312240907400306. PMID: 20161 350; PMCID: PMC2776742.

Hearn, J. (2004). From Hegemonic Masculinity to the Hegemony of Men. *Feminist Theory, 5*(1), 49–72.

Henwood, et al. (2012). 'Why aren't you at work?' Negotiating Economic Models of Fathering Identity. *Fathering, 10*(3), 274–290.

Houborg, E., Kronbæk, M., Kappel, N., Relsted Fahnøe, K., Mørch Pedersen S., & Schepelern Johansen, K. (2022). Marginaliserede stofbrugeres hverdagsliv i København – stofmiljøer og velfærdstilbud. https://www.researchgate.net/publication/362932106_Marginaliserede_stofbrugeres_hverdagsliv_i_Kobenhavn_-stofmiljoer_og_velfaerdstilbud

Hübgen, S. (2018). Only a Husband Away from Poverty'? Lone Mothers' Poverty Risks in a European Comparison. In L. Bernardi & D. Mortelmans (Eds.), *Lone Parenthood in the Life Course.* Springer Link.

Hughes, K. (2007). Migrating Identities: The Relational Constitution of Drug Use and Addiction. *Sociology of Health & Illness, 29*, 673–691. https://doi.org/10.1111/j.1467-9566.2007.01018.x

Hughes, K., & Emmel, N. (2012). *Analysing Time: Times and Timing in the Lives of Low-Income Grandparents,* Timescapes Methods Guides Series 2012 Guide No. 9. file:///Users/anna/Downloads/analysingtimeandtimingshughesandemmel.pdf

Hughes, K., & Tarrant, A. (2020). *Qualitative Secondary Analysis.* London: Sage.

Hughes, K., Goodwin, J., & Hughes, J. (2016). Documenti e reperti umani come figurazioni. *Cambio. Rivista Sulle Trasformazioni Sociali, 6*(11), 123–138. https://doi.org/10.13128/cambio-18788

Hughes, K., Hughes, J., & Tarrant, A. (2020). Re-approaching Interview Data Through Qualitative Secondary Analysis: Interviews with Internet Gamblers. *International Journal of Social Research Methodology, 23*(5), 565–579.

Hughes, K., Hughes, J., & Tarrant, A. (2022). Working at a Remove: Continuous, Collective, and Configurative Approaches to Qualitative Secondary Analysis. *Quality & Quantity, 56*, 375–394.

Hunt, J. (2018). Grandparents as Substitute Parents in the UK. *Contemporary Social Science, 13*(2), 175–186.

Hunt, J., Waterhouse, S., & Lutman, E. (2008). *Keeping Them in the Family: Outcomes for Abused and Neglected Children Placed with Family or Friends Carers Through Care Proceedings.* BAAF.

Irwin, S. (2013). Qualitative Secondary Data Analysis: Ethics, Epistemology and Context. *Progress in Development Studies, 13*(4), 295–306.

Irwin, S., & Winterton, M. (2011a). *Debates in Qualitative Secondary Analysis: Critical Reflections*, Timescapes Working Paper No. 4. http://www.timescapes.leeds.ac.uk/assets/files/WP4-March-2011.pdf

Irwin, S., & Winterton, M. (2011b). *Qualitative Secondary Analysis: A Guide to Practice*, Timescapes Working Paper, Guide 19. chrome-extension://efaidnbmnnnibpcajpcglclefindmkaj/https://timescapes-archive.leeds.ac.uk/wp-content/uploads/sites/47/2020/07/timescapes-irwin-secondary-analysis.pdf

Irwin, S., Bornat, J., & Winterton, M. (2012). Timescapes Secondary Analysis: Comparison, Context and Working Across Data Sets. *Qualitative Research, 12*(1), 66–80.

Jensen, T. (2014). Welfare Commonsense, Poverty Porn and Doxosophy. *Sociological Research Online, 19*(3), 277–283.

Joseph Rowntree Foundation. (2022). Poverty Report. https://www.jrf.org.uk/report/uk-poverty-2022

LaPlaca, V., & Corlyon, J. (2015). Unpacking the Relationship between Parenting and Poverty: Theory, Evidence and Policy. *Social Policy and Society, 15*(1), 11–28.

Layte, R., & Whelan, C. T. (2003). Moving in and out of Poverty. *European Society, 5*, 167–191.

Leisering, L., & Walker, R. (1998). *The Dynamics of Modern Society: Poverty, Policy and Welfare*. Policy Press.

Lichtenwalter, S. (2005). Gender Poverty Disparity in US Cities: Evidence Exonerating Female-Headed Families. *Journal of Sociology and Social Welfare, 32*(2), 75–96.

Lister, R. (2005). *Poverty*. Polity Press.

MacDonald, R. (1997). *Youth, the 'Underclass' and Social Exclusion*. Routledge.

MacDonald, R., Shildrick, T., Webster, C., & Simpson, D. (2005). Growing Up in Poor Neighbourhoods. *Sociology, 39*(5), 873–891.

Mann, R., Tarrant, A., & Leeson, G. (2016). Grandfatherhood: Shifting Masculinities in Later Life. *Sociology, 50*(3), 594–610.

McArthur, D., & Reeves, A. (2019). The Rhetoric of Recessions: How British Newspapers Talk about the Poor When Unemployment Rises, 1896–2000. *Sociology, 53*(6), 1005–1025.

McDowell, L. (2000). The Trouble with Men? Young People, Gender Transformations and the Crisis of Masculinity. *International Journal of Urban and Regional Research, 24*(1), 201–209.

McKenzie, L. (2015). *Getting By: Estates, Class and Culture in Austerity Britain*. Policy Press.

McLanahan, S. S., & Kelly, E. L. (2006). The Feminization of Poverty. In *Handbook of the Sociology of Gender. Handbooks of Sociology and Social Research*. Springer. 10.1007/0-387-36218-5_7

Mendola, D., Busetta, A., & Milito, A. (2011). Combining the Intensity and Sequencing of the Poverty Experience: A Class of Longitudinal Poverty Indices. *Statistics in Society, 174*(4), 953–973.

Millar, J. (2007). The Dynamics of Poverty and Employment: The Contribution of Qualitative Longitudinal Research to Understanding Transitions, Adaptations and Trajectories. *Social Policy and Society, 6*(4), 533–544.

Millar, J. (2019). Self-Responsibility and Activation for Lone Mothers in the United Kingdom. *American Behavioural Science, 63*(1), 85–99.

Millar, J. (2021). Families, Work and Care: Qualitative Longitudinal Research and Policy Engagement. *Social Policy and Society, 20*(4), 629–634. https://doi.org/10.1017/S1474746420000482

Millar, J., & Ridge, T. (2009). Relationships of Care: Working Lone Mothers, Their Children and Employment Sustainability. *Journal of Social Policy, 38*(1), 103–121.

Mills, C. W. (1959). *The Sociological Imagination*. Oxford: Oxford University Press.

Mincy, R. B., Jethwani, M., & Klempin, S. (2015). *Failing Our Fathers: Confronting the Crisis of Economically Vulnerable Fathers*. Oxford University Press.

Morgan, D. (1996). *Family Connections: An Introduction to Family Studies*. Cambridge: Polity.

Morgan, D. (2011). Locating Family Practices. *Sociological Research Online, 16*(4), 14.

Morrow, V. (2013). Troubling Transitions? Young People's Experiences of Growing Up in Poverty in Rural Andhra Pradesh, India. *Journal of Youth Studies, 16*(1), 86–100. https://doi.org/10.1080/13676261.2012.704986

Neale, B. (2016). Introduction: Young Fatherhood: Lived Experiences and Policy Challenges. *Social Policy and Society, 15*(1), 75–83.

Neale, B. (2020). *The Craft of Qualitative Longitudinal Research*. Sage.

Neale, B., & Lau Clayton, C. (2014). Young Parenthood and Cross Generational Relationships: The Perspectives of Young Fathers. In J. Holland & R. Edwards (Eds.), *Understanding Families Over Time*. Palgrave Macmillan.

Neale, B., & Patrick, R. (2016) Engaged Young Fathers? Gender Parenthood and the Dynamics of Relationships, *FYF Working Paper Series no. 1*. https://followingfathers.leeds.ac.uk/wp-content/uploads/sites/79/2015/10/FYF-Working-Paper-Engaged-young-fathers.pdf

Neale, B., Lau Clayton, C., Davies, L., & Ladlow, L. (2015) Researching the Lives of Young Fathers: The Following Young Fathers Study and Dataset, Briefing Paper no. 8. https://followingfathers.leeds.ac.uk/wp-content/uploads/sites/79/2015/10/Researching-the-Lives-of-Young-Fathers-updated-Oct-22.pdf

Nelson, T. J. (2004). Low-Income Fathers. *Annual Review of Sociology, 30*, 427–451. https://doi.org/10.1146/annurev.soc.29.010202.09594

O'Laughlin, B. (2008). Missing Men? The debate over rural poverty and women-headed households in Southern Africa. *The Journal of Peasant Studies, 25*(2), 1–48.

Parton, N. (2012). Reflections on 'Governing the Family': The Close Relationship Between Child Protection and Social Work in Advanced Western Societies –

The Example of England. *Families, Relationships and Societies, 1*(1), 87–101. Retrieved November 12, 2022, from https://bristoluniversitypressdigital. com/view/journals/frs/1/1/article-p87.xml

Pearce, D. (1978). The Feminization of Poverty: Women, Work and Welfare. *Urban and Social Change Review, 11*, 28–36.

Portes, J., & Reed, H. (2018). *The Cumulative Impact of Tax and Welfare Reforms.* Manchester, England: Equality and Human Rights Commission. https:// www.equalityhumanrights.com/sites/default/files/cumulative-impact-assessment-report.pdf

Public Health England. (2018). A Review of Recent Trends in Mortality in England, PHE Publications Gateway Number: GW-686. https://assets.pub-lishing.service.gov.uk/government/uploads/system/uploads/attachment_data/file/827518/Recent_trends_in_mortality_in_England.pdf

Ray, L. (2018). *Violence and Society* (2nd ed.). SAGE.

Ridge, T. (2009). *Living with Poverty: A Review of the Literature on Children's and Families' Experiences of Poverty,* Department for Work and Pensions Research Report No 594. http://www.bris.ac.uk/poverty/downloads/keyofficialdocu-ments/Child%20Poverty%20lit%20review%20DWP.pdf

Ridge, T., & Millar, J. (2008). *Work and Wellbeing Over Time: Lone Mothers and Their Children,* Department for Work and Pensions Research Report No 536.

Rose, W., & McAuley, C. (2019). Poverty and its Impact on Parenting in the UK: Re-defining the Critical Nature of the Relationship Through Examining Lived Experiences in Times of Austerity. *Children and Youth Services Review, 97*, 134–141.

Roy, K. (2014). Fathering from the Long View: Framing Personal and Social Change Through Life Course Theory. *Journal of Family Theory and Review, 6*, 319–335.

Roy, K., & Jones, N. (2014). *Pathways to Adulthood for Disconnected Young Men in Low-Income Communities.* Wiley.

Shildrick, T., MacDonald, R., Webster, C., & Garthwaite, K. (2012). *Poverty and Insecurity: Life in Low Pay, No Pay Britain.* Policy Press.

Smethers, S. (2015). What Are the Issues Affecting Grandparents in Britain Today? *Quality in Ageing and Older Adults, 16*(1), 37–43.

Stack, C. B. (1974). *All Our Kin: Strategies for Survival in a Black Community.* Harper & Row.

Stanko, E. A. (2001). The Day to Count: Reflections on a Methodology to Raise Awareness about the Impact of Domestic Violence in the UK. *Criminal Justice, 1*(2), 215–226. https://doi.org/10.1177/1466802501001002005

Stewart, K., Reeves, A., & Patrick, R. (2021). *A Time of Need: Exploring the Changing Poverty Risk Facing Larger Families in the UK.* https://sticerd.lse. ac.uk/CASE/_NEW/PUBLICATIONS/abstract/?index=8275

Sullivan, M. L. (1989). *Getting Paid: Youth Crime and Work in the Inner City.* Cornell University Press.

Tarrant, A. (2014). Negotiating Multiple Positionalities in the Interview Setting; Researching Across Gender and Generational Boundaries. *The Professional Geographer, 66*(3), 493–500.

Tarrant, A. (2015) Domestic ageing masculinities and grandfathering, in Gorman-Murray, A. and Hopkins, P. (eds.) Masculinities and Place, Surrey, Ashgate. Chapter 15, pp. 241-255.

Tarrant, A. (2016) The spatial and gendered politics of displaying family: exploring material cultures in grandfathers' homes. Gender, Place and Culture, 23 (7): 966–982.

Tarrant, A. (2017). Getting Out of the Swamp? Methodological Reflections on Using Qualitative Secondary Analysis to Develop Research Design. *International Journal of Social Research Methodology, 20*(6), 599–611.

Tarrant, A. (2021). *Fathering and Poverty: Uncovering Men's Participation in Low-Income Family Life.* Policy Press.

Tarrant, A., & Hughes, K. (2019). Qualitative Secondary Analysis: Building Longitudinal Samples to Understand Men's Generational Identities in Low Income Contexts. *Sociology, 53*(3), 538–553.

Tarrant, A., & Hughes, K. (2020). Collective Qualitative Secondary Analysis and Data-Sharing: Strategies, Insights and Challenges. In K. Hughes & A. Tarrant (Eds.), *Qualitative Secondary Analysis* (pp. 101–118). Sage.

Tarrant, A., & Hughes, K. (2021). Qualitative Data Re-use and Secondary Analysis: Researching In and About a Crisis. In H. Kara & S.-M. Khoo (Eds.), *Qualitative and Digital Research in Times of Crisis.* Policy Press.

Tarrant, A., Terry, G., Ward, M.R., Ruxton, S., Robb, M., & Featherstone, B. (2015). Are Male Role Models Really the Solution?: Interrogating the 'War on Boys' Through the Lens of the 'Male Role Model' Discourse. *Boyhood Studies, 8*(1), 60–83.

Tarrant, A., Featherstone, B., O'Dell, L., & Fraser, C. (2017). "You Try to Keep a Brave Face on But Inside You Are in Bits": Grandparent Experiences of Engaging with Professionals in Children's Services. *Qualitative Social Work, 16*(3), 351–366.

Tarrant, A., Ladlow, L., & Way, L. (Eds.). (2023). *Men and Welfare.* Routledge.

Treanor, M. (2020). *Child Poverty: Aspiring to Survive.* Bristol: Policy Press.

Wacquant, L. (2004). Decivilizing and Demonizing: The Weakening of the Black American Ghetto. In S. Loyal & S. Quilley (Eds.), *The Sociology of Norbert Elias* (pp. 95–121). Cambridge University Press.

Whelan, C. T., Layte, R., & Maître, B. (2003). Persistent Income Poverty and Deprivation in the European Union. *Journal of Social Policy, 32,* 1–18.

Whelan, C. T., & Maitre, B. (2006). Comparing Poverty and Deprivation Dynamics: Issues of Reliability and Validity. *The Journal of Economic Inequality, 4,* 303–323.

Whitaker, E. M., & Atkinson, P. (2022). *Reflexivity in Social Research.* Springer Link.

Women's Budget Group. (2018). The Female Face of Poverty. https://wbg.org.uk/analysis/the-female-face-of-poverty/

CHAPTER 2

Men in Poverty in Families: Missing or a Case of Smoke and Mirrors?

INTRODUCTION

In this chapter we account for our engagement with existing social sciences literature and consider how men might, often inadvertently, be rendered 'absent', through the discursive and theoretical framing of men's relationships to and in their families in research on family poverty. Engaging with existing evidence concerning the dynamic lifecourse trajectories of men through families in poverty from multiple family identities has been a case of 'smoke and mirrors', whereby we are able to 'see' men in some aspects of family life and participation, and from specific family identities (namely as fathers), but somewhat fragmented and partial views of men and their wider family participation as these change over their lifecourse. Our challenge has been to situate our own empirical observations of men, as they appear and are presented in the data on which we draw, in existing theoretical frameworks. Here we synthesise the literature about family and poverty where men do have a presence, both to determine the value of this for our own work and to identify how our empirically driven analyses may contribute to these debates.

We begin with a brief overview of poverty in the UK to situate our discussions, and to clarify who these men are, where we might find them, and why it is important to take a locality-based approach in understanding their family participation over their lives. Outlining theoretical approaches to

K. Hughes, A. Tarrant, *Men, Families, and Poverty*, Palgrave Macmillan Studies in Family and Intimate Life, https://doi.org/10.1007/978-3-031-24922-8_2

and treatments of the relationship between poverty and family in existing literatures, we identify and explore how men have so far been understood to navigate and experience the longitudinal dynamics of *poverty* from a literature in which qualitative accounts of men are rare. Next, we consider social sciences perspectives of men in *families*, which offer a rich seam of analysis. Our synthesis of this literature identifies an overfocus on men as fathers, which constrains more complex explanations of men's intergenerational family participation through multiple generational identities (e.g. as father, son, brother, cousin, and so on). In our final section, 'men in the margins', we elaborate how the overfocus on men as fathers is replicated in the hyper-visibility of men in low-income contexts manifested especially through discursive framings of 'absent' fathers in social policy (see also Tarrant, 2021). Such focus has limited utility for explanations of how and why enduring poverty shapes opportunities and limits for family participation for men. Taken together, we demonstrate how existing theoretical frameworks both in the sociology and social policy of families in low-income contexts, limit engagement with men's family participation from multiple generational positions across the lifecourse.

Poverty in the UK

In the UK, at the time of writing, an estimated 22% of the UK's population are living in circumstances of poverty. This percentage equates to 14.5 million people, of which 8.1 million are working-age adults, 4.3 million are children, approximately 1 in 3 of the child population; and 2.1 million are pensioners (Joseph Rowntree Foundation, 2022). Statistical data on poverty demonstrate that poverty is on the rise for all age groups. The rates of children in poverty are rising quickly, and a period of relative security against poverty for pensioners has ended (ibid.). Poverty, in the UK, is therefore less an experience of the marginalised few, but is instead the experience of roughly a quarter of the nation's population.

Early social sciences engagement in making sense of poverty established that, rather than a state of being, poverty is experiential, dynamic, and processual. Rowntree, in 1901, for example described a poverty 'cycle' which changes over the individual lifecourse, leading to alternating periods of want and plenty. Such observations indicated the need for longitudinal capture of such dynamics, and there have been significant investments in the UK towards research of this nature. For example, from the 1990s onwards (the 1980s in the US), the collation and analysis of large-scale longitudinal data (e.g. British Household Panel Survey and the US Panel

Study of Income Dynamics) have enhanced our ability to understand broad trends in low-income life—who lives in what kind of hardship and for how long. Importantly, such research establishes that there is no discrete category of 'the poor', no fixed 'underclass', and no unitary experience of hardship (Bane & Ellwood, 1986, pp. 1–23; Leisering & Walker, 1998). Experiences of low-income life, then, are varied and dynamic, and there is some evidence to suggest that hardship may be temporary, recurrent, or persistent, with differential effects across the lifecourse and in varied circumstances (Leisering & Walker, 1998; Stephens & Leishman, 2017; Shildrick et al., 2012).

Accompanying these large-scale surveys tracing and collating broad-level trends, there has been a solid phalanx of scholars tracking these trends through qualitative longitudinal research engagement (see Chap. 1), and we would identify our own research as falling within this corpus. The relevance of these studies continues to grow as the consequences of several decades of worsening welfare provision, recession, the unfolding impacts of Brexit and more recently, the COVID-19 pandemic, contribute to rising levels of poverty in the UK context, manifesting as a cost of living crisis with broad implications for low-income families (Garthwaite et al., 2022). Qualitative research demonstrates the everyday work, negotiation, and management required to address associated effects of poverty, such as hunger and lack of resources (see for example, Lister, 2005; Ridge, 2009; Shildrick et al., 2012; Erhard, 2020). Qualitative longitudinal methods enable researchers to identify and engage with these people to understand how and which everyday experiences comprise longitudinal dynamics of poverty for them and their families, and thereby support insight into precisely *how* dynamic poverty processes are variously experienced (Ridge & Millar, 2008; Millar & Ridge, 2009; Emmel & Hughes, 2010, 2014) and produced. Such approaches are critically important for problematising voluntaristic understandings of poverty, often those underscoring the very policies designed to address hardship. These are exemplified by policy engagement that de-emphasises local-level interventions to address hardship in favour of those that frame and treat people as inadequate and having failed and thereby creating conditions of poverty for themselves and their children (see Cooper, 2021; Tyler, 2013; Jensen, 2014). Situating our work alongside these debates, our empirical analyses address specifically how such policies and their enactment may sometimes serve to amplify or worsen experiences of hardship, and even work to shape intergenerational family configurations.

The Longitudinal Dynamics of Poverty

A central concern for this book is how qualitative longitudinal approaches may identify, and provide the means to address, an increasingly pertinent question: if populations of those in hardship are shifting, how might we account for areas of stubborn intergenerational poverty, again without recourse to an over-individualisation and responsibilisation of those living in these locales? This question is particularly relevant for the four linked studies on experiences of low-income life on which we draw. Rather than moving in and out of hardship over time, the localities in which these studies were conducted have experienced over three decades of worsening economic decline, exacerbated by a retreat of industry and employment, loss of area-level resources such as healthcare centres and effective transport infrastructure (Emmel & Malby, 2000), and community-level investments such as community and children's centres. This decades-long deprivation at area level has resulted in experiences of entrenched and stubborn poverty for the people living and ageing there. Consequently, the participants in the four studies we analyse churn between low-paid low-skill employment, underemployment, and unemployment (Shildrick et al., 2012) with lives characterised by high levels of insecurity in all measures of economic, social, and cultural life (Berthoud & Bryan, 2011; Savage et al., 2013; Emmel & Hughes, 2014). However, these people have been engaged with somewhat unevenly in social sciences interrogation of poverty. Poverty scholarship has predominantly focused on women, and family poverty has often been interrogated at household level. These approaches are driven by evidence, and utility. A predominant empirical emphasis on women in poverty research, for example, reflects how women are typically at a higher risk of living in stubborn poverty across the lifecourse (Bennett & Daly, 2014) and are more likely to be challenged in achieving financial security for themselves and their families (Ridge & Millar, 2008; Ridge, 2009). Focusing on the household level in research on poverty allows for a more detailed and nuanced understanding of the specific factors that contribute to poverty and how poverty affects individuals and families across households. Additionally, household-level research can demonstrate patterns of intergenerational transmission of poverty and how different interventions impact specific household types. Overall, household-level research can contribute to the development of more targeted and effective poverty reduction policies and programs. However, these foci also serve to obscure important dimensions of lives through poverty. A focus on the household as a unit of analysis serves to preclude wider analysis of resource and income distributions within family settings (e.g. Daly, 2018; Dermott, 2016), as well as gendered and generational interdependencies and family processes across households (Tarrant, 2021). This methodological approach therefore has the effect of conflating 'the effects of living arrangements on poverty with those of gender' (Bennett & Daly, 2014, p. 7). Furthermore, a focus on women, while empirically justifiable, disguises the precise character of the gendered dynamics of poverty especially as they relate to poverty through an empirical omission of men.

Where men have been considered, this too has been somewhat uneven. There is some evidence to suggest that life in the UK has become increasingly insecure and impoverished for men (Ruxton, 2002; Dermott & Pantazis, 2014) but attention to men and poverty tends towards identifying risk groups of men in poverty or focuses on men in singular generational positions. Poverty trends in the UK since 2012 indicate that gender disparities between and among some men and women are less stark than historically assumed. Non-resident fathers are a particularly vulnerable group in this regard, and as more likely to be parenting across households and in contexts of poverty and disadvantage (Dermott, 2016; Poole et al., 2016). In general, there has been a lack of empirical attention to the experiences of non-resident fathers, or of fathers who parent alone (Burgess & Davies, 2017; Gatrell et al., 2015). A notable body of sociological scholarship has explored the diverse biographies and transitions of young adult men in low-income localities, from youth to adulthood (e.g. MacDonald, 1997; Ward, 2015; McDowell, 2017), and some empirical attention to men as fathers in low-income families (e.g. Edin & Nelson, 2013) including more recently focus on men in different generational positions (Tarrant, 2021). However, patchy engagement with men in low-income families has meant that few of these literatures have connected the key themes explored in this book.

To set out our challenges in empirically 'seeing' the complexities of low-income family life for men and their family participation, we begin by synthesising three key areas of scholarly debate concerning possible relationships between family, poverty, and men, namely: theories of families and poverty; men in families from social sciences perspectives; and the discursive constructions and gendered problematisation of men in policy. By synthesising these literatures, we demonstrate how and why men have come to be regarded as 'missing' from families (O'laughlin, 2008). In doing so, we establish the importance of a more comprehensive understanding of men's family participation, consider the value of a processual approach for our own work and identify fresh areas for scholarship and research.

Men's Participation in Low-income Families: A Case of Smoke and Mirrors

Our preoccupation with questions of how and why men might be absent from families in low-income contexts was initially prompted by Anna's Leverhulme Fellowship study, 'Men, Poverty and Lifetimes of Care' (Men, Poverty and Care study), described in more detail in Chap. 1. Via a dialogic programme of analysis, including collective qualitative secondary analysis (Hughes et al., 2022) of existing datasets from research with families in low-income contexts (Chap. 3), Anna's Fellowship provided an opportunity to examine whether, how and in which ways, men were involved in family life. Although aspects of men's family participation had been explored by Kahryn and the research teams in the other studies, the very design of the Men, Poverty and Care study involved detailed engagement with questions of where men may be present or absent, both in the data and in narratives of families.

Despite observing diverse forms of family participation by men in the various datasets on which Men, Poverty and Care study drew, analytical engagement with existing literature and policy established that men's 'visibility' in low-income families is partial and unsatisfactory (see Tarrant, 2021 for a detailed review). Only men as fathers appear to be of concern to research and policy and, even then, it is men in low-income contexts who are typically described as absent from family life. This observation prompted new questions that form the basis of this book: if empirical accounts demonstrate that men's participation is integral to family life in low-income contexts, *why* are they so frequently discursively constructed as absent? This suggested a further question: is there anything distinctive about the character of family participation by men in *low-income contexts* that may serve to support this idea of their 'absence'?

Synthesising across the three key debates concerning families, poverty, and men, we sought to achieve a Venn Diagram effect (Fig. 2.1), whereby the conflation of the various established literatures would, ultimately, bring the men, and the diverse forms of family participation across the

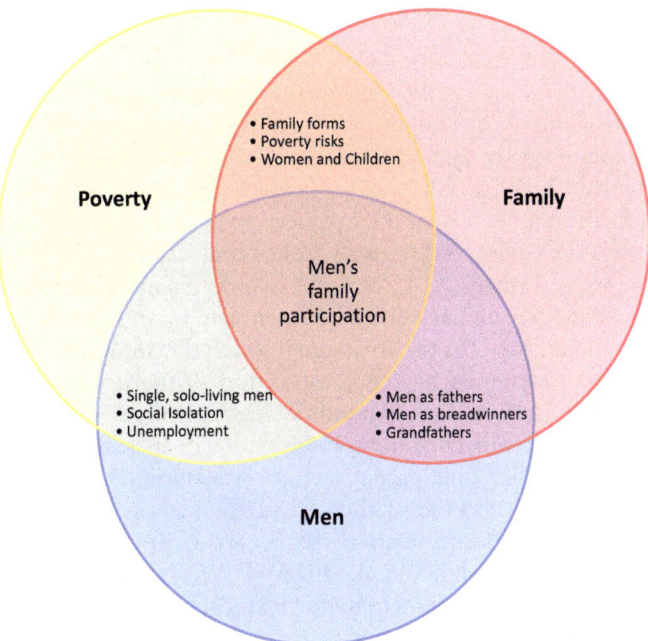

Fig. 2.1 Venn diagram of pertinent academic literatures about men's family participation

lifecourse observable in our data, into scholarly view. However, each time we turned to established bodies of scholarship, it became a case of smoke and mirrors where men emerged in some ways (e.g. as single men, bread-winners, and/or fathers), but disappeared in others (e.g. as brothers, uncles, cousins, sons). Importantly, these methodological, discursive, the-oretical, analytic, and empirical absences constrained our considerations of men's family participation in the round, and obscured vital aspects of their 'doing' of family life through low-income circumstances. Without a clear analytic framework, we were required instead to interrogate how and in which ways men in these circumstances have been 'absented' from schol-arship and policy concerning their participation, and we outline our argu-ments for why this is the case in the sections below.

Theories of Families and Poverty

We quickly established that while certain debates have significantly advanced theories about the relationship between family and poverty, albeit with recognition that both are contested concepts (Daly, 2018), specific experiences of family for men are often obscured. This happens inadvertently via the parcelling up of 'families' and 'poverty' as discrete yet overlapping themes that subsequently need to be analytically resynthesised (see Edwards & Gillies, 2012; also Hughes et al., 2022).

According to Daly (2018), there are two dominant models for understanding formative interrelations between family and poverty, namely structural and cultural. In the structural model, she argues that poverty is conceived as determined by the composition of the demographic unit, which has implications for economic status, resource, and consequent poverty risk for members of households. Individuals living in units with certain structures like lone parent families (statistically more likely to be headed by lone mothers than fathers), large families, cohabiting families, and so forth tend to be at a relatively higher risk of poverty than the wider population (see also Culliney et al., 2013). Poverty risks for individuals in these family types have been heightened by recent welfare reforms, such as the introduction of the two-child benefit cap which disproportionately affects large families, for example (e.g. Patrick et al., 2021). Yet family structures may also mitigate against the risks of poverty, such as when elderly relatives live with extended family (Farthing, 2014). Daly (2018) critiques these implied causal relationships for being relatively simplistic, whereby characteristics such as size and composition of the collective unit, combined with the number of earners vis-à-vis 'dependants', are posited as pivotal in poverty risks. While the structural approach avoids the tendency to blame individuals, namely parents, for their poverty and the poverty of their household, it nevertheless obscures the everyday dynamics of living through and managing poverty by family members. In other words, it fails to address the (often feminised) 'work' involved in poverty including parenting, money management, family support, and local engagement (Daly & Kelly, 2015). In addition, parenting that happens across households, such as non-resident parenting, is ignored.

Alternatively, cultural models of poverty conceptualise the transmission of (poor) norms, values, and practices as the main determinant of poverty risk. This model largely underscores much policy development, but has been subject to sustained sociological critique and analysis (e.g. Shildrick et al., 2012; Jensen & Tyler, 2012). From this perspective, because families are deemed to be the primary legitimate sites of child socialisation, policy focus is on 'cycles of deprivation' and the intergenerational perpetuation of poverty through reproductive cycles of 'bad practices' within families (Wilson, 1985; Welshman, 2006). Recent UK policy, driven by a politics of 'austerity', strives to inhibit such 'cycles' through interventions such as welfare conditionality. These are designed to encourage financial 'independence', and to counter presumed assumptions by those with impoverished family norms, living in impoverished localities, that the state will 'provide', or compensate for their inadequacies (Tyler, 2013; Jensen, 2018; see also Tarrant, 2021). Such rhetoric is also cyclical and most strongly directed (problematically) at children, such as those from single-mother families where a father or male role model is absent. Blue collar men in, or absent from, these families have also long been castigated as 'drunk, criminal, aimless, feckless and hopeless. And perhaps claim to suffer from low self-esteem, brought on by unemployment' (e.g. Boris Johnson, 1995). Here, men as fathers are treated as implicitly responsible for 'failing families' and 'failing areas', for transmitting 'bad' practices to their sons by shirking their responsibilities as breadwinners, caregivers, and agents of socialisation, and conspicuous in their ostensible absence from households and localities.

Father absence is frequently posited as an explanatory factor for many of society's ills from those with a variety of different political and theoretical perspectives (Williams, 1998; Tarrant, 2021). The growth of fatherless families, for example, was explicitly linked to increasing crime rates in areas of the UK in the early 1990s (Dennis & Erdos, 1992). At this time, the erosion of the breadwinning-father identity was considered symbolic of the loss of a patriarchal family figure, and in turn the demise of normative family relationships responsible for the successful socialisation of young men into acceptable socially responsible behaviour (ibid.). Consequently, it was argued, there was an increase in the criminality of young men in low-income localities, less as a result of hardship and more because of bad or absent fathering. We return to these arguments later in Chap. 7, where a young man, Joe, discusses both his father, who was violent and died prematurely from alcoholism, and his step-father, one of the few supportive people in his life. A simplistic reading of his narrative might be used to support the blaming of absent or inadequate fathers for the vulnerabilities of their sons. However, our analyses of Joe's case alongside other low-income young men across the datasets, support a more complex account of how his experiences of hardship and family life intersect with and influence his transitions to adulthood, including his trajectories in and through poverty and place and his relationships with other men.

More recently, parent blame has reemerged in austerity discourses, which have served to absent men through emphasis on their assumed absence from households and/or framing as 'failing' breadwinners and role models for younger male relatives. The allocation of blame to absent fathers (and lone mothers by implication) during the urban riots in 2011 replicated explanations used by politicians for socio-economic crises decades before. Distinctively, during austerity, the weaponisation of discursive framings of failing fathers by policy makers served to legitimise more punitive, conditional policy responses towards people in need of social welfare support (explored later in the chapter, see also De Benedictis, 2012; Jensen & Tyler, 2012). Tarrant (2021) argues that in a context where low-income fathers are hyper-visible through their representation in policy as bad or absent dads, qualitative accounts of the mundanities of family life and diverse forms of family participation by low-income men are rarely developed. Consequently, these literatures lack empirical counterparts of the men in our own datasets, and they provide limited support for the theoretical interpretation of our empirical observations.

In working through the complex of causal relationships linking poverty and family, Daly (2018) identifies a growing emphasis in political rhetoric on 'jobless or low work intensity' households, which combines economic and cultural conceptualisations of worklessness as a norm, an idea which has also been strongly criticised (Shildrick et al., 2012). To redress the somewhat static and normative rendering of both 'family' and 'poverty' in such approaches, Daly introduces lifecourse and intergenerational perspectives. Such perspectives conceptualise circumstances of family poverty as contingent on dynamic and complex social processes, with a repeated or persistent character. Possible relationships between families and poverty are consequently theorised in numerous ways (Daly, 2018). Firstly, socialisation practices may be seen to be cumulative, resulting in dependencies produced through the transmission of disadvantage. Secondly, that lifecourses are shaped by factors in people's social background which may operate as relatively permanent influences. Thirdly, poverty can be caused by broader socio-economic changes affecting lifecourses such as significant global economic crises, social policy reform and, we would add, global pandemics (e.g. Garthwaite et al., 2022), as well as risks associated with other life transitions. Thus, she concludes that these two perspectives (namely *worklessness*, and *lifecourse and intergenerational*) remain in their infancy, especially empirically (Daly, 2018). It is to this tranche of work that we explicitly contribute.

To begin with, lifecourse perspectives are especially valuable for understanding how the risks of, and routes in and out of poverty over time, are gendered, with different implications for men and women and without obscuring either. Empirical emphasis on women's experiences of poverty reflects the gendered nature of poverty processes, whereby women tend to be disproportionately at risk of living and remaining in poverty across the lifecourse (Bennett & Daly, 2014). More broadly, however, in the UK between 1999 and 2012, analyses of poverty from nationally representative data demonstrate an overall convergence of poverty rates for some men and women over time (Dermott & Pantazis, 2014). This work establishes that poverty rates among female lone parents continue to be exceptionally high but also identifies an emerging group of poorer men living alone (ibid., 2014). These data illustrate divergent trajectories and outcomes of poverty for men and women dependent on household and relationship circumstances longitudinally. Taking the long view, women are more likely to experience persistent or recurrent spells of poverty across the lifecourse while men tend to be more socially isolated, and by implication, segregated from family contexts (ibid., 2014). Retrospective life histories research conducted with single, middle-aged men by Demey et al. (2013) demonstrates that delayed family formation is more likely to be experienced by men, and disadvantages them compared to some women. In their empirical attention to men via life history interviews, these sources are unusual in a wider literature examining possible relationships between poverty, gender, and families, as well as the 'feminisation of poverty' (Pearce, 1978; Chant, 2006). However, even here, the very language of 'single men' serves conceptually to absent them from families by conflating 'families' with men's domiciliary residence with their spouses/partners, and children. Furthermore, it serves to imply an absence of broader family or kin relations more generally by focusing on men solely in terms of their family identities as fathers. From these longitudinal perspectives, then, the dynamic relationship between gender and poverty is often less visible *within* household contexts and struggles to engage with families *across* households, particularly in relation to the distinctive challenges poverty creates for both men and women for family participation. A need for a more nuanced engagement is especially important for families that do not reflect the traditional nuclear form, such as those who are solo-living, reconstituted families, families headed by grandparents or other family members providing kinship care, and families—especially those in poverty—that are sustained across households and generations (Emmel & Hughes, 2014).

A central tension in the poverty and families literature is that 'families' are often treated as somewhat static forms. Categorical proxies for family, especially that of *household*, are often used as 'catch alls', rendering complex relational nexuses comprising families and family relations as overly simplistic units. The conflation of families with households and between poverty, living arrangements and gender (Bennett & Daly, 2014), noted earlier, is another example here. This further serves to exclude consideration of men's situations, whilst simultaneously obscuring relational dynamics gendering differing forms of family participation for women. Dermott (2016), for example, has highlighted the empirical omission of fathers who are non-resident (Dermott, 2016), men who are also more likely to be experiencing socio-economic disadvantage. Thus, where there is literature that focuses on family and poverty as well as gender, the framing of each, obscures particular aspects of men's family participation and their wider familial interdependencies, or alternatively distinctive features of their experiences of hardship. Consequently, these debates sit somewhat in tension with two decades of intensive scholarship concerning family diversity and dynamics (Neale, 2000). Indeed, although conceptions of family have expanded to allow for the inclusion of relationships beyond discrete households, as well as for a much broader diversity of family identities than those typically associated with the parent/child identities comprising traditional nuclear families (see below), this literature also lacks sustained attention to men's family participation across the lifecourse, particularly in low-income contexts, as we now move on to discuss.

Men in Families: Social Sciences Perspectives

Since the mid-1990s, in the social sciences, there has been a steady theoretical withdrawal from views of 'the family' as an hermeneutic form of social institution, such as those proposed by Parsons (1952), wherein families are considered to be self-contained, biologically determined, 'units'. In this earlier normative and functionalist perspective, which reified the model of a heterosexual, two-parent nuclear family, men's family participation was relatively straightforward. Framed around gendered stereotypes, fathers were breadwinners and mothers were caregivers. Here, 'care' and 'work' were separated as different spheres of activity, and through their association with, and relationship to, paid work and employment beyond the home men were conceptually, empirically, and physically absented from the caring work of family life. Thus, while men were very much observed within families as social units as breadwinners, this breadwinner model resulted in the overlooking of men's work within families and homes as well as producing a conceptual problematic in family-focused research for apprehending unemployed men and men in low-income families where such breadwinning is often unavailable.

As noted, sociological critique of static conceptualisations of the family resulted in an intensified focus on family dynamics and diversity, presaged by a paradigmatic shift from conceiving of the family as a functional social institution and instead towards recognising the 'family' as a set of relational practices, a shift articulated most effectively in the work of David Morgan (1996, 2011, 2020). Rather than normative framings of family members dependent on characteristics such as generational identity (child, parent), or roles (mother, father), new sociological engagement sought to explore the experiences of those comprising the family, and to understand their 'inner worlds' (Daly & Kelly, 2015). Underpinned by innovations in methods of qualitative engagement, attention was also given to people's ongoing emotional reflexivity around the 'meanings' and 'doing' of family in different socio-economic circumstances (see also Charles et al., 2008). The language of 'doing' produced its own offspring, such as 'mothering' and 'fathering', terms reflecting the intentions, meanings and social practices involved in what were formerly treated as given roles (e.g. Morgan, 1996). Here, families are also acknowledged as sites of performance, agency, and negotiation (Daly, 2018). Consequently, assumptions of rigid gender roles have more recently been replaced by empirically nuanced engagement with questions of gender diversity, performativity, fluidity, and changing gender relations (Daly & Kelly, 2015). Even more recently, analyses of men's family involvement have been formulated through studies of fatherhood and the development of related conceptual languages such as caring masculinities (Elliott, 2016), discussed in greater detail towards the end of this chapter.

This unpicking of taken-for-granted ideas of traditional ties and family forms gave rise to a variety of new conceptual languages and approaches for capturing and explaining the increasingly diverse relationships and cohabitations that have emerged over the last few decades, formerly conflated under the umbrella of 'family'. Such language includes 'intimacy' (Jamieson, 1999, 2011) and 'relatedness' (Carsten, 2004), but also extends to comprehend 'personal life' (Smart, 2007). These concepts and others seek to explicate relational complexity, diversity, and dynamics without using collective terms that obscure individuals, and in this way avoid the static reification of 'family' as an arbitrary, yet analytically cogent, social unit. Despite emphases on a diversity of relationships, identities, and choices in such literature, the wider gamut of men's family relationships and identities (as sons, brothers, uncles, nephews, and so on), as well as their family participation across the lifecourse, have only partially been brought into analytic 'view'.

Where there has been attention to men in families, researchers have been oriented to distinguishing men as fathers from their identities as men as husbands (e.g. Henwood & Proctor, 2003; Dermott, 2008; King, 2015; Shirani et al., 2012; Strange, 2012, see also Tarrant, 2021). Indeed, there is a rich body of scholarship in this vein and attention to fatherhood is now well established as an area of international scholarship (Roy, 2014, Dermott & Miller, 2015). One key approach by fatherhood researchers has been to measure and/or assess the extent to which men's participation in families is accessible or otherwise, for particular groups of fathers in context of emerging cultural models of father involvement and engagement (Dermott, 2008; Miller, 2010). For example, sociologists have recently begun to examine the lives of men who are not commonly interrogated in fatherhood research, a field more traditionally dominated by the voices and experiences of largely white, heterosexual, middle-class, employed men who also happen to be fathers (Dermott & Miller, 2015; Roy et al., 2015). More recent work has sought to embrace a more extensive range of fatherhoods through empirical attention to men on a low-income (Tarrant, 2021), men and religion (Britton, 2019), men of colour (Abdill, 2018; Scourfield & Lewinson, 2016), men fathering with a disability or fathering for children with a disability (Kilkey & Clarke, 2010), and non-resident fathers (Scourfield, 2006; Dermott, 2016). However, while these offer important empirical insight into a diversity of men's experiences, this sometimes 'factorial' approach treats the diversity of men's family involvement as premised on *types* of men categorised along axes of difference and inequality and/or by types of context (i.e. non-resident, separated, divorced, and so on). In addition, considering men as fathers from these categorical positions only permits a 'view' of men through a specific framing, namely *as* fathers. We see this replicated in policy focus and debates about family and poverty, as discussed earlier in this chapter. Analytical constraints in understanding men's family participation in the round are often introduced via an overfocus on, or unpicking of, certain generational identities, for example, men as fathers, which obscures their identities and how they 'do kinship' more generally. Thus, while a wider constituency of men as fathers is being empirically and analytically 'recovered' in nuclear family contexts, the broader sets of familial interdependencies in which they are embedded over time and across the lifecourse, continue to require theoretical elaboration.

Attention to family interdependencies is integral to bringing such diversity of men's broader family participation across the lifecourse back into analytic view. Nevertheless, we make the case for retaining the language of 'family' and its salience for providing for the analytic capture of particular forms of relational engagement and participation. In sociological approaches to engaging with questions of choice and change in the composition of personal ties, there has been a tendency to destablise and decentre the idea of 'family' (Morgan, 1996; Williams, 2003), such that its theoretical value has been lost. As Gilding (2010) suggests, privileging the open-endedness of intimate relations may result in losing analytic sight of the institutional embeddedness of family relationships. In other words, an over-focus on individuals serves to obscure the relationships, policy contexts and processes through which families, and family identities, are produced and shaped over time. This is especially important as legislative and policy processes are based on normative models of family life that frequently serve to disadvantage particular social groups and family forms. Edwards and Gillies (2012, p. 67), for example, note that working-class and minority families, whose disadvantage sets them apart from such normative models of family life, are more likely to find themselves positioned within 'socially excluded' and 'antisocial' family discourses and therefore subject to particular forms of governance, regulation, and surveillance. To abandon the language of 'family', then, renders invisible foundational social processes productive of peoples' lives, *and their family relationships,* as they are lived and ordered through place and over time.

Challenges to the conceptual vitality of the 'family' have ushered in a repertoire of concepts to capture the doing and making of families, and to consider how families are sustained and remain important to them. A key concept that retains elements of family and its multigenerational significance for people is that of 'kinship'. Kinship allows for simultaneous engagement with the broader, multi-, and intergenerational complex of relationships, ties and practices, sustaining families over time. Invoking such language has potential to facilitate theoretical engagement with the broader family participation of men in our datasets. By avoiding the naturalisation of kinship (Comas d'Argemir & Soronellas, 2019), and a conceptual separation of kinship from care, we can observe in our datasets how men's participation may constitute particular forms of caregiving, both for and on behalf of their families. Arguing that 'care is kinship', Comas d'Argemir and Soronellas (2019, p. 316) suggest that 'in a context of social change, a crisis of care, and economic crisis, kinship becomes a primary factor in the attribution of care, while gender roles remain secondary'. In this book, through the empirical chapters we present, we develop related, but somewhat different arguments. For low-income families there are always crises associated with longitudinal circumstances of constrained, low-, or no income, both across families and their localities. Therefore, the very contexts of low-income for families motivate specific sorts of family participation by men, which cannot be understood solely through considerations of gender, whether gender *roles* (breadwinner), or *behaviours* (masculinities). By retaining the language of family, we remain able to understand such participation over time, from a range of familial identities, alongside different forms of collectivity, identification, and meaning across localities, without subsuming attention to inequalities and power dynamics embedded in individual experience and motivations. Understanding these complexities is better facilitated through a processual, temporally oriented framework.

In summary, while men have an empirical presence in family scholarship, existing theoretical and discursive framings of family life including across the lifecourse predominantly foreground the accounts of women and/or fathers as a generational position. Attention to men as fathers is also replicated in the research and policy focus on men in low-income contexts, as we now explore in more depth.

Men, Families, and Social Policy: Men in the Margins

As noted earlier, emerging work continues to identify and address gaps in fatherhood research, typically in relation to social and relational inequalities. While piecemeal in its factorial approach to exploring diversity, this work is beginning to provide important insights about men's participation in low-income life, albeit again from the perspectives of the father generation. This is not a drawback, because we continue to know little about fathering in contexts of poverty or disadvantage (see also Bennett & Daly, 2014; Ridge, 2009) or of men engaging in family life in other generational positions (although see Tarrant, 2021).

Providing a comprehensive review elsewhere of how fathers in low-income contexts have been constructed by policy makers and in public discourse, Anna argues that men in low-income families are hyper-visible in representational contexts, for example, as 'absent', 'feckless', and thus 'uncaring fathers', and framed as a problem for policy to address (Tarrant, 2021). However, the very framing of these men as absent, and of low-income families and localities as fatherless, serves to obscure consideration of their voices and experiences. Policy approaches to contemporary father-hood have been shaped by two linked trends: increasing rates of parental break-up whereby fathers are non-resident and reside in different house-holds from their children, and an increased emphasis on paternal involve-ment in the lives of young children (Skevik, 2006; Tarrant, 2021). These processes have been translated into corresponding binary questions con-cerning father absence and presence (or involvement), and a moral dis-course that categorises 'good' and 'bad' fathers. These binaries additionally articulate conflicting societal expectations for men in relation to their fam-ily participation. Consequently, the rising prevalence of non-resident fatherhood has been conflated with 'absent fathers', and often interpreted by public and political commentators as a 'crisis of fatherlessness' (Williams, 1998), thought to be specific to families ostensibly embodying a 'culture of poverty'. Such fatherlessness is therefore not simply an articulation of impoverished parental norms (Jensen, 2018; see also Brooks & Hodkinson, 2020), but a perpetuation of such, and of family poverty more generally. Reflecting academic interests in men as fathers, therefore, policy debates and discourses betray a set of anxieties about the role of fathers, encapsu-lated in a contemporary crisis of paternity, centred predominantly on men who might be described as 'in the margins' (Abdill, 2018; Roberts & Elliott, 2020).

In response, and especially through a conceptual language of masculini-ties, there have been efforts to understand and analyse how men partici-pate in families in new ways. The language of caring masculinities (Elliott, 2016), for example, often describes what 'modern' men do as something novel or transformative, obscuring longer histories of men's caring in and for their families. With distinct parallels to fatherhood research, in these discussions middle-class men are often treated theoretically as the van-guards for progress, an issue Roberts and Elliott (2020) take to task.

Roberts and Elliott (2020) argue that marginalised men and 'men in the margins', namely working-class men and boys, men of colour, and/or men with disabilities, are often denied recognition that they are able to perform caring masculinities, creating the impression that they are somehow 'lagging behind' their white, middle-class counterparts.

These arguments are particularly relevant for the research we present here in challenging the difficulties of formulating histories of families and masculinities, and masculinities and *poverty*, wherein men in low-income contexts can be simultaneously perceived as *poor* and *caring*. Unfortunately, existing policy frameworks appear to support the idea that men in low-income contexts struggle to care, or formulate new masculine identities predicated on their caring ability. For example, in research on young fathers, Neale and Davies (2015), found that in healthcare settings or in encounters with social workers, the young fathers in their study were systematically marginalised or sidelined from decision-making about the care and management of their child/ren (see also Philip et al., 2020; Donald et al., 2021). The social disadvantages experienced by men in low-income contexts are therefore often translated as 'risks', precluding support premised on a strengths-based approach (Tarrant & Neale, forthcoming). Importantly, these empirical observations illustrate how men's experiences of, access to, and participation in families through circumstances of poverty are regulated in distinctive ways (see also Tarrant & Hughes, 2019), based on normative framings of their *capacity to care*, or *interest in participation*. In effect, such observations raise questions not only about how and whether men are absent from families, but also how men may be marginalised, sidelined, and excluded *from* family contexts, such as through maternal gatekeeping (Allen & Hawkins, 1999; Neale & Lau Clayton, 2014; Abdill, 2018). Such questions necessitate a mode of analytic engagement which allows for the interrogation of the longitudinal dynamics of men's broader family involvement or otherwise, the character of such, in which circumstances and—where the evidence is available—for what purposes. These and associated questions underscore the need for a more comprehensive engagement with men's family participation—including beyond fatherhood—in low-income contexts, and over time.

Roy's (2006) life history study with 40 African American men in low-income families in the US is an exemplar of methodological innovation in this direction, wherein he situates his findings in the context of fatherhood research and, drawing on a temporal framework, simultaneously examines men's experiences of being fathered and fathering their children. Roy

(2006) addresses a similar empirical gap, responding to a lack of academic attention to fathers and sons in minority and/or low-income families. Through a temporal framework, underscored by the tools offered by a lifecourse perspective, he illustrates how the broader study of men in families has been driven by recognition that fathering experiences have become more dynamic and complex over time. He argues that men's movements in and across households, intimate family relationships, and family-supportive employment, alongside altered norms for men within families across generations, have produced increasingly transitory experiences, reflective of men's varying responses to paternity (2006, p. 32). In the life history interviews conducted for his study, Roy explored how men constructed narratives and specific meaning about their own fathers' movements in and out of their lives, along a spectrum of stability, liminality, and inquiry, and linked these to patterns of their own paternal involvement. The first two narratives, stability and liminality, were premised on accounts of involved fathers but reflected variation in the extent of their fathers' involvement. Constructed narratives of stability were rarer among the participants but these narratives were used to characterise fathers who held normative commitments to marriage and employment. Narratives of liminality and ambiguous expectations described fathers who were never truly in or out of their son's lives. These men were described as sacrificing their family lives and household ties to the demands of employment. Reflecting a narrative of absence, the third narrative, inquiry, characterised fathers who were never known. Despite mothers' attempts to model paternal identities, young men who did not know their fathers described having experienced distinct difficulties in creating their own paternal identities. Roy's approach addresses questions concerning the gendering of familial relationships through hardship, demonstrating how broader socio-economic processes constrain or impinge upon father and son relationships. Our own work contributes to these insights by considering the porous and interconnected character of families and their localities, demonstrating how these are mutually identifying and constitutive relational contexts.

In addition to providing substantive insights about the intergenerational effects of fathering, of significance for this book, Roy's study provides a methodological justification for the analytical strategies we develop in our own work and present here, namely accessing multigenerational narratives, experiences, and descriptions to provide a more comprehensive account of the broader gamut of men's family participation in low-income contexts.

Conclusion: Marginalising Low-income Men in Families

We began this chapter by seeking to reframe the family participation of men in low-income contexts who are often represented as participating either 'from the margin' (Abdill, 2018) or not at all. We did this to account for, and explain, the contributions of the men in our datasets who could be seen to be engaging in vital but often overlooked and undervalued roles in sustaining their families. What we encountered were representations of low-income men in literature orientated towards questions of family life that actively, albeit unintentionally, marginalised them, either as a group or population or treated them analytically in singular generational/familial positions (especially as fathers). Men's broader contribution to, or importance in, families was consequently obscured either through limited empirical engagement and/or such constrained conceptual framing. In seeking to draw on this literature for our own analyses, we observed that a lack of a developed sociology of family participation from the perspectives of uncles, sons, cousins, and so forth, precluded consideration of the wider gamut of men's intergenerational and familial identities. Consequently, both the practices and distinctive challenges that men in low-income contexts engage in and experience to sustain their family members and other relatives, observable in our datasets, disappear from analytic view, or remain only partially 'visible' from limited familial positions. In consequence, we lack explanations of how and why men may indeed be absent from low-income families, which prohibits consideration of why this is the case, and questioning where else they may be.

Rather than arguing for specific empirical engagement with 'men in the margins', we suggest that existing literature inadvertently marginalises low-income men where substantive, or policy, concern focuses on family participation. Men in low-income circumstances do not constitute a marginal population, up to 14.5 people were living in circumstances of poverty before the COVID-19 pandemic, and a significant percentage of these are men.[1] Nevertheless, we encounter men in existing literature on

---

[1] Up to 18% of men in the UK live in households of below average income 2016–2018, DWP figures, https://assets.publishing.service.gov.uk/government/uploads/system/uploads/attachment_data/file/789997/households-below-average-income-1994-1995-2017-2018.pdf.

family life as either marginal to the research, or through the various forms of framing outlined above, as 'men in the margins'.

Consequently, existing debates are ill equipped to address two key questions. First, what might be the longitudinal character of men's broader family participation in low-income contexts? And, second, what are the distinctive challenges of persistent poverty for the possibilities of family participation for men? Such questions are critical to understanding poverty more broadly. For example, existing approaches to conceiving of men's family participation in low-income contexts mute or obscure particular forms of family participation by men and thus fail to support insight into the dynamics of family life through circumstances of poverty *for* men, women, and children. Ultimately, these limitations constrain our ability theoretically to engage with how poverty shapes the everyday lives of families, and the multiple related questions of how, whether, and why poverty may persist across families over time.

To address these questions, we develop a theoretical family lifecourse analytic framework to bring men 'back in' empirically, interrogate the longitudinal, inter- and multigenerational dynamics of family participation, and capture something more of the complexities of family lives, their constraints and their dynamics in and for the broader nexus of relationships of which families are comprised. Across our four empirical chapters (Chaps. 4, 5, 6, and 7) we use this framework to synthesise multiple accounts and perspectives of men in low-income contexts in different generational positions so as to develop a complex understanding of the dynamics of their family participation over time.

We also concern ourselves with considering how men describe their encounters with policy-related professionals, in terms of the impacts, effects, understandings, and interpretations of men in relation to the policy-driven framing of men's family participation in its broadest sense (Tarrant, 2021; Tarrant & Neale, forthcoming). Our definition of social policy as it pertains to our discussions here may be at first glance relatively narrow, specifically policies concerned primarily with the wellbeing, functioning and responsibilities of families with children (Daly, 2018). However, our empirical attention is towards interrogating peoples' own understandings and experiences of policy, whether through welfare payments, social housing arrangements, health and social care interventions, and social institutions including schools. We draw back from individuals within families, to consider their movement across and within broader intergenerational family networks, to account simultaneously for how social policy intersects with, but also disrupts, shapes and reorganises, families as sets of individuals and as 'collective structures' (Mätzke & Ostner, 2010). While we do not provide a policy analysis, we nevertheless seek to account for how families may be shaped through a broader 'organized field of social practices' (Appadurai, 1996, p. 29), involving hegemonic power balances and diverse discourses of men and family life in policy-related encounters.

We conclude that the normative constitution and discursive framing of families in circumstances of poverty in scholarship and policy, in particular, have produced forms of *male* absence from low-income family life (Tarrant, 2021). This, often unintentional, absenting of men, which positions and represents them as 'men in the margin' (Roberts & Elliott, 2020), has consequences for how and even whether men are included or 'seen' in empirical research on families in poverty contexts. In contrast, however, the four studies described more fully in Chap. 1 are saturated with accounts from and by men concerning their family participation. To contextualise these empirical accounts, this chapter has addressed the question of how and why men have come to be described, and treated, as absent from their families in sociological research and social policy on low-income family life across the lifecourse. Somewhat paradoxically, then, we carve out our rationale and a research agenda for exploring men's accounts of low-income family life directly *from* the very debates that serve to render them less visible.

References

Abdill, A. (2018). *Fathering from the Margins: An Intimate Examination of Black Fatherhood*. Columbia University Press.

Allen, S. M., & Hawkins, A. J. (1999). Maternal Gatekeeping: Mothers' Beliefs and Behaviors That Inhibit Greater Father Involvement in Family Work. *Journal of Marriage and the Family, 61*(1), 199–212.

Appadurai, A. (1996). *Modernity at Large: Cultural Dimensions of Globalization*. University of Minnesota Press.

Bane, M., & Ellwood, D. (1986). Slipping Into and Out of Poverty: The Dynamics of Spells. *Journal of Human Resources, 21*(1), 1–23.

Bennett, F., & Daly, M. (2014). *Poverty Through a Gender Lens: Evidence and Policy Review on Gender and Poverty*. Joseph Rowntree Foundation Report.

Berthoud, R., & Bryan, M. (2011). Income, Deprivation and Poverty: A Longitudinal Analysis. *Journal of Social Policy, 40*(1), 135–156.

Britton, J. (2019). Muslim Men, Racialised Masculinities and Personal Life. *Sociology, 53*(1), 31–51.

Brooks, R., & Hodkinson, P. (2020). *Sharing Care: Equal and Primary Carer Fathers and Early Years Parenting*. Policy Press.

Burgess, A., & Davies, J. (2017). *Cash or Carry? Fathers Combining Work and Care in the UK*, (Full Report). Contemporary Fathers in the UK series. Marlborough: Fatherhood Institute.

Carsten, J. (2004). *After Kinship*. Cambridge University Press.

Chant, S. H. (2006). Re-thinking the "Feminization of Poverty" in Relation to Aggregate Gender Indices. *Journal of Human Development, 7*(2), 201–220.

Charles, N., Aull Davies, C., & Harris, C. (2008). *Families in Transition: Social Change, Family Formation, and Kin Relationships*. Policy Press.

Comas-d'Argemir, D., & Soronellas, M. (2019). Men as Carers in Long-Term Caring: Doing Gender and Doing Kinship. *Journal of Family Issues, 40*(3), 315–339.

Cooper, K. (2021). Are Poor Parents *Poor* Parents? The Relationship between Poverty and Parenting among Mothers in the UK. *Sociology, 55*(2), 349–383.

Culliney, M., Haux, T., & McKay, S. (2013). *Family Structure and Poverty in the UK: An Evidence and Policy Review*. Joseph Rowntree Foundation report.

Daly, M. (2018). Towards a Theorization of the Relationship Between Poverty and Family. *Social Policy & Administration, 52*(3), 565–577.

Daly, M., & Kelly, G. (2015). *Families and Poverty: Everyday Life on a Low-Income*. Policy Press.

De Benedictis, S. (2012). Feral Parents: Austerity Parenting Under Neoliberalism. *Studies in the Maternal, 4*(2).

Demey, D., Berrington, A., Evandrou, M., & Falkingham, J. (2013). Pathways into Living Alone in Mid-Life: Diversity and Policy Implications. *Advances in Life Course Research, 18*(3), 161–174.

Dennis, N., & Erdos, G. (1992). *Families Without Fatherhood*. Wiltshire: The Cromwell Press.

Dermott, E. (2008). *Intimate fatherhood: A sociological analysis* (2nd ed.). Routledge.

Dermott, E. (2016). Non-resident Fathers in the UK: Living Standards and Social Support. *Journal of Poverty and Social Justice, 24*(2), 113–125.

Dermott, E., & Miller, T. (2015). More Than the Sum of its Parts? Contemporary Fatherhood Policy, Practice and Discourse. *Families, Relationships and Societies, 4*(2), 183–195.

Dermott, E., & Pantazis, C. (2014). Gender and Poverty in Britain: Changes and Continuities between 1999 and 2012. *Journal of Poverty and Social Justice, 22*(3), 253–269.

Donald, L., Davidson, R., Murphy, S., Hadley, A., Puthussery, S., & Randhawa, G. (2021). How Young, Disadvantaged Fathers Are Affected by Socioeconomic and Relational Barriers: A UK-Based Qualitative Study, *Families, Relationships and Societies* (published online ahead of print 2021). Retrieved July 3, 2022, fromhttps://bristoluniversitypressdigital.com/view/journals/frs/aop/article-10.1332-204674321X16321468785082/article-10.1332-204674321X16321468785082.xml

Edin, K., & Nelson, T. J. (2013). *Doing the Best I Can: Fatherhood in the Inner City*. University of California Press.

Edwards, R., & Gillies, V. (2012). Farewell to Family? Notes on an Argument for Retaining the Concept. *Families, Relationships and Societies, 1*(1), 63–69.

Elliott, K. (2016). Caring Masculinities: Theorizing an Emerging Concept. *Men and Masculinities, 19*(3), 240–259.

Emmel, N., & Hughes, K. (2010). 'Recession, It's All the Same to Us Son': The Longitudinal Experience (1999-2010) of Deprivation. *Twenty-First Century Society, 5*(2), 171–181.

Emmel, N., & Hughes, K. (2014). Vulnerability, Intergenerational Exchange and the Conscience of Generations. In R. Edwards & J. Holland (Eds.), *Understanding Families Over Time: Research and Policy*. Palgrave Macmillan.

Emmel, N., & Malby, B. (2000). *Meeting Health Needs in Gipton — Regeneration and Health*. East Leeds Primary Care Group.

Erhard, F. (2020). The Struggle to Provide: How Poverty Is Experienced in the Context of Family Care. *Journal of Poverty and Social Justice, 28*(1), 119–134.

Farthing, R. (2014). What's Wrong with Being Poor? The Problems of Poverty, as Young People Describe Them. *Children and Society, 30*(2), 107–119.

Garthwaite, K., Patrick, R., Power, M., Tarrant, A., & Warnock, R. (2022). *Covid Collaborations: Researching Poverty and Low-Income Family Life During the Pandemic*. Policy Press.

Gatrell, C. J., Burnett, S. B., Cooper, C. L. & Sparrow, P. (2015). The Price of Love: The Prioritisation of Childcare and Income Earning among UK Fathers. *Families, Relationships and Societies, 4*(2), 225–238.

Henwood, K., & Proctor, J. (2003). The 'Good Father': Reading Men's Accounts of Paternal Involvement During the Transition to First-Time Fatherhood. *British Journal of Social Psychology, 42*(3), 337–355.

Hughes, K., Hughes, J., & Tarrant, A. (2022). Working at a Remove: Continuous, Collective, and Configurative Approaches to Qualitative Secondary Analysis. *Quality & Quantity, 56*, 375–394.

Jamieson, L. (1999). Intimacy Transformed? A Critical Look at the 'Pure Relationship'. *Sociology, 33*(3), 477–494.

Jamieson, L. (2011). Intimacy as a Concept: Explaining Social Change in the Context of Globalisation or Another Form of Ethnocentrism? *Sociological Research Online, 16*(4), 151–163.

Jensen, T. (2014). Welfare Commonsense, Poverty Porn and Doxosophy. *Sociological Research Online, 19*(3), 277–283.

Jensen, T. (2018). *Parenting the Crisis: The Cultural Politics of Parent-Blame*. Policy Press.

Jensen, T., & Tyler, I. (2012). Austerity Parenting: New Economies of Parent-Citizenship. *Studies in the Maternal, 4*(2), 1.

Joseph Rowntree Foundation. (2022). Poverty Report. https://www.jrf.org.uk/report/uk-poverty-2022

Kilkey, M., & Clarke, H. (2010). Disabled Men and Fathering: Opportunities and Constraints. *Community, Work and Family, 13*(2), 127–146.

King, L. (2015). *Family Men: Fatherhood and Masculinity in Britain, C. 1914-1960*. Oxford University Press.

Leisering, L., & Walker, R. (1998). *The Dynamics of Modern Society: Poverty, Policy and Welfare*. Policy Press.

Lister, R. (2005). *Poverty*. Polity Press.

MacDonald, R. (1997). *Youth, the 'Underclass' and Social Exclusion*. Routledge.

Mätzke, M., & Ostner, I. (2010). Introduction: Change and Continuity in Recent Family Policies. *Journal of European Social Policy, 20*(5), 387–398.

McDowell, L. (2017). Youth, Children and Families in Austere Times: Change, Politics and a New Gender Contract. *Area, 49*(3), 311–316.

Millar, J., & Ridge, T. (2009). Relationships of Care: Working Lone Mothers, Their Children and Employment Sustainability. *Journal of Social Policy, 38*(1), 103–121.

Miller, T. (2010). *Making Sense of Fatherhood: Gender, Caring and Work*. Cambridge University Press.

Morgan, D. (1996). *Family Connections: An Introduction to Family Studies*. Polity.

Morgan, D. (2011). Locating Family Practices. *Sociological Research Online, 16*(4), 14.

Morgan, D. (2020). Family Practices in Time and Space. *Gender, Place and Culture, 27*(5), 733–743.

Neale, B. (2000). *Theorising Family, Kinship and Social Change*, Workshop Paper 6 Prepared for Workshop Two: Statistics and Theories for Understanding Social Change. https://www.leeds.ac.uk/cava/papers/wsp6.pdf

Neale, B., & Davies, L. (2015). *Hard to Reach? Re-thinking Support for Young Fathers*, Briefing Paper no. 6. https://followingfathers.leeds.ac.uk/wp-content/uploads/sites/79/2015/10/Brieifing-Paper-6-V7.pdf

Neale, B., & Lau Clayton, C. (2014). Young Parenthood and Cross Generational Relationships: The Perspectives of Young Fathers. In J. Holland & R. Edwards (Eds.), *Understanding Families Over Time*. Palgrave Macmillan.

O'Laughlin, B. (2008). Missing Men? The debate over rural poverty and women-headed households in Southern Africa. *The Journal of Peasant Studies, 25*(2), 1–48.

Parsons, T. (1952). *The Social System*. Routledge.

Patrick, R., Treanor, M., & Wenham, A. (2021). Introduction: Qualitative Longitudinal Research for Social Policy – Where Are We Now? *Social Policy and Society, 20*(4), 622–628.

Pearce, D. (1978). The Feminization of Poverty: Women, Work and Welfare. *Urban and Social Change Review, 11,* 28–36.

Philip, G., Youansamouth, L., Bedston, S., Broadhurst, K., Hu, Y., Clifton, J., & Brandon, M. (2020). "I Had No Hope, I Had No Help at All": Insights from a First Study of Fathers and Recurrent Care Proceedings. *Societies, 10*(4), 89–105.

Poole, E., Speight, S., O'Brien, M., Connolly, S, & Aldrich, M. (2016). Who are Non-Resident Fathers?: A British Socio-Demographic Profile. *Journal of Social Policy, 45*(2), 223–250.

Ridge, T. (2009). *Living with Poverty: A Review of the Literature on Children's and Families' Experiences of Poverty,* Department for Work and Pensions Research Report No 594. http://www.bris.ac.uk/poverty/downloads/keyofficialdocuments/Child%20Poverty%20lit%20review%20DWP.pdf

Ridge, T., & Millar, J. (2008). *Work and Wellbeing Over Time: Lone Mothers and Their Children,* Department for Work and Pensions Research Report No 536.

Roberts, S., & Elliott, K. (2020). Challenging Dominant Representations of Marginalised Boys and Men in Critical Studies on Men and Masculinities. *Boyhood Studies, 13*(2), 87–104.

Roy, K. (2006). Father Stories: A Life Course Examination of Paternal Identity Among Low-income African American Men. *Journal of Family Issues, 27*(1), 31–54.

Roy, K. (2014). Fathering from the Long View: Framing Personal and Social Change Through Life Course Theory. *Journal of Family Theory and Review, 6,* 319–335.

Roy, K., Palkovitz, R., & Waters, D. (2015). Low-income Fathers as Resilient Care-givers. In J. A. Arditti (Ed.), *Family Problems: Stress, Risk, and Resilience* (pp. 83–98). Wiley Blackwell.

Ruxton, S. (2002). *Men, Masculinities and Poverty in the UK.* Oxfam.

Savage, M., Devine, F., Cunningham, N., Taylor, M., Li, Y., Hjellbrekke, J., Le Roux, B., Friedman, S., & Miles, A. (2013). A New Model of Social Class? Findings from the BBC's Great British Class Survey Experiment. *Sociology, 47*(2), 219–250.

Scourfield, J. (2006). The Challenge of Engaging Fathers in the Child Protection Process. *Critical Social Policy, 26*(2), 440–449.

Scourfield, J. B., & Lewinson, E. (2016). Engaging Black Fathers in Child Protection Services. In C. Bernard & P. Harris (Eds.), *Safeguarding Black Children: Good Practice in Child Protection* (pp. 165–176). Jessica Kingsley.

Shildrick, T., MacDonald, R., Webster, C., & Garthwaite, K. (2012). *Poverty and Insecurity: Life in Low Pay, No Pay Britain.* Policy Press.

Shirani, F., Henwood, K., & Coltart, C. (2012). Meeting the Challenges of Intensive Parenting Culture: Gender, Risk Management and the Moral Parent. *Sociology, 46*(1), 25–40.

Skevik, A. (2006). 'Absent Fathers' or 'Reorganized Families'? Variations in Father-child Contact After Parental Break-up in Norway. *The Sociological Review, 54*(1), 114–132.

Smart, C. (2007). *Personal Life*. Polity Press.

Stephens, M., & Leishman, C. M. (2017). Housing and Poverty: A Longitudinal Analysis. *Housing Studies, 32*(8), 1039–1061. https://doi.org/10.1080/02673037.2017.1291913

Strange, J.-M. (2012). Fatherhood, Providing, and attachment in Late Victorian and Edwardian Working-class Families. *The Historical Journal, 55*(4), 1007–1027.

Tarrant, A. (2021). *Fathering and Poverty: Uncovering Men's Participation in Low-Income Family Life*. Policy Press.

Tarrant, A., & Hughes, K. (2019). Qualitative Secondary Analysis: Building Longitudinal Samples to Understand Men's Generational Identities in Low Income Contexts. *Sociology, 53*(3), 538–553.

Tarrant, A., & Neale, B. (forthcoming). *Following Young Fathers: Lived Experiences, Policy Challenges*. Policy Press.

Tyler, I. (2013). The Riots of the Underclass?: Stigmatisation, Mediation and the Government of Poverty and Disadvantage in Neoliberal Britain. *Sociological Research Online, 18*(4), 6.

Ward, M. R. M. (2015). *From Labouring to Learning: Working-Class Masculinities, Education and De-Industrialization*. Basingstoke: Palgrave Macmillan.

Welshman, J. (2006). The Concept of the Unemployable. *The Economic History Review, 59*(3), 578–606.

Williams, F. (1998). Troubled Masculinities in Social Policy Discourses: Fatherhood. In J. Popay, J. Hearn, & J. Edwards (Eds.), *Men, Gender Divisions and Welfare* (pp. 63–100). Routledge.

Williams, F. (2003). *Rethinking Families. Calouste Gulbenkian Foundation*.

Wilson, W. J. (1985). Cycles of Deprivation and the Underclass Debate. *Social Service Review, 59*(4), 541–559.

CHAPTER 3

Qualitative Secondary Analysis: Establishing a theoretical family lifecourse framework

INTRODUCTION

The first two chapters of this book identify a significant gap in existing understandings of men's family participation in low-income contexts (see also Tarrant, 2021). Problematically, existing public, policy, and academic debate serves mainly to absent these men, to argue they are failing their children, and at worst that their absence is provoking a crisis in families. Specifically, we have observed how existing theoretical frameworks either in the sociology, or social policy, of families and those in low-income contexts, struggle to engage with men's family participation from multiple generational positions across the lifecourse. Whilst this literature provides us with the tools and concepts to understand aspects of men's lives in families, or men living through poverty, existing approaches facilitate only a partial explanation of men's experiences of family through circumstances of poverty. This is additionally exacerbated by a persistent tendency to view men from specific generational positions, namely as fathers. Indeed, it was these partial accounts that provoked us to ask the fundamental question underpinning this book: how have men come to be considered as absent from their families? In contrast to the scant evidence on men, our empirical data are replete with accounts of a diverse range of men's family participation across households and families and across the lifecourse. Instead of being absent, our data assert a somewhat more general

K. Hughes, A. Tarrant, *Men, Families, and Poverty*, Palgrave Macmillan Studies in Family and Intimate Life, https://doi.org/10.1007/978-3-031-24922-8_3

incontestable claim: that men are integral to all elements of family life, including in low-income family contexts. However, men's family participation in low income families is, as yet poorly understood and, as we discuss in Chap. 2, existing approaches have the tendency to reinforce assumptions of men's 'absence' or actively 'absent' them through specific, gendered, framings of proscriptive roles of the men and women comprising families in circumstances of poverty.

To redress these omissions, and to produce a theoretically grounded exposition of men's family lives and circumstances, we develop and refine a novel theoretical family lifecourse framework that supports an intergenerational analysis of the longitudinal dynamics of family lives through poverty. This chapter details the methodological strategies involved in this development, as well as a more detailed account of the specific approaches to data analyses we have taken. The empirical chapters of this book, namely Chaps. 4, 5, and 6, build from this methodological innovation and analytic framework, and combined support new conceptualisations of the diversity, dynamics, and particularities of men's family participation across the lifecourse and over time.

To elaborate our analytic approach, we briefly introduce methods of reusing qualitative research data, or as we term this, Qualitative Secondary Analysis. We introduce the methodological innovations of this work, including the family lifecourse framework used to make sense of, and explain, our findings. In describing these, we found it necessary to outline our own histories as researchers as these are so integral to the central approaches we present here.

QUALITATIVE DATA REUSE AND THE POSSIBILITIES OF DATA ARCHIVES

Our collaboration builds out of a longer history that coincided with the establishment of the Timescapes Archive, which marked a time when scholars were only just beginning to embrace the possibilities of methods of qualitative data reuse rather than caution against them (e.g. Mason, 2007; Moore, 2007). A 'data turn', towards qualitative data reuse, was reflective of a broader history of changing resources, technology, analytic interest, and investment in the UK. The Timescapes Archive was not only a part, but also a product, of such advances. It is worthwhile to provide a brief overview of the history of these investments as they articulate the interlayered character of socio-technological change, social sciences interest, and methodological innovation. The work here directly reflects such histories, and addresses the key concerns of these debates.

The digitisation of research data, alongside an increasing imperative to reuse it by major European and UK funding councils stimulated a more concerted and self-conscious engagement with the methodological complexities of reusing data, including those with which researchers have had no prior relationship. An early investment in data resources for the purposes of reuse in the UK was the Qualitative Data Archival Resource (originally named QUALIDATA, and now the UK Data Service), developed to make qualitative data available for reuse at a national scale for the first time (Moore, 2007; Bishop & Kuula-Luumi, 2017). The Economic and Social Research Council (ESRC)[1] also began to require funded researchers to deposit copies of their data into QUALIDATA. These developments followed an ESRC scoping review by Jennifer Mason (2002) which identified existing data resources for the purposes of data sharing and reuse and the potential for capacity building in this area (see also Holland et al., 2006; Mason, 2007).

The establishment of the UKDA also occurred alongside a broader dialogue concerning the methods of Qualitative Longitudinal (QL) research, methods predicated on the need to 'go back' to existing data. Such methods ushered in debates around how existing data might be reused by researchers over time, and repurposed for new research questions and interests. Combined, these developments created the conditions for the development of a new satellite repository of QL data in the UK: the Timescapes Archive.

The Timescapes Archive was produced as part of the *Timescapes: Changing Lives and Times* Qualitative Longitudinal Programme of research (Neale et al., 2012). Both the Archive and the original datasets that began its data holdings represented the largest investment by the ESRC in QL research at that time. The *Timescapes Programme* used a unique model of working wherein the Timescapes 'team' constituted a consortium of researchers and their studies from across the UK. This involved the researchers working both in their own teams, but also across the Timescapes 'team' more generally. This pioneering design was

---

[1] The Economic and Social Research Council is the major funder of social sciences research in the UK.

developed to facilitate an ethical and collaborative approach to 'sharing' in activities across the three main strands of work that comprised the overall programme. These were: first, the carrying out and linking of seven QL studies with shared substantive interests and questions, albeit with different empirical foci and samples, and each building out of earlier, heritage, studies. Second, a programme of QSA involving the sharing of data from the seven empirical studies (Irwin & Winterton, 2011a, 2011b; Irwin et al., 2012). Third, the development of the Timescapes Archive (Neale & Bishop, 2012).[2] The principle of data sharing thus underscored the whole *Timescapes Programme* in terms of design, conduct, and outputs at the time, but also created a legacy for future data reusers, supported the possibilities for new collaborations and methodological innovation both in QL and qualitative data reuse, or QSA research methods. Some of the key features of debates concerning methods of QSA are covered below, to illustrate our contributions and provide a backdrop for the more specific methodological innovations on which the analyses for this book have been based.

METHODS OF QUALITATIVE SECONDARY ANALYSIS

At its simplest, Qualitative Secondary Analysis (hereafter QSA) refers to the reuse of existing qualitative data generated for previous research studies, for new purposes (Bishop & Kuula-Luumi, 2017). Despite improved accessibility of qualitative data, QSA continues to be a contested methodological field where debate often coalesces around epistemological, contextual, practical, and ethical questions (Irwin, 2013). Epistemological questions have concerned contexts of data production, wherein originating teams have inevitably shaped the types and content of data via their theoretical and methodological modes of research engagement. Early debate argued that qualitative research data are distinctive from other data, for example, quantitative data, because they are co-constructed between the researcher and researched (Mauthner et al., 1998; see also Hammersley, 2010). These concerns touch also on the *contextual* embeddedness of those data, and the contexts of the lives of the participants from

---

[2] Although the original *Timescapes Programme* came to an end in 2012, the Timescapes Archive, under Kahryn's Directorship, continues to accrue internationally accessible datasets and now includes resources for teaching and research methods training.

which such data are drawn. Concerns include criticism of the lack of primacy of personal research engagement for data reusers, and subsequent constraints on the possibilities for researchers' contextual understanding (Mauthner et al., 1998). The process of 'getting to grips' with the contextual embeddedness of data also raises questions of *practicality*, such as the need for the researcher to identify, access, and familiarise themselves with large datasets and the samples from which they were drawn, and the consequent impact this has on budgets and time. In other words, given the specificity of qualitative data, how could they be repurposed to answer new research questions, or even to answer similar questions by new researchers in new contexts? The idea that new researchers could simply stroll into an existing dataset and unproblematically reuse it for their own ends was held to express a 'naive realism', wherein the complexities of context, of temporal immanence of human dynamics and engagement were either erased or ignored.

In 2007, in response to these arguments, Jennifer Mason significantly moved debate forwards by advocating a shift beyond questions of whether we *should* reuse qualitative data, to questions of *how* we can. Advancing an 'investigative epistemology', Mason's intervention paved the way for greater innovation and creativity in methods of qualitative data reuse (ibid., 2007, p. 2) including 'energetically and creatively seeking out a range of data sources to answer pressing research questions in quite distinctive ways'. In the same special issue, led by Mason, Moore (2007) also questioned the distinction between primary and secondary analysts, pointing out that for analysis to become 'secondary', data must become 'secondary' too. She argued that to conceive of 'pre-existing data' is to be blind to how data are coproduced in new contexts (ibid.). She proposed instead that (re)using data involves primary analysis of a different order of data (Moore, ibid.; see also Henderson et al., 2006; Hughes et al., 2022). Here, if we indeed accept that data are coproduced, the challenge for QSA researchers is to develop strategies for the comprehensive capture of *how* this occurs (Hughes et al., 2022). This involves researchers reflecting on the 'embedded contexts' of both their own and the previous study (Irwin et al., 2012) to 'make sense' of what those data are and how their 'usefulness' may be understood. Reflexive engagement is required concerning how we may bring differently constituted datasets into analytic conversation and alignment (Irwin, 2013). Thus, recontextualising data/sets involves recasting them as theoretical objects, identifying not only how they were produced, but how they may be repurposed for new questions and research aims (see also Tarrant, 2017; Tarrant & Hughes, 2019a; Hughes & Tarrant, 2020; Hughes et al., 2022).

The QSA strand of the *Timescapes Programme* ushered in a host of methodological innovations in reusing qualitative research data that have continued to proliferate across widening disciplinary fields. While impossible to do justice to the breadth and richness of creativity in developments in QSA, it is worth mentioning notable interventions that demonstrate the huge potential for substantive and theoretical advance, knowledge production, and methodological development. These include bringing new questions to research data; developing new interpretations by analysing existing datasets; gaining new methodological insights by bringing existing studies into analytic conversation; using existing research data to inform the design of new empirical studies; or any combination of these (e.g. Irwin & Winterton, 2011a, b; Tarrant, 2017; Davidson et al., 2018; Jamieson & Lewthwaite, 2019; Edwards et al., 2020; Hughes & Tarrant, 2020; Tarrant & Hughes, 2020; Hughes et al., 2022).

In our own work, we conceptualise QSA as a process wherein researchers seek to *apprehend* data of different orders. This approach treats repositories, resources, and data as offering researchers opportunities for enhanced engagement with questions of *how* we determine whether and how data generated can be used as evidence to inform on the social world (Hughes et al., 2022). QSA involves careful and critical engagement with the 'embedded contexts' both of previous studies and the subsequent contexts of researchers seeking to make sense of existing data and the extent of their usefulness (Hughes & Tarrant, 2020). From this position, temporal and epistemic 'distance' from original study contexts are not inevitable analytic deficits. Instead they offer opportunities for new insights in ways not always available to those researchers proximal to the formative contexts of research. In effect, the language of QSA is one infused with temporal modes of epistemological reflexivity. Indeed, seeing data with a new temporal perspective can enhance understandings of social processes (Duncan, 2012; Hughes et al., 2022).

As noted in Chap. 1, we also describe the methods in this book as a form of data ethnography using methods of QSA and casing (Emmel & Hughes, 2009) from across multiple datasets. The data ethnography we develop involves tracking across two decades of research via the QSA of four datasets (these are (1) *Accessing Socially Excluded People*, (2) *Midlife Grandparents* (3) Following Young Fathers and (4) *Men, Poverty and Care*, see also Chap. 1, Fig. 1.1 for a description of each). This enables us to capture peoples' accounts of the longitudinal histories of place, for the careful building of narrative trajectories about people and place. We situate the interview narratives from these datasets within additional forms of evidence and scholarship to support theoretical engagement in questions concerning the character of social life as it is recounted and described over time. In this respect, we have sought to establish multidirectional analyses to simultaneously trace the trajectories of individuals through families, the longitudinal trajectories of changing family configurations over time, and the interrelationship of these various trajectories through placed-based poverty and disadvantage. Establishing the analytic complementarity of the four datasets has been critical to the epistemological work we have done to appropriately apprehend and synthesise these data.

Establishing Analytic Complementarity

Our connections to the datasets, to our shared programme of research, and to the broader community of researchers—especially those from the *Timescapes Programme*—were instrumental in shaping our ideas of how we might reuse existing data, as well as the substantive questions we have continued to pursue. However, it is important to clarify how the linked character of these datasets *permits* the approaches to QSA we take and have developed. In other words, we need to address questions concerning how working across datasets that were differently constituted, albeit with linked samples in the same localities over an extended period of intermittent fieldwork engagement, and at different time points, allows us to develop analytic trajectories of men's family lives through poverty.

Addressing these questions forms the bedrock of our reflexive engagement to support our claims to new knowledge and clarify how our theoretical advances are both possible and rigorous. We are particularly keen to stress how having multiple, linked studies (see also Irwin & Winterton, 2011a; pp. 4–5) has engendered opportunities to 'scale up' our findings in ways that extend understanding and explanation of social processes (Neale, 2013). Throughout the empirical chapters we discuss the complexities and affordances of bringing multiple datasets from different research teams into 'meaningful analytical conversation' and translating evidence across them (Irwin et al., 2012), and consider whether amalgamating data in the way we do supports cumulative findings (e.g. Fielding, 2004; Irwin,

2013, see also Davidson et al., 2018; Edwards et al., 2020). A key strand of the QSA work for this book, therefore, involves a reflexive process of establishing the complementarity and 'linked' character of the datasets.

The three key areas of overlapping, and distinctive, connection across the four datasets we identified were longitudinal, thematic, and contextual. Firstly, the longitudinal linkages were diverse, in and of themselves, and included shared pragmatic, design based, and thematic characteristics inherent to each of the studies and their datasets and that played out simultaneously across them. In terms of pragmatic connections, several of the studies built directly out of others. Findings from the 'Methods for Accessing Socially Excluded People' study provided an empirically driven intellectual case on which the 'Midlife Grandparents' study was based, for example, and both 'Midlife Grandparents' and the 'Following Young Fathers' study were baseline studies for 'Men, Poverty and Lifetimes of Care'. Through their various connections to each other and the Timescapes Programme, the four studies also shared comparable longitudinal designs.

All used a specific longitudinal methodology in terms of how they engaged with participants. Methods for Accessing Socially Excluded People' used life history interviews, repeat interviews with gatekeepers, and relational mapping techniques, to build understandings of people's lives over time in their locality. 'Following Young Fathers' and 'Midlife Grandparents' both had qualitative longitudinal designs and engaged with participants over multiple waves of interviews, in which family trees and family life histories were produced. Developing both the methods and findings of 'Following Young Fathers' and 'Midlife Grandparents', in the 'Men, Poverty and Lifetimes of Care' study Anna developed an extended longitudinal sample involving engagements both with previous study partners and participants (Tarrant, 2017). The combined data from 'Following Young Fathers' and 'Midlife Grandparents' were used to bring new questions to bear about men's care responsibilities in low-income family contexts on existing data, while also generating new empirical data and questions taken forward with new research participants (Tarrant, 2021). Finally, all four studies had a shared orientation towards time and temporality, either because of their connections to the Timescapes Programme or because of the substantive questions that the studies were interrogating. All Timescapes Programme studies shared questions that privileged the temporal phenomena in people accounts, such as futures, turning points, tipping points, and transitions (Neale, 2015), a framing that meant all studies produced data orientated towards specific temporal subjects (Tarrant & Hughes, 2019a). In our QSA work, we were therefore able to work across multiple layers of time and temporality in the life trajectories of the sampled cases in each of the empirical chapters. We brought each of the datasets into 'meaningful analytic conversation' (Irwin, 2013) via the participants' thematic life history narratives. It was this analytic process that alerted us to the men and the multigenerational positions they hold, aiding us with identifying, recovering, and foregrounding the complexities of men's familial roles and identities, whether expressed by the women or the men in the samples (Tarrant & Hughes, 2019a). By situating the life history accounts of men of different ages and in different intergenerational positions alongside each other, we were also able to build complex and dynamic analyses of low-income family life from a lifecourse perspective.

Secondly, via their longitudinal connections, the four studies also shared several thematic concerns. As we summarise elsewhere (Tarrant & Hughes, 2019a), the extended insights afforded across the studies demonstrated the persistent character of poverty over the lifecourse; how little room there is for change and diversity in low-income circumstances; and how limited the scope is for alternative lifecourse trajectories, albeit with different implications and manifestations for men of different generations (Tarrant & Hughes, 2019a). Robust findings from 'Methods for Accessing Socially Excluded People' demonstrated the importance of support services and legal systems in ameliorating or exacerbating vulnerability in the lives of our samples and this was also apparent in the later studies, albeit for a much broader and extended participant sample.

Thirdly, there were also shared contextual connections across the four studies. The geographical context of each of the studies was especially pertinent. All four studies were conducted in the same UK city. The study sample therefore shared salient socio-economic and geographical factors. This included residing in low-income localities with similar health ward data profiles and research access through gatekeepers working in comparable organisations in these localities (Emmel & Hughes, 2010; Neale et al., 2015). More specifically, participants' socio-economic and geographical contexts were materially similar with regard to life expectancy, high prevalence of teenage births, and high rates of miscarriage and neonatal deaths (Emmel & Hughes, 2010, 2014). Population heterogeneity across the four datasets reflects broader population heterogeneity across the localities in which the participants for each study live. This addresses a key challenge in QSA, namely the question of how far selected cases from extant datasets are expressive of the contexts of their production, or how far they are distinct from them. As noted, via the 'Men, Poverty and Care' study, Anna also took forward relationships with project partners from the three originating studies and was able to access the 'Young Fathers' and 'Midlife Grandparents' participants (Tarrant, 2017).

The QSA involved analytical synthesis not only across the datasets but also the outputs and associated materials from the originating studies and research teams (see also Hughes et al., 2022). Such synthetic modes of analysis facilitate the tracking backwards and forwards in time, across these datasets, and across the broader literature, to develop critical data histories of men's family participation. Foregrounding the analytic opportunities offered through the temporal reach of these combined datasets, provided heightened opportunity for engagement with how data are able to speak of the social world and 'tell about society' (Becker, 2007).

Place as a Case

In moving beyond individualised accounts of poverty, we drew on earlier work to treat the localities themselves as 'cases' across which we could interrogate continuities and change in people's experiences of locality-based hardship. This is critical to shifting our attention to how poverty shapes the places in which people live their lives over time. As part of this we are able to identify trajectories for men through poverty with attention to the consequences of these for their family participation, as well as how locality-driven poverty produces distinctive intergenerational family patterning. We therefore develop place as a case as a key point of analytic alignment across the datasets. In this next data extract, Dianne, wife of Bob whose case was used to open this book, vividly describes the dynamic character and profound change of the place in which she lives and of which she is a part, highlighting processes of deinvestment and policy intervention associated with recession:

Interviewer: And, so, you obviously have a lot of memories and knowledge of [Estate] and?
Dianne: Yeah how it's changed.
Interviewer: Right. How has it changed like?

Dianne: Knocking houses down and rebuilding 'em.
Interviewer: Do you think there is an area, I mean, is it, would you say
               it was different between [the south and north parts] of
               the estate?
Dianne: I don't know why they split it up because it were all one
               rent office..... point, it all dealt round here. But Estate
               North rent office, all' rent offices were all merged into one
               but because they've split it up now, Estate South's rent
               office is just on [Centre] there.
Interviewer: Right.....and back in the days when you were growing up
               on [your] Road
Dianne: There were all the shops up there, there's only one shop
               now and that's the off licence standing, all the rest of them
               have gone.
Interviewer: What on the Centre there were?
Dianne: Ermmm No, [road name], as you come out of our house
               where my nana lived, and then if you went up to the shop
               there wor fish shop, then there were fruit shop up on the
               corner, then there were the bun shop, then there wor.....
               cheap shop where you could get your shopping and all that
               if you didn't want to go on't [road name]. Then there were
               hairdressers and then Post Office, and off licence. There is
               only the off licence what is standing. All the rest of them
               have gone so there's nowt there. So.
Interviewer: Yeah, where, because I know where the community centre
               is, was a school wasn't it?
Dianne: [school name], yeah, that's where I went, yeah.
Interviewer: That's right.
Dianne: Yeah, my school, and then you come up to [area name].
               Infants and middle and then last year, and then go up to do
               this year here. We stayed there until I was sixteen and then
               you left. So..... that's all changed now.
               Bob and Dianne, Accessing Socially Excluded

The original research sites for 'Accessing Socially Excluded' and 'Midlife Grandparents' studies were several low-income urban social housing estates in a city in the north of England (Emmel & Hughes, 2010). The localities of the 'Following Young Fathers' and the Men, Poverty and Care' studies intersected with these and similar estates in the same geographical area. At the time of the research, approximately two-thirds of homes across these estates were rented from the local authority and housing associations, and the majority of those living in these localities are white. The estates were primarily built in the mid-1930s as slum clearance sites. Their purpose was to supply ready labour to nearby manufacturing sites, many of which had closed down by the economic recession of 1980/1981. The remainder closed in the following five years. Over the 20 years covered by the aggregated datasets, these areas have experienced progressively high levels of unemployment and remain in the top 10% of communities receiving some form of additional welfare to redress unemployment according to the Index of Multiple Deprivation. The City Council's calculation of the Jarmen Underprivileged Area Score (UPA8) for the longitudinal experience (1999–2010) of deprivation. The local council data demonstrate there an exceptionally high proportion of households in these areas claim council administered benefits (free school meals, council tax rebate, and housing benefit). According to the City Observatory (2019),[3] of the 17 streets that comprise the ward where our studies took place, 1 street features in the top 1% of the most deprived in the country, 7 streets are in the top 3%, and 12 in the top 5%. All but one street in this ward feature in the top 10% most deprived.

The inequalities and experiences of deprivation recorded have been exacerbated and underscored by policy changes that have adhered to a trajectory of austerity, the rolling back of the welfare state and an increasing emphasis on punitive forms of welfare conditionality (Dwyer et al., 2020). Changes include those of welfare rights, cuts in child benefits, and the introduction of the two-child benefit gap which is estimated to have resulted in 200,000 children moving into poverty (CPAG, 2021).

These families living in social housing estates and neighbourhoods describe the microexchanges across their families and therefore across various localities in which they live, whereby exceptionally modest sums of money become critical to everyday living. We speculate that more recent policy changes, including those such as the shift to a monthly payment schedule to families through Universal Credit (UC), will be productive of the further intensification of hardship, more frequent experiences of chaos, and disruption to everyday life provoked through the lack of the barest necessities, such as food, school necessities such as school uniform, nappies for babies, towels and curtains, bedding for unexpected grandchildren

---

[3] Not referenced to preserve anonymity.

needing either temporary or more permanent residential care. While these may be speculations, they are nevertheless based on descriptions of experiences across all four datasets over the 20-year period in these localities. The consequences of these policy changes have elsewhere been demonstrated to plunge families into a cycle of debt, compounded by further fluctuations in UC as a result of precarious employment, volatile earnings, and the high UC taper rate (63p of every £1 earned in addition to UC) (Garthwaite et al., 2022).

More generally, and tying into our discussion around the civic and interpersonal forms of ordering of these localities, such as through violence, Dianne's account describes the consequences of processes of social disinvestment (Wacquant, 2004) and instances of civic intervention. These include a carving up and shifting of different council wards and their boundaries, which exacerbated the deprivation of resources in the locality, including healthcare centres, shops, and transport. The men who participated in Men, Poverty and Care had observed these processes, identifying how the pharmacy and gambling shop had become the only spaces available to men in the locality (Tarrant, 2021). In this way, civic interventions produced architectures of deprivation (Elias, 1997; Foucault, 1976). Consequently, the dual-fold retreat of industry and the exacerbation of locality-based deprivation created 'estate enclosures', where mobility in and out of these areas was constrained through lack of transport infrastructure. While the wider city experienced a long-term decline in rates of violence, as part of longer social processes, these areas demonstrate the unevenness of a decline in violence (see also Ray, 2018), in response to deindustrialisation (Soja, 2000) as well as the gentrification of selective streets on the outskirts of these areas. While historical scholarship has associated locality-based violence with a breakdown or weakening of 'social solidarity', exemplified by higher rates of 'personal disorganization, mental breakdown, suicide, delinquency, crime, corruption, and disorder' (Wirth, 1938, p. 23), these were often also aligned with a weakening of family and kinship ties and disposable local relations (see Desmond, 2012). Conversely, in our own data, hardship has intensified people's familial interdependencies, involving the sharing of micro resources, time, support, and care across the localities. Even where family estrangement has occurred, this has been gendered, and experienced as a significant loss with potentially catastrophic effects, such as suicide in men and mental illness in women, although not exclusively so. Furthermore, place-based hardship has intensified people's longer-term dependencies on local services, producing experiences of family, and family arrangements, that express these relational entanglements.

The consequences of intergenerational hardship for these families include shorter life expectancy and higher rates of midlife morbidity, manifested through distinctive inter/generational patterning. The families in these low-income localities were not simply closely layered generationally (namely intergenerational spacing, referring to narrow age gaps between grandparents, parents, and child generations) but were generationally interlayered—where the children of the midlife grandparents are growing up alongside their nephews and nieces, who are either of similar ages, or generationally contiguous. These families were also larger in the earlier studies but a shift in birth rate was observable down the generations towards fewer children. Policy changes, therefore, have driven changes in family formation decisions, including size and composition, in ways we have yet to identify. Even though these patterns are expressive of poverty, we lack the requisite theoretical frameworks for understanding how and why these family formations emerge and what the implications of poverty for these family formations have been. To pursue our own questions, we were required to develop a family theoretical framework that explains how these patterns emerge over time and their interconnections between poverty, family patterning, and place.

DEVELOPING A FAMILY LIFECOURSE FRAMEWORK

A lifecourse perspective was necessary to grasp the complexities of families where generational positions, responsibilities, and roles are not necessarily age-differentiated. By this we mean that age-differentiated identities, such as 'parent' or 'grandparent' were less easy to enact separately because they were often intermeshed for research participants. Responsibilities, particularly towards younger relatives, did not always shift either 'up' or 'down' the generational ladder (Settersten, 2003) as participants aged. Instead, people might be parent and grandparent at the same time, perhaps having children at the same time as their oldest child, yet in the same household. Distinctively, too, poverty disrupts peoples' age-differentiated and age-integrated understandings of family, their generational identities in these families, and their shifting intergenerational responsibilities, illustrated in detail across our empirical chapters.

In contrast to the framing and representation in sociological research and social policies of men as absent, the men who are included—either in women's accounts of their family lives, or who speak for themselves in interview—were involved in their families in endlessly different ways. Josie's son, Lewis—a son of one of the women described in Chap. 4—protected her from her abusive ex-partner and acted as a guardian for his younger brother while Josie was in prison. Bob, one of the men whose interviews we draw on for Chap. 5, did deliveries for his elderly sister, provided healthcare and support for his wife, and was an unofficial kinship carer for a grandson. Sheila's sons walked their younger brothers and sisters to school (see Chap. 7) and then later, as their siblings began having children and the extended family grew, they walk their nieces and nephews. These sorts of practices are essential to the doing and sustaining of low-income family life, and reflect the kinds of ordinary and extraordinary practices involved in constructing and managing family and relationships in low-income circumstances (Daly & Kelly, 2015). These are perhaps more usefully conceived of as 'doing kinship'. Comas d'Argemir and Soronellas (2019) suggest that 'doing kinship' involves more than just caregiving. They suggest that when women provide care, as mothers, wives, daughters, and relatives by marriage, they can be seen as simultaneously sustaining families more broadly. By avoiding the 'naturalisation' of kinship (Gupta & Featherstone, 2020; Alber & Thelen, 2021), involved in reducing these to biological relations and biologically driven imperatives, and conceptually separating kinship from care, we can observe in our datasets how men's commitments vary across different family configurations and at different stages of their lifecourse. These observations underscore our commitment to a lifecourse approach, as this supports a more comprehensive engagement in questions of what men do in and for families, across a range of family identities (Milardo, 2010), over time, as uncles, brothers, sons, and so on providing more insightful understandings of family dynamics in the round.

Our analytical framing also underscores an endeavour to shift analytical foci from gendered and binary conceptualisations of breadwinning/caregiving to family participation for either men or women. In response to what we have observed in the datasets, our theoretical family lifecourse approach has been developed to capture the complexity of how men in low-income contexts consider themselves as integral to the everyday lives of families through diverse employment, relationship, or residence circumstances. As noted in Chap. 1, this framework enables explanation of men's efforts to sustain 'biographical careers' (MacDonald et al., 2005) that articulate long histories of distancing from 'poverty' identities (Lister,

2005; see also Shildrick et al., 2010; Shildrick et al., 2012), through narratives of and engagements in 'provisioning' (Neysmith et al., 2010).

Furthermore, as illustrated in Chaps. 5 and 6, it captures the increasing professionalisation in men's approaches to, and language for, formal health and social care services in securing necessary resources *and* family identities, such as foster carer, step-father, and grandparent kinship carer. Our framework is essential to establishing a simultaneous analytic frame of both family and governmental relationships as they interweave over time. In turn, we are able to unpick how the multiple intersections of family, governmental, policy, health and social care, and judicial services shape the ongoing formation and sustaining of these men's work and family relationships and identities, and—to some degree—the 'life-worlds' of poverty in these localities (Erhard, 2020). These processes are constitutive of the 'civic' ordering we elaborate in Chap. 1, whereby professional relationships may be supportive in providing the necessary services and resources for making ends meet on a day-to-day basis, serving to sustain families in hardship over time. However, they are not universally benign, involving as they do uncertainty, threat, and punitive repercussions such as the withholding of benefits or removal of younger relatives from their families. Such relationships with professionals are imbued with multiple normative beliefs which are variously passed on, enforced, and enacted through family relationships, serving to support some family arrangements and connections, while (sometimes simultaneously) severing or rendering impossible others (see Chaps. 5 and 6).

There is a more general point here worth considering, relating to qualitative research approaches more broadly, which clarifies the need for a theoretical framework that provides for the relational analysis work we undertake here. Strategies such as qualitative interviewing, for example, may encourage an overwhelming theoretical orientation towards questions of intentional agency and rational action accruing to the individual, rather than the emergence of social processes consisting of the unintentional interlacing of peoples' (rather than *a single* person's) intentions and actions. Indeed, qualitative research almost inevitably requires us to focus on individuals because the intention is usually to develop detailed explanations of why people behave in the ways they do that give rise to, or express, broader social patterns. However, this tends to individualise participants in ways that atomise them from their broader social contexts, even when engaged in understanding the particularities of such 'contexts'.

Unintentionally, we may treat people *as* individuals by foregrounding questions of identity, selfhood, agency, and so forth, and in doing so, erase the multiple, social, relational character of social-ness. This has been a challenge in our own analyses where we have observed that working from one specific generational position obscures broader family experiences in the round, as well as the diversity of men's (and women's) participation in and across families (see also Emmel & Hughes, 2014). Simultaneously, to engage with family forms more generally (see also Edwards et al., 2012; McCarthy, 2012) without engaging with the individuals that comprise them, is equally analytically limiting, because this ignores how families are produced through a complex of shifting multigenerational relationships where people hold multigenerational identities (see also Mare, 2014).

More broadly, we develop and use this theoretical framework to interrogate both *the experience of family life*, that is, the complex and dynamic positioning of individuals within families, their transitions in and through different family configurations and generational positions and their interdependencies over time, and *the lives of families*, that is, the shifting, complex of longitudinal trajectories of family networks shaped through, and shaping, peoples' involvements, transitions, and trajectories (see also Chap. 1). In relation to the use of interview data, we develop a view of interview encounters as at once social arenas with their own emergent dynamics and affordances, and, simultaneously, as nexuses of relationships which extend across space and time considerably beyond the immediate contexts of data production (Fink & Lomax, 2016; Tarrant & Hughes, 2019b; Hughes et al., 2022). In relation to the specific substantive and theoretical challenges of our intellectual endeavour, we advance a new family lifecourse framework which facilitates simultaneous analytic engagement with the intersecting longer-term processes of the lives of family members, their family relational nexuses, and the localities in and through which people live, and described more fully below. Accordingly, we use methods of QSA to interrogate features of participants' research involvement, and to consider how these are structured by particular relational dynamics, but not reducible to such. We therefore explore how participants actively engage in interviews in articulating their own interests (Thapar-Björkert & Henry, 2004; Karnieli-Miller et al., 2009; Rodríguez-Dorans, 2018), to understand how their lives, and those of the others they describe, may be shaped through, and reflective of, broader relational contexts and processes (Tarrant & Hughes, 2019b; Hughes et al., 2022).

To return, then, to the three key questions underpinning this book:

1. How and why men have come to be described, and treated, as 'absent' from their families?
2. How do enduring and intergenerational experiences of poverty shape and constrain men's intra- and intergenerational family participation across the lifecourse and in place? How might we observe these?
3. How and in which ways are the interactions of policy and place implicated in men's trajectories through poverty and what are the consequences for their family participation?

In formulating our analyses in response to these questions, and in dialogue with existing literature and the datasets, we established the following temporally driven orientations, constitutive of our family lifecourse framework: *Multigenerational, Intergenerational, Intragenerational,* and *Lifecourse*. The analytic foci and purpose of each of these main components are described in more detail in Table 3.1, including an explanation of the kind of analyses each facilitates.

Each are temporal categories variously foregrounding certain dimensions of family dynamics and engagement with specific viewpoints, either for families or the individuals within them. As researchers the framework also supports us to engage with empirical accounts in particular ways, for example casing within studies and across datasets (Emmel & Hughes, 2009; Tarrant & Hughes, 2020) to critically interrogate the complex dynamics of various modes of relating across families without reifying individuals within a family, nor the experiences they describe. In other words, this framework supports a constant multiperspective and multidirectional approach that is vital to a longitudinal understanding of the complex processes of how poverty shapes family lives.

CONCLUSION

In this chapter, we elaborate the novel longitudinal research process noted in Chap. 1, that underscores our data ethnography, that has both prompted and underscored the development of a new family lifecourse framework for developing a nuanced, fine-grained sociological explanation of how the longitudinal dynamics of poverty shape family lives over time. While developed using existing qualitative data, we anticipate that the theoretical framework will nevertheless support theorisation of the dynamics of

Table 3.1 A theoretical family lifecourse framework

Analytic foci	Purpose	Facilitates
Multigenerational identities	Empirical engagement with the range of generational identities different participants in the research may hold.	Temporal analysis of the shifting processes through which people transition through different generational identities, how and whether these accrue particular meanings, responsibilities, constraints; How different generational positions produce conflict or tension or individuals, or for how families may themselves.
Intergenerational	Interchanges and connections between generations (e.g. father/child; grandparent/ grandchild)	Analysis of how in familial contexts, people may describe themselves from particular generational positions, the normative they ascribe to these. Also, families, themselves, are treated through policy and legislation as comprised of different generations, each ascribed particular sets of intergenerational responsibilities to those in other generational positions. Distinctive processes of intergenerational exchange and responsibility are normative but also enshrined in law and policy (e.g. inheritance tax, parental duty, payments such as spousal support).
Intragenerational	A cohort perspective, across a generation whether familial or historical, a locality, a family, across households	A methodological strategy of casing across particular contexts. How and whether people invoke notions of collective age groups, what's meaningful to them about the broader lateral relationships through which they live their lives May facilitate locality-based analyses
Lifecourse	A dynamic and processual shift of generational identities, families over time.	An empirical capture of families and change over time.

longitudinal family poverty for ongoing research endeavors. Our work constitutes a sustained eight-year programme where we have refined ideas in conversation with each other (and with our colleagues), with several earlier datasets, with literature (which has also developed hugely in that time), and with new phases of fieldwork that share numerous connections with the earlier datasets. This long-term analytical project has involved both the reformulation of our analytical foci and sustained methodological innovation, particularly in Qualitative Secondary Analysis (see also Hughes & Tarrant, 2020). In developing our analyses prior to, and in the writing of, this book, these innovations continue. For example, our work here has involved an extended period of methodological consideration of how and in which ways we might be able to recover men's experiences of family, not just from the perspectives of men but also through the accounts of women and other family members across the datasets on which we draw. The scholarship in this book is therefore built on a foundation of careful, creative, and long-term reflexive engagement with existing sources to refine new substantive, methodological, and theoretical advances that continue to have contemporary relevance and are capable of speaking to contemporary debates and concerns.

Throughout the empirical chapters of this book we recover a place-based view of men in their families that seeks to engage with family life-courses, where families are produced and sustained through members who always hold multigenerational identities and positions. Specifically, we establish an intergenerational, multigenerational approach that also accommodates diversity and change across the lifecourse and enables analytic engagement with how and why men are included, or indeed, absented in research and in broader considerations of family life. This approach enables us to engage thematically across the lifecourse of families to observe where men are absent or present, and how and for whom they become so.

References

Alber, E., & Thelen, T. (2021). *Politics and Kinship: A Reader.* Taylor & Francis Ltd.

Becker, H. (2007). *Telling About Society.* University of Chicago Press.

Bishop, L., & Kuula-Luumi, A. (2017). Revisiting Qualitative Data Reuse: A Decade On. *Sage Open, 7*(1), 2158244016685136.

Comas-d'Argemir, D., & Soronellas, M. (2019). Men as Carers in Long-Term Caring: Doing Gender and Doing Kinship. *Journal of Family Issues, 40*(3), 315–339.

CPAG. (2021). *200,000 More Children Pushed into Poverty the Year Before the Pandemic - Dismal Data Warning.* https://cpag.org.uk/news-blogs/news-listings/200000-more-children-pushed-poverty-year-pandemic-dismal-data-warning

Daly, M., & Kelly, G. (2015). *Families and Poverty: Everyday Life on a Low-Income.* Policy Press.

Davidson, E., Edwards, R., Jamieson, J., & Weller, S. (2018). Big Data, Qualitative Style: A Breadth-and-Depth Method for Working with Large Amounts of Secondary Qualitative Data. *Quality & Quantity, 53,* 363–376.

Desmond, M. (2012). Disposable Ties and the Urban Poor. *American Journal of Sociology, 117*(5), 1295–1335.

Duncan, S. (2012). Using Elderly Data Theoretically: Personal Life in 1949/1950 and Individualisation Theory. *International Journal of Social Research Methodology, 15*(4), 311–319.

Dwyer, P., Scullion, L., Jones, K., McNeill, J., & Stewart, A. B. R. (2020). Work, Welfare, and Wellbeing: The Impacts of Welfare Conditionality on People with Mental Health Impairments in the UK. *Social Policy & Administration, 54*(2), 0144–5596. https://doi.org/10.1111/spol.12560

Edwards, R., Davidson, E., Jamieson, L., & Weller, S. (2020). Theory and the Breadth-and-Depth Method of Analysing Large Amounts of Qualitative Data. *Quality and Quantity, 55,* 1275–1280.

Edwards, R., McCarthy, J., & Gillies, V. (2012). The Politics of Concepts: Family and Its (Putative) Replacements. *The British Journal of Sociology, 63*(4), 730–746.

Elias, N. (1997). Informalization and the Civilizing Process. In J. Goudsblom & S. Mennell (Eds.), *The Norbert Elias Reader.* Blackwell.

Emmel, N., & Hughes, K. (2010). 'Recession, It's All the Same to Us Son': The Longitudinal Experience (1999-2010) of Deprivation. *Twenty-First Century Society, 5*(2), 171–181.

Emmel, N., & Hughes, K. (2014). Vulnerability, Intergenerational Exchange and the Conscience of Generations. In R. Edwards & J. Holland (Eds.), *Understanding Families Over Time: Research and Policy.* Palgrave Macmillan.

Emmel, N., & Hughes, K. (2009). Small-N Access Cases to Refine Theories of Social Exclusion and Access to Socially Excluded Individuals and Groups. In D. Byrne & C. Ragin (Eds.), *The SAGE Handbook of Case-Centered Methods.* SAGE.

Erhard, F. (2020). The Struggle to Provide: How Poverty Is Experienced in the Context of Family Care. *Journal of Poverty and Social Justice, 28*(1), 119–134.

Fielding, N. (2004). The Shared Fate of Two Innovations in Qualitative Methodology: The Relationship of Qualitative Software and Secondary Analysis of Archived Qualitative Data. *FORUM: Qualitative Social Research, 1*(3), Art. 22.

Fink, J., & Lomax, H. (2016). Sharing Images, Spoiling Meanings? Class, Gender, and Ethics in Visual Research with Girls. *Girlhood Studies: An Interdisciplinary Journal, 3,* 20–36.

Foucault, M. (1976). *Discipline and Punish.* Allen Lane.

Garthwaite, K., Patrick, R., Power, M., Tarrant, A., & Warnock, R. (2022). *Covid Collaborations: Researching Poverty and Low-Income Family Life During the Pandemic.* Policy Press.

Gupta, A., & Featherstone, B. (2020). On Hope, Loss, Anger, and the Spaces in Between: Reflections on Living with/in Adoption and the Role of the Social Worker. *Child & Family Social Work., 25,* 165–172. https://doi. org/10.1111/cfs.12674

Hammersley, M. (2010). Can We Re-Use Qualitative Data via Secondary Analysis? Notes on Some Terminological and Substantive Issues. *Sociological Research Online, 15*(1), 5.

Henderson, S., Holland, J., McGrellis, S., Sharpe, S., & Thomson, R. (2006). *Inventing Adulthoods: A Biographical Approach to Youth Transitions.* Sage.

Holland, J., Thomson, R., & Henderson, S. (2006). *Qualitative Longitudinal Research: A Discussion Paper,* London Southbank University. Retrieved May 20, 2019, from www.researchgate.net/publication/242763174_Qualitative_ Longitudinal_Research_A_Discussion_Paper

Hughes, K., & Tarrant, A. (2020). *Qualitative Secondary Analysis.* London: Sage.

Hughes, K., Hughes, J., & Tarrant, A. (2022). Working at a Remove: Continuous, Collective, and Configurative Approaches to Qualitative Secondary Analysis. *Quality & Quantity, 56,* 375–394.

Irwin, S. (2013). Qualitative Secondary Data Analysis: Ethics, Epistemology and Context. *Progress in Development Studies, 13*(4), 295–306.

Irwin, S., Bornat, J., & Winterton, M. (2012). Timescapes Secondary Analysis: Comparison, Context and Working Across Data Sets. *Qualitative Research, 12*(1), 66–80.

Irwin, S., & Winterton, M. (2011a). *Debates in Qualitative Secondary Analysis: Critical Reflections,* Timescapes Working Paper No. 4. http://www.times-capes.leeds.ac.uk/assets/files/WP4-March-2011.pdf

Irwin, S., & Winterton, M. (2011b). *Qualitative Secondary Analysis: A Guide to Practice,* Timescapes Working Paper, Guide 19. chrome-extension://efaidn-bmnnnibpcajpcglclefindmkaj/https://timescapes-archive.leeds.ac.uk/wp-content/uploads/sites/47/2020/07/timescapes-irwin-secondary-analysis.pdf

Jamieson, L., & Lewthwaite, S. (2019). *Big Qual – Why We Should Be Thinking Big About Qualitative Data for Research, Teaching and Policy.* https://blogs. lse.ac.uk/impactofsocialsciences/2019/03/04/big-qual-why-we-should-be-thinking-big-about-qualitative-data-for-research-teaching-and-policy/

Karnieli-Miller, O., Strier, R., & Pessach, L. (2009). Power Relations in Qualitative Research. *Qualitative Health Research, 19*(2), 279–289.

Lister, R. (2005). *Poverty.* Polity Press.

MacDonald, R., Shildrick, T., Webster, C., & Simpson, D. (2005). Growing Up in Poor Neighbourhoods. *Sociology, 39*(5), 873–891.

Mare, R. D. (2014). Multigenerational Aspects of Social Stratification: Issues for Further Research. *Researching Social Stratification and Mobility., 1*(35), 121–128. https://doi.org/10.1016/j.rssm.2014.01.004. PMID: 24748709; PMCID: PMC3987910.

Mason, J. (2002). *Qualitative Researching*. Sage.

Mason, J. (2007). 'Re-Using' Qualitative Data: On the Merits of an Investigative Epistemology. *Sociological Research Online, 12*(3). https://doi.org/10.5153/sro.1507

Mauthner, N. S., Parry, O., & Beckett-Milburn, K. (1998). The Data Are Out There, or Are They?: Implications for Archiving and Revisiting Qualitative Data. *Sociology, 32*(4), 733–745.

McCarthy, R. (2012). The Powerful Relational Language of 'Family': Togetherness, Belonging and Personhood. *The Sociological Review, 60*(1), 68–90.

Milardo, R. M. (2010). *The Forgotten Kin: Aunts and Uncles*. Cambridge University Press.

Moore, N. (2007). (Re)-using Qualitative data? *Sociological Research Online, 12*(3), 1–13.

Neale, B. (2013). Adding Time into the Mix: Stakeholder Ethics in Qualitative Longitudinal Research. *Methodological Innovations Online, 8*(2), 6–20.

Neale, B. (2015). Time and the Lifecourse: Perspectives from Qualitative Longitudinal Research. In N. Worth & I. Hardill (Eds.), *Researching the Lifecourse*. Bristol: Policy Press.

Neale, B., & Bishop, L. (2012). The Timescapes Archive: A Stakeholder Approach to Archiving Qualitative Longitudinal Data. *Qualitative Research, 12*(1), 53–65.

Neale, B., Henwood, K., & Holland, J. (2012). Researching Lives Through Time: An Introduction to the Timescapes Approach. *Qualitative Research, 12*(1), 4–15.

Neale, B., Lau Clayton, C., Davies, L., & Ladlow, L. (2015). Researching the Lives of Young Fathers: The Following Young Fathers Study and Dataset, Briefing Paper no. 8. https://followingfathers.leeds.ac.uk/wp-content/uploads/sites/79/2015/10/Researching-the-Lives-of-Young-Fathers-updated-Oct-22.pdf

Neysmith, S. M., Reitsma-Street, M., Baker-Collins, S., Porter, E., & Tam, S. (2010). Provisioning Responsibilities: How Relationships Shape the Work That Women Do. *Canadian Review of Sociology, 47*(2), 149–170.

Ray, L. (2018). *Violence and Society* (2nd ed.). SAGE.

Rodríguez-Dorans, E. (2018). Reflexivity and Ethical Research Practice While Interviewing on Sexual Topics. *International Journal of Social Research Methodology, 21*(6), 747–760.

Settersten, R. (Ed.). (2003). *Invitation to the Life Course: Towards New Understandings of Later Life*. Baywood Publishing.

Shildrick, T., MacDonald, R., Webster, C., & Garthwaite, K. (2010). *The Low-Pay, No-Pay Cycle: Understanding Recurrent Poverty*. Joseph Rowntree Foundation.

Shildrick, T., MacDonald, R., Webster, C., & Garthwaite, K. (2012). *Poverty and Insecurity: Life in Low Pay, No Pay Britain*. Policy Press.

Soja, E. W. (2000). *Postmetropolis: Critical Studies of Cities and Regions*. Blackwell.

Tarrant, A. (2017). Getting Out of the Swamp? Methodological Reflections on Using Qualitative Secondary Analysis to Develop Research Design. *International Journal of Social Research Methodology, 20*(6), 599–611.

Tarrant, A. (2021). *Fathering and Poverty: Uncovering Men's Participation in Low-Income Family Life.* Policy Press.

Tarrant, A., & Hughes, K. (2019a). Qualitative Secondary Analysis: Building Longitudinal Samples to Understand Men's Generational Identities in Low Income Contexts. *Sociology, 53*(3), 538–553.

Tarrant, A., & Hughes, K. (2019b). The Ethics of Technology Choice: Photovoice Methodology with Men Living in Low-Income Contexts. *Sociological Research Online, 25*(2), 289–306. https://doi.org/10.1177/1360780419878714

Tarrant, A., & Hughes, K. (2020). Collective Qualitative Secondary Analysis and Data-Sharing: Strategies, Insights and Challenges. In K. Hughes & A. Tarrant (Eds.), *Qualitative Secondary Analysis* (pp. 101–118). Sage, London.

Thapar-Björkert, S., & Henry, M. (2004). Reassessing the Research Relationship: Location, Position and Power in Fieldwork Accounts. *International Journal of Social Research Methodology, 7*(5), 363–381. https://doi.org/10.1080/1364557092000045294

Wacquant, L. (2004). Decivilizing and Demonizing: The Weakening of the Black American Ghetto. In S. Loyal & S. Quilley (Eds.), *The Sociology of Norbert Elias* (pp. 95–121). Cambridge University Press.

Wirth, L. (1938). Urbanism as a Way of Life. *The American Journal of Sociology, 44*(1), 1–24.

CHAPTER 4

Women's Accounts of Men in Low-income Families

Introduction

In the first of our four empirical chapters, we present accounts of men in poverty through the voices and perspectives of women. These accounts illustrate both how men are anything but absent from their families, and how poverty shapes the possibilities and limits for family with different implications for men and women. A broad literature establishes how poverty is gendered both in its prevalence (Dermott & Pantazis, 2014; Women's Budget Group, 2018) and effects across a range of dimensions including the lifecourse (see for example, Lister, 2005; Gillies, 2006; Bastos et al., 2009; Bennett & Daly, 2014; Daly & Kelly, 2015). In terms of prevalence, women's relationships to paid work, welfare, and family responsibilities combine to render them both statistically more vulnerable to be living in poverty than men, as well as more likely to be in single parent households in hardship. Women's experiences of deprivation manifest in multiple ways (see also Bastos et al., 2009). Limitations in choices of living locations—for example because of dependency on cross-family support, care, and resourcing—mean that women's access to family support may be compromised, which was certainly apparent across our four datasets (Women's Budget Group Report, 2018, p. 7). Job opportunities for women and educational choices for their children are constrained in circumstances of hardship. Combined, these serve to trap them in violent or

K. Hughes, A. Tarrant, *Men, Families, and Poverty*, Palgrave Macmillan Studies in Family and Intimate Life, https://doi.org/10.1007/978-3-031-24922-8_4

abusive relationships. Women spend longer periods in poverty than men (Bastos et al., 2009; Bennett & Daly, 2014) and face distinctive challenges concerning their physical vulnerability to violence, their health, and mental wellbeing (Golin et al., 2016). Simultaneously, economic changes disproportionately affect working-class men, including older men, such that their position is a consequence of the same series of economic restructuring that have driven disaffected young men to the streets (McDowell, 2000). Attention to the implications of this for men's family dynamics and relationships is much less developed in the literature.

Through these analyses, we provide additional insight into these gendered trends of poverty by engaging at the level of 'family'. We foreground accounts of men by women to provide context to, and interrogate, the formation of interior logics of poverty expressed by women when describing the work involved in strategising, managing, navigating, and ameliorating hardship over time (Lister, 2005; Ridge, 2009; Hughes and Emmel, 2012; Shildrick et al., 2012). We also interrogate how managing, or enduring, the additional risks to personal safety, health, and wellbeing poverty is often associated with women *in family contexts*. In doing so, we contribute to existing evidence and debate by describing, albeit only partially, specific risks associated with sustaining families that women are more likely to experience. The findings in this chapter identify such dangers, particularly through violent relationships with partners and husbands. We use the women's broader narratives to recover the often overlooked or partially understood forms of family participation by men from multiple generational standpoints. Additionally, this chapter provides the bases for later discussions, such as those in Chap. 7, concerning the distinctive dangers associated with being excluded from families disproportionately experienced by men.

In this chapter, we focus on four cases from just one of our linked datasets, the Midlife Grandparents study. This dataset consists of repeat interviews, collected over a period of four years, with women about family life in low-income contexts. We use these cases both to demonstrate the key methodological advances described in Chap. 3, and through these, how we were able to build new empirical insights. To do so, we first illustrate how we 'retrieved', 'recovered', and interpreted accounts of men's participation in low-income families from the perspectives of women. Second, we show how this analytic attention enables us to demonstrate a more complex picture of the longitudinal and multigenerational character of men's family participation. In drawing on the women's accounts, this chapter variously reflects and troubles the traditional mode of reporting on family and family poverty. As Chap. 2 illustrates, this is predominantly through theoretical, policy or empirical foci empirically rooted in women's experiences of both (Chant, 2006; Ridge, 2009). However, a key departure in our methodological approach is the foregrounding of women's accounts of male relatives to trouble a sometimes simplistic reading of men as 'absent' from their families and households, to ask the following sub-questions:

1. Are men 'absent' in women's accounts of the longitudinal dynamics of family lives through low-income circumstances?
2. If so, which men and when are they 'absent' and 'present'?
3. How might men be rendered as 'absent' through an empirical focus on women's accounts?
4. Which men are we able to 'see' through women's narratives?

It is important to note here that we approach these questions with caution, in order not to deny or discount women's perspectives of a lived reality. What we observe is that, while women themselves may also develop discourses of men's 'absence' in their narratives about their partners and husbands, their interviews are nevertheless replete with accounts of different forms of men's family participation both in their presents, and in their family histories (see also Harman, 2001). Such participation constitutes the sustaining of family, even if women do not ascribe this character to what it is that men do in and for families. It is worth noting that researchers rarely follow up questions of women about the men they mention, beyond children and partners, so in Qualitative Secondary Analysis (QSA) we are always observing partial accounts. The 'Midlife Grandparents' study data is distinctive in that its substantive focus on following the lives of families in poverty facilitated detailed attention to the longitudinal trajectories, such as through employment, education, parenting, and other family situations, of a diverse range of family members, including men.

In paying analytic attention to the myriad ways men feature in women's accounts, we thus become able to redress hitherto somewhat partial empirical descriptions of the broader range of men in these families. Thematically structured around men's generational positions, we move from a focus on partnering relationships, to intergenerational roles of fathers and sons, and then to the broader family relationships including those with/as uncles, brothers, and so on (see also Milardo, 2005, 2010). Capturing the diversity of these diverse familial roles men may simultaneously hold prevents us developing a categorical over-emphasis on men as partners and fathers. All too often, accounts of men in these roles depend on reductive binary narratives in which men are cast as 'present' or 'absent' (e.g. Tarrant, 2021), risk or resource (Featherstone, 2009), 'good' or 'bad' (Bailey, 2010), 'angels' or 'demons'. Instead, our analytic approach underscores and facilitates a sociological account of the contexts and processes that shape men's family participation in low-income contexts, as well as the possibilities for, and constraints of, relationships between family members (see particularly Chaps. 6 and 7).

A Brief Overview of the Cases

The cases we predominantly focus on in this chapter are with four women: Sheila, Carolyn, Josie, and Susan. Below are brief overviews of each, taken from pen portraits developed at the time the study was conducted. These portraits are elaborated to provide context to the analyses presented in the chapter:

Sheila: At the time of the Midlife Grandparents study, Sheila is aged **43** years old, has 8 children, and 18 grandchildren. She is living in social housing, with her two eldest sons, and is unemployed. One of the rooms in her home downstairs has been adapted with the addition of a walk-in shower due to a series of health conditions. Sheila has been forcibly moved from her previous home, also council-owned, when the street she lived on was demolished. Sheila's ex-partner, and father of her children, Ben was abusive to her until her twin sons were adult enough to force him out of the home. Ben dies on his mother's sofa during the course of the study, at the age of 46 from alcohol-related illness and after this, Sheila says that she does not want to speak ill of the dead. Sheila is extensively involved with her children and grandchildren, but describes her life in her locality as highly constrained, with few friends and few opportunities and little inclination to move beyond her home. Sheila was one of the least resourced women of these four but, because of her centrality in her family, and her disinclination to leave her home, arranging interviews with her was reasonably straightforward, and she was reliably available on the agreed dates. Her interviews contain conversations with various adult children as they arrive and leave during the recording. In the fourth-round interview, her third eldest son talked for over half an hour about his own relationship with his partner, their child, and his partner's pregnancy.

Carolyn: Carolyn was **39** years old when first interviewed for the Midlife Grandparents study. Her current partner Victor is in his early forties, and they met when he was working as a taxi driver and he would transport Carolyn and her children to and from school. Carolyn's ex-partner Paul lived a separate life of pubs, friends, and criminal activity and they had separate finances even when they lived together. This had potential consequences for the welfare payments to which she was entitled. For example, Carolyn had to work to support the family whilst at the same time raising four children, and not declare that Paul was living with them because he would not provide. Carolyn also spent a period of time living in a hostel, while pregnant with her first daughter, which she explains is because Paul was violent and not providing financially. She has four children from her first marriage, and Victor has one son who lives with his mother but visits regularly. They have one grandchild, aged two years old through Carolyn's eldest daughter from Carolyn's first marriage. Generally, they also have two foster children living with them. At the point of the first interview, they were providing Carolyn's second eldest daughter with extensive support after several life crises, including relationship breakup, loss of housing, and the death of a child. They are also acting in an informal capacity as kinship carers providing care for their grandson. Carolyn and Victor presented a very stable relationship and expressed a high degree of confidence in their capacity to care, evidenced by their roles as foster parents. Victor was present during Carolyn's interviews and contributed to them.

Josie: Josie is **42** years old when she is first interviewed. She has four children and three grandchildren and has been living with a new partner for three years after a lengthy period in a relationship with a very violent and controlling man. Much of her interview focuses on her experiences of rebuilding her life after this relationship as well as the personal history beforehand that led her into it which include family neglect, abuse, and bullying at school. She also spent a period in care, and described her social worker as a strong mother figure. Josie ended up in prison having been prosecuted for an armed robbery her former partner perpetrated. Being in prison was hard for her because her kids were vulnerable to her partner and indeed suffered a great deal, but she was able while inside to secure a divorce, seek counselling and begin to rebuild her life. Prison was in many ways a positive experience for her. She is now fully disconnected from her former partner although she knows he only lives nearby and has degenerated into further drug and alcohol use. Josie was the least resourced of these four women and was the most difficult to interview because of the chaotic nature of her life meaning that booking an interview more than one or two days in advance was unfeasible. This meant that the study only secured two interviews with Josie. Josie's eldest daughter, Naomi, was present in her interviews and contributed to them. We also found this useful as a means of distinguishing in our reporting between the presents they described, and their past histories. **Susan** is **46** years old, living in social housing, with three adult children and six grandchildren, and is divorced from her abusive ex-husband. At the beginning of the 'Midlife Grandparents' study, Susan had residential care of four of her five grandchildren from her daughter, Nicky. During the course of the study, her daughter Nicky died, the fifth child moved in with Susan and Susan withdrew from the study. This meant Susan was only interviewed for three of the four rounds of data collection in the Midlife Grandparents study. Susan had extremely high levels of health and social care involvement in her family life. This is because the various grandchildren in her care were each assigned a different social worker, resulting in a total of five social workers for one family. Susan had a well-resourced upbringing, was emotionally close to her parents and grandparents, and is the most financially resourced of these four women. Susan's interviews are extensive and describe extended family networks. Ethan, Susan's eldest son, makes only occasional comments in her first interview, but nothing sufficient to support our analyses here.

In reporting on these cases throughout the chapter, although we are drawing on historical data, we retain the present tense used by the women in their interviews, as it reflects the presents they were describing. We also found this useful as a means of distinguishing in our reporting between the presents they described, and their past histories. Through the use of changing tenses, we have been better able to articulate the temporality, particularly the longitudinal dynamics, of the relationships and family circumstances the women described.

PARTNERS AND EX-PARTNERS: DISRUPTING 'ANGELS' AND 'DEMONS' NARRATIVES

We begin with a focus on how women discuss the fathers of their children in their narratives, who they describe predominantly as either their ex- and/or current partners. Where academic literature and policy focus tend to emphasise men's absence as fathers, framing them as 'bad dads', by implication, they are also considered absent from the household and from partner relationships. Non-resident fatherhood and separation and repartnering work against a broader policy commitment to nuclear family and dual earner structures, underscored and reinforced through current UK social care and welfare provision.

In our QSA, we engaged with the longitudinal narratives comprising the cases of these women, which we describe as 'emblematic' cases (Hughes & Tarrant, 2020). These were produced across the various waves of interviews and included detailed life and family histories, described in Chap. 3. The women's personal circumstances also represent a broad continuum of family poverty, as well as a diversity of family networks in terms of intergenerational connectedness and size. These cases were developed and used to gain insight into the more complex emotional trajectories of women's various partner relationships. Through building and interrogating these cases, we observed a diversity of men's participation from a broad range of generational positions, such as sons, fathers, uncles, brothers, as a central feature of family life, that were considerably more varied than could be captured in discourses of 'bad' men, husbands, and dads.

Partner relationships were far from unproblematic. The original Midlife Grandparents team identified common patterns of partnering in sometimes disrupted or challenging family relationships in the early life trajectories of these women. In our QSA we looked at these afresh to consider the distinctive character of men's participation in these. For Sheila, Josie, and Carolyn, all of whom described more troubled family backgrounds, the men were a little older than the women when they met. In all three relationships, the couples moved in together in their mid- to late teens, with the men's relatives (Sheila, Josie), quickly began having children, and then gained their own social housing. Over time, the men became increasingly violent, controlling, and inconsistent in their relationships. In the cases of Sheila and Carolyn, this was linked to second or third pregnancies, unemployment, mental illness and/or addictions. Josie's partner was violent, abusive, and controlling from the outset.

Sheila, aged 43 at the time of this interview, provides a succinct summary of this partner relationship/family trajectory below:

> I met Ben, and I think it was within what, four weeks, five weeks I'd moved in with his mum and dad. I think I moved with him to get away from home basically. But we did have a really good relationship at first. I mean when the twins came along it was great. Er, but then I fell pregnant with [eldest daughter] and I don't think he could cope...he started drinking a lot when

I first, erm, he was drinking when I had the twins, but he started drinking more when I fell on again[1] with [second daughter/fourth child]. Ben did what he wanted, when he wanted. You know? And I can't explain, I can't, 'cause to me he missed out on a hell of a lot of the kids. I mean, with the way he was, he missed them growing up. He missed a lot of their lives but now he's trying to get back into their lives and the kids aren't particularly bothered about it. *Sheila, Midlife Grandparents Study, Round 2 interviews*

Sheila's case includes a detailed account of the changing dynamics of her partner relationship. Sheila's childhood had been continuously disrupted; she describes attending 13 different schools in different low-income localities of the city, was in and out of care, and she and her half siblings (one of whom she took for medical attention on several occasions) experienced abuse at the hands of her step-mother. When her own mother died, her grandparents withdrew, they lost contact with Sheila and her siblings, and there was no further support from them. She had no older relatives to turn to. She met Ben when she was 16 and he was 19 and they moved out together to live with his parents. Ben offered her an escape from caring for younger siblings, the possibility of a stable relationship in which she would be cared for, and the prospect of a future life together.

When she fell pregnant, Sheila and Ben were allocated social housing. Sheila said about this housing that it was her first stable home and one from which she refused to move until it was demolished by the local council. Had Sheila been interviewed after the birth of her first children, Ben would have figured as her saviour, the father of her children, the enabler of her having a family. However, as the children keep coming, Ben's employment becomes increasingly precarious. The clothing industries that have provided work and incomes to the residents of the purpose-built estate disappear. Ben withdraws, begins to drink, and becomes violent and absent. Within this one narrative, Ben is thus saviour and abuser, the man with whom Sheila has eight children and creates a family, but also somebody who reduces her 'to a mouse', and ultimately figures as an absent father and an abusive husband. Sheila concludes:

I was thinking the other day when our [granddaughter] was born, she was born on what would have been mine and Ben's 30th anniversary. We'd have been together 30 years on the [date], and I thought, "30 years. If I'd killed

---

[1] A colloquialism meaning to become pregnant.

him when I met him, I'd been out now." You know?[2] *Sheila, Midlife Grandparents Study, Round One Interview*

Carolyn's case articulates a similar narrative of her previous abusive relationship, but at the time of interview she is in a new relationship with somebody who has a 'saviour' role in rescuing her and her children. While Sheila's case describes the same man as saviour and abuser, Carolyn's begins to articulate how, over different relationships, women might move from one to the other.

At the time of Carolyn's first interview, she is living with Victor, a man with whom she has formed a new relationship having left an abusive and neglectful relationship with the father of her four children. Carolyn met her ex-partner through a friend and later discovered that he had been in jail for Grievous Bodily Harm (GBH). She explains that he lived a separate life of pubs and friends and lived more like a lodger than a partner. When he stopped working, for example, he secured a flat somewhere else so that he could get a jobseeker's allowance, and began dealing in illegal substances such as cannabis, speed, and coke. He is described as both violent and unsupportive (financially and emotionally). She says he was both a 'crap' partner and dad, defining his absence both in terms of their marital relationship and his relationships with his children:

> He was just crap. He was a crap dad, he was a crap partner, he was just, he was really….he just needed a bedsit with somebody else to pay the bills. That was it. And, I mean, he even admitted it himself, he wan't cut out to be a dad, and he really wasn't… *Carolyn, Midlife Grandparents Study, Round One*

In detailing the longitudinal dynamics of their changing partner relationships, the women situate these changes within complex housing journeys, different family settings and compositions, and poor/low/un/employment trajectories for working age family members shaped by the economic fortunes of the wider locality (Emmel & Hughes, 2010).

However, analysing the men's trajectories as described in these accounts, we can observe similarities in how the ex-partners, as younger men, struggle to cope through circumstances of precarious employment, while at the same time experiencing intensifying emotional and financial responsibilities for increasing numbers of children. Here, Carolyn describes Paul's

---

[2] Ben's family trajectory is discussed in more detail in Chap. 7.

trajectory which characterises these processes whilst at the same time illustrating how these, and associated violent behaviours, contribute towards the increasing presence of low-income women and children in safe hostels (e.g. Maycock et al., 2012):

Carolyn: Yeah. I went to live in a hostel for a while, erm, I was still seeing him, I were pregnant with Lucy at the time. Erm, because he'd got in with a bad lot, and wasn't working as much as he should have been, he wasn't doing anything, basically. And he got into drugs and stuff, and he was in a band, and basically, he was, like, doing his own thing and I was just bringing up…

Interviewer: Bringing up three kids?

Carolyn: Yeah. Er, so I had [younger daughters, and we got a house on a local road in social housing], and then he… He was just, sort of, in and out of the relationship, basically, then, erm, I had [youngest son] in 1992… and, I was still working part time, he wasn't working at all now, although he was still there. But he had a flat somewhere else, but he never lived there, he just had a flat somewhere else so that he could get, erm, jobseekers allowance and things like that. So he had his own money still, but he was spending it all on drugs and quite a lot of money that came to the house, my money, for the kids and stuff, he was, like, using, on drugs and stuff. So I still had to have a part time job, I had various jobs in pubs and chip shops and things like that.

               Carolyn and Victor, Midlife Grandparents, Round One

Paul's trajectory, as described by Carolyn, is a counterexample to a lot of men across the datasets, whose cases we elaborate in Chap. 7 and combine with further observations from Victor about what it means to be a good father and step-father in low-income localities. With young men, we see them become increasingly involved with drugs, as users and dealers, develop addictions and begin to sofa surf when they are expelled from families. They consequently enter increasingly precarious phases of their lives during which they are vulnerable to violence from other men, or punitive involvements with surveillance and regulating agencies such as the police, and court systems. With older men, such as Sheila's partner, Ben, they may be expelled from the family later in life in response to their violence towards their children and/or partner. As a counterexample Paul has settled and stable housing, separate from his partner and children, with a secure income, albeit an allowance. Paul's case introduces us to key themes taken up later around the importance of men's relationships to people across the locality and how these intersect with family relationships. While for the commonality of younger men the consequence of leaving families is to render them increasingly vulnerable, in this relationship, it is Carolyn and her children who become increasingly precarious, because they have to move into hostels to escape Paul's violence and unpredictability.

Where men's violence, abuse, and absence lead to relationship break-down, which is not always inevitable, these men emerge in women's accounts as figures of contempt and disdain in their families more generally, often isolated from their families, or experiencing reluctant or infrequent contact with adult children (see Stack, 1974, see also Chap. 7). When ex-partners leave the family home, these departures are fraught, often involving contestation around financial support for their children (see Chap. 5), or repeated returns where men are threatening or violent (see Josie's case below).

It is at this point that we step back from an overfocus on men and moralities, as either 'good' or 'bad' partners/husbands/fathers, and focus instead on the broader contexts of hardship through which these relationships and families evolve. We suggest that, in considering men's behaviours and family dispositions in the context of poverty scholarship, rather than solely with an eye to either the sociology or social policy of the family and fathers, it is possible to contextualise the men's behaviours in relation to multiple forms, or expressions, of deprivation. This includes their low pay, un- or underemployment (e.g. Shildrick et al., 2012) traditionally analysed in existing research as their failure to fulfil a breadwinner role and thus a 'good' father identity (e.g. Liebow, 1967; Nelson, 2004; Tarrant, 2021); increased involvement in drug and alcohol misuse and dependency (e.g. Staley, 1992; Wacquant, 1995; Crutchfield & Wadsworth, 2003; Manhica et al., 2021); crime (e.g. Newman & Peeples Massengill, 2006; Wikström & Treiber, 2016); and high rates of repartnering (e.g. Corlyon et al., 2009).

While scholars identify demonstrable statistical correlations between, say, crime and poverty, or substance misuse and poverty, such as those mentioned above, the authors of such studies take pains to illustrate how the directional character of the relationships is not clear. We would make the same point. Our observations introduce the possibility of observing men's family participation as pertaining to something more than solely a lack of moral character, so often the key explanatory framework in public and policy arenas (Dorey, 2010; Jensen, 2018; Tarrant, 2021). Particularly in the context of the four cases we are using for this chapter, we remain mindful and cautious in drawing links between, say, domestic violence and unemployment, or domestic violence, multiple children, and poverty, and have no intention to imply causality in these (see also Harding, 2009; Newman & Peeples Massengill, 2006; Dobash & Dobash, 2004). Instead, our aim is to provide a contextualised and nuanced account of longitudinal experiences of poverty, without either retreating to a singular moral explanation, obscuring or condoning domestic violence, or dismissing gendered power asymmetries and inequalities.

Additionally, our approach seeks to highlight how partner/spouse relationships such as those described by the women above often feature in family poverty research to support descriptions and explanations of men's absence. However, we suggest that this may be a result of a perhaps inadvertent taken-for-granted assumption that men as fathers/partners *are* absent consequent on researchers' endeavours to elucidate otherwise invisible experiences of women who describe them as such. This focus additionally serves to obscure the broader gendered processes that shape men's trajectories in and through low-income family contexts, the multiple ways that men may be present, and the situations, and relationships, from which men are absent or actively absented (see Chap. 7). Thus, as we argue in Chap. 2, men are doubly marginalised by public and policy accounts, and in research based on an empirical snapshot, at a single time point, from a single person's perspective (e.g. women as wives, mothers, grandmothers).

In illustration of the need to resist or trouble simplistic explanations of casual relationships between poverty and violence, or solely ascribe to circumstances of poverty an explanation that has its roots in a critique of the moral character of people, and their behaviours, we present Susan's case. Similar to Sheila, Carolyn, and Josie, Susan married young, lived for one and a half years with her in-laws, and describes experiences of violence by her mother-in-law. Here, Susan explains her ex-husband's absence both from their relationship and her children's lives as a father, and that she was able to decide to leave that relationship:

> I would say that it was difficult in the beginning, because obviously mixed race marriage all that time ago was, you know, wasn't acceptable.... But I

really did try. I was determined that it was gonna work. But, erm, it didn't, sadly. Erm, but the type of person that I am, I felt that, and despite our relationship, [ex-husband] still needed a relationship with his children, albeit wasn't, he wasn't as forthcoming as we would have liked him to be. It was, it was quite difficult really. Sadly he had a lot of affairs. And he only ever turned up when the children did anything good. *Susan, Midlife Grandparents Study, Round One*

Susan's decision to leave her marriage sits in contrast to the experiences of the other three women. Sheila's relationship with Ben ended when her oldest sons were physically strong enough to expel him from the house (see also Chap. 7). Carolyn was effectively constrained to remain in her abusive relationship by family and friends, until 'rescued' by Victor. Josie, whom we discuss later in this chapter, was only able to secure a divorce from her abusive husband from prison, and after having received counselling which supported her to develop a language to describe her 'self'. Carolyn and Josie additionally experience neighbourhood systems of surveillance, involving friends and relatives (see also Klein, 2012).

These surveillance systems contribute to highly constrained opportunities for movement for women (e.g. where the women are allowed to work, how far away the workplace is, how they travel to their place of work, where they go more generally in their locality, and who they see or speak to). In these three cases, the women required the support of others to leave or escape the relationship, but also to *decide* to leave. Susan, who still lives with the physical and emotional scars of the violence she endured, similarly required support to leave her violent relationship. However, while the interviews of the other three women are saturated with discourses of powerlessness, constraint, and endurance, Susan's interviews articulate discourses of identity and choice, wherein she expresses a degree of authority over her own decision-making, and legitimacy in her decision to leave. Distinctively, Susan's broader interview account articulates her involvement in a broad set of family relationships beyond those of her husband's family, which are well-resourced emotionally and financially. Susan's father, in particular, helped her to move out of her marital home when she decided to leave with her children, carried furniture, hired a removal van, and organised her move. He also supported her financially and pragmatically in setting up her new home. This support from Susan's father exemplifies invisible forms of family participation by men we observe in empirical research but are rarely pursued in analyses as distinct subjects of inquiry.

MAKING A CASE FOR MULTIGENERATIONAL PERSPECTIVES: DADS AND SONS

To explore these and other obscured forms of family participation by men, we use a multigenerational approach in the next section to consider the varied modes of support men provide in the doing and sustaining of families as fathers and sons, including where they may hold both identities simultaneously. To begin this analytic recovery of the longitudinal dynamics of men's family participation through circumstances of poverty, we elaborate an extended analysis of Josie, focusing on the parallels her case provides for other cases in the Midlife Grandparents study. Literature typically focuses on the father-son relationship, the intergenerational transmission of parenting and behaviours across the lifecourse and/or men as role models (e.g. Hofferth et al., 2012; Bjørnholt, 2014; Brannen, 2015), but rarely focuses on how men hold simultaneous familial generational standpoints. Here, Josie's case is emblematic because, through her explanations of the processes through which she escapes her abusive ex-partner, her son Lewis takes on a particularly significant role.

Josie was 42 years old when first interviewed, and like Sheila, begins by describing a childhood where she was estranged from her main parent (in Josie's case, her mother) when she repartnered. She repeatedly moved in and out of care and left home at age 14, had a child at 15, and moved in with her partner, Phil's, older sister until she and Phil were able to secure stable housing. Phil was violent from the outset, but became increasingly violent both to herself and her children, to the extent that in her mid-forties, like Susan, she still experiences kidney problems from beatings. Josie's narrative focuses predominantly on her time in prison after getting mixed up in a robbery perpetrated by her violent husband. The two most valuable sources of support provided through her prison experience were counselling and practical legal advice which enabled her to secure a divorce while there.

Unlike Susan, Josie was unable to leave Phil, despite having escaped to women's refuges on a number of occasions. However, Josie explains how the counselling she received enabled her to develop new ways of thinking about herself, to the extent that she gained a new sense of self, and belief in her right to independence, which challenged her former sense of guilt and responsibility for having been beaten by her husband. We observe here that professional counselling intervention for Josie, and legal support from prison, was productive of a reordering (ending) of her marriage, her dependency on Phil and therefore of her children's family. Indeed, Josie described this counselling as emancipatory, giving her a new language to talk about and analyse her feelings, to develop explanations about her life and how it was turning out, as well as explanations about her daughter's relationships and circumstances. Furthermore, Josie said the counselling, through her, gave her children new forms of emotional resilience and freedom from the belief that being beaten was either deserved or inevitable:

Josie: ...got my independence... 'Cause I went, I was in [name of jail], which was a closed jail, for like 15 months. I did an 8-week course of thinking skills, confidence building. Once I got that I went to open [prison]. Then I was allowed home. So I came home to my son's who only lived up the road at the time, for weekends. And then I got day releases so I could come home to the children. And then I ended up going out to work from the prison, so I had money when I came home. But through that there was so much. Because they, he couldn't get at me, he was doing it to the kids. I mean [Naomi, middle daughter], she went down to 5 and a half stone. Went in, at 16 ended up going into, erm, a hostel for battered wives at 16. And that's when my mam took her. And that's when me and my mam sort of got together. Cos at the end of the day she took my daughter. *Josie, Midlife Grandparents Study, Round One*

In contrast to Susan's identity and choice narrative, above, about how and when or even whether she could leave her violent partner, Josie describes how prison was the *only* place where she received the support she needed, both emotional and legal, to leave him. Prison also removed her from her children. During her time in prison, Josie's children bore the brunt of their father's brutality, and so for Josie, keeping the family together was no longer a form of protection for her or for them. The emphasis, then, became one of getting her children away from their father. Without Josie in the picture, daughter Naomi's experience with her own dad became one of intergenerational violence also requiring legal intervention:

I mean my daughter Naomi, she's had three injunctions out with him.
Three times he's broke' it. Three times he's gone to prison for breaking it.
Josie, Midlife Grandparents Study, Round One

At this juncture, the period through which Phil's violence towards Josie is
transferred to Naomi, his daughter, we observe the limits of family for managing and regulating violence. Naomi draws on two forms of support in
order either to distance herself from her father or distance him from her.
First, like other women, including Carolyn above, Naomi sought to distance
herself by removing to a hostel for victims of domestic violence. However,
this is only a temporary solution for a young woman trying to sustain friendship and family relationships. Over time, Naomi is required to rely on legal
interventions, injunctions, to remove Phil from her physical sphere, and
inhibit his persistent attempts at abuse. Prison becomes the key mode of
'civic' reordering in this family, but with different effects. For Josie, in prison,
it is protective, supportive and empowering, yet renders her family vulnerable
to Phil's violence. For Phil, it is constraining and separating, but empowering, supportive and protective for his children, especially for Naomi.

In seeking to disrupt the intergenerational transmission of violence, Josie
identifies three key areas of activity: first, managing long-term emotional/
psychological effects for the targets of violence, second, managing attitudinal
orientations for those who have witnessed/experienced violence and rework-
ing or disrupting any accommodation of violence in their own intimate partnerships, and third, managing the perpetrator of violence. In discussing how
these various dimensions may be managed, Josie's account exemplifies the
complex blend of formal and informal involvements and regulatory interventions involved in these various activities. The first intervention is that of counselling, and as we mention above, Josie describes how she 'passes on' her
learning from the counselling she has had. The second is dealt with within
the family, through mutually supportive means. The third returns us to the
court system, where injunctions are used, and the prison system for the forc-
ible removal of perpetrators of violence. Josie's narrative continually expresses
a desire to 'live normally', and for her this is primarily violence free. For this
to happen, the violent men in her family's life need to be forcibly removed.

Interviewer: So Naomi's relationship has caused you some concern with
                regard to [1st child].
Josie: Yeah, yeah, and [2nd child], yeah, and I still, and I think…
                I mean, me and [Josie's current partner] talked about it. I
                do keep a really close eye on her 'cause if it… I love Naomi

to bits, do you know what I mean, and I'm not saying she's a bad mum, cos she's not, but sometimes I feel I need to do more, or if I... Just, if that carries on, then I'm gonna just take 'em out of the house. I have come... (overlapping)

Interviewer: So you would, you would be willing to take them away if things got too (inaudible). (overlapping)

Josie: Yeah, definitely. Oh, definitely, yeah.

Interviewer: So would you feel happier if Naomi was in, not in that relationship?

Josie: Yeah, definitely.

Interviewer: You think she would be coping better if she didn't have...

Josie: Yeah, because when Greg [Natalie's partner] has been in prison, she's been much happier, much contented, she's got on with everything, the kids seem better, plus having more money for herself as well. But just much bouncier person than she is now. I mean, he does pull her down. He does pull her down.

Interviewer: Yes, so in a sense, is she in a similar situation to what you were in ten years ago? (overlapping)

Josie: Yeah, yeah.

Interviewer: I think that's about right, isn't it.

Josie: Yeah, yeah. Definitely, and that's what I say cos I can see that her relationship, what I was in, I mean it wasn't as bad, but I'm not saying it, it might get worse, mighten it. You just don't know, and I can see how it's pulling her down. I mean, "Oh, I'm depressed, I'm depressed," and crying all the time, and that's what I was, but like I said to Naomi, "You need to get out of it because it still haunts, it'll still haunt you." I mean it still haunts me. I mean I see a psychiatrist. I have support workers now because of it, because I can't get on with life normally because of all the stuff I went through.

Interviewer: Yeah. So I guess that makes it doubly hard for you, doesn't it, having been there yourself?

Josie: Yeah. Yeah, I mean, that's what I say to the... I say it to her about [Naomi's two young children], because my children remember it, and still they talk about it. So obviously it's still affecting 'em. Do you know what I mean, and that's what it's gonna do to [Naomi's two children].

Josie, Midlife Grandparents, Round Two

Josie reflects here on what she perceives as the inevitability of violence as part of the intergenerational transmission of poverty trajectories. We examine the consequences of men's removal from families for men in more detail in Chap. 7. Here however, we see how as well as accounting for intergenerational processes of violence inherent in longitudinal processes of hardship, Josie's narrative of Naomi's biography details when men are far too present, when and how service intervention is essential for ensuring men's absence from women's lives, and consequently the limits of family for managing violence.

Beyond the support she received in prison, two key people were integral to Josie's success in leaving her marriage and supporting her children during her forced absence. The first was her mother, their grandmother, who 'stepped in', and rescued Naomi from her father. Josie's relationship with her mother had always been ambivalent, but these actions produced a moderate reconciliation between them, which continued through the three-year period of research contact. The second person, and of relevance to our analyses, was Josie's oldest son, Lewis, who was essential in 'keeping the family together'. In this excerpt, Josie discusses the joint care she and Lewis took of Rory, her youngest son:

> Rory was under the hospital 'cause he had bowel trouble. He had asthma, but he [ex-husband] had 'em sleeping in a tent with no blankets so they could go rob shops, to bring it back to sell it on. Do you know what I mean? I mean, I ended up going through court for custody of Rory while I was in jail. So, me and Lewis got custody of him. So, he went to live at Lewis's. But obviously Lewis couldn't do too much without my consent 'til I came back out. And then I got full custody of Rory when I come back out. *Josie, Midlife Grandparents Study, Round One*

In effect, Lewis became a kinship carer in his mother's absence, a position occupied by men in families that rarely receives empirical attention (although see Tarrant, 2021; see also Chap. 7), yet is often a role that exacerbates, and is reflective of, circumstances of poverty. As Roy et al. (2014) observe, young and teenage boys in economically disadvantaged households may experience a process of adultification that involves providing critical caregiving and financial support for members of their families and playing a kinkeeper role. Lewis's support of his mother and siblings continues beyond the period his mother is in prison. When Josie left prison, she move into Lewis's accommodation, rented with his girlfriend, and was supported by her son until she secured social housing of her own.[3] Lewis, who became a father himself at age 17, is therefore critical to Josie's survival post-prison, providing emotional and financial support. For a period of time, he was also a *de facto* coparent with Josie, responsible for his younger siblings. Josie and her children remain vulnerable to violence from Phil, against whom Lewis is often called upon to act as protector on behalf of both his sister and his mother:

> He [Phil] phoned Lewis, … and Lewis turned round and said, "Dad, I don't wanna know. It's your problem." And then he [Phil] sort of took offence then. So really he knows not to sort of confront me. Which I feel safe now, in that we, that I know somebody will sort of… *Josie, Midlife Grandparents Study, Round One*

As mentioned, Josie is the most vulnerable and marginalised of the four women selected for this chapter and the multiple deprivations and difficulties she experiences, a violent partner, a lack of wider family, intense poverty, chronic illness in her children, combined intensify her and her children's experiences of hardship. To be a young dad at 17, responsible for the protection of his siblings and his mother, is an especially distinctive situation for Lewis. Nevertheless, we observe parallels between this and other cases in young men's trajectories, not only in the Midlife Grandparents study, but also from the perspectives of young fathers in the Following Young Fathers study (Neale et al., 2015). For example, as we mention above, Sheila gains independence from Ben only when her eldest sons can physically intervene on her behalf, in effect when they become collectively stronger than their father. Although Lewis's responsibilities are considerable and distinctive, Josie's case is nevertheless significant in aiding analytic interrogation of the multi- and intergenerational character of men's family participation. We see Lewis sustaining his family not just as a son but also as a brother and, as the next section illustrates, as an uncle, in his longitudinal involvement and contribution to the broader nexus of family relationships of which he is so demonstrably a part.

---

[3] See Edin and Lein (1997), for further discussion on how women 'make ends meet' through informal supplementary financial support from 'absent' fathers but also other men in their families.

Uncles, Brothers, and Other Relatives

Our attention to men as partners, ex-partners, dads, and sons in women's accounts introduces us to the multifaceted character of men's family participation in low-income contexts. This includes attention to men in familiar generational and familial positions in which that researchers have traditionally explored them, but also provides insight into the broader complex familial interdependencies and dynamics that characterise the longer family histories of these women (see also Milardo, 2005). In our attention to accounts of both intra- and intergenerational family relations, we also begin to recover a multimodal view of men's family participation in their everyday lives across the lifecourse including as brothers, uncles, grandfathers, and so on.

Returning to Lewis, Josie's eldest son, we get a partial yet crucial insight into how he participates in family in myriad ways as a teenage father, a brother, a son, and latterly an uncle. By the second interview, his protective role in the family is reconfirmed. Josie and Naomi's relationship has become more troubled, and Josie argues that Naomi needs to take more responsibility for her children. Josie suggests that Naomi has been using her son, Josie's grandson, as a weapon in this mother/daughter relationship. Here, Josie describes how Lewis extends his protection towards his nephew:

> At that time, to me it felt like she were just using [grandson] as a weapon because if we'd argued, 'cause she used to go into town a lot and in the bus station, and drink with her mates, and take [grandson] with her, and he was only a baby. I mean, our Lewis once was going out, and he was going to a nightclub, and he didn't go out while half past nine. He got off the bus at the market, seen Naomi, and he ended up taking ... [his nephew] from her and taking him home, and never went out, because she was in town. She wanted to be with her mates. *Josie, Midlife Grandparents Study, Round Two*

We reserve further analysis of Lewis's role here to avoid an over-romanticisation and individualisation of his practices in ways which replicate or even amplify the 'saviour' narrative that Josie associates with him. This is not to obscure Lewis's contributions to the family, which are critical in supporting his younger siblings during Josie's time in prison and continue to be vital to Josie in managing Phil, Lewis's father. Yet Lewis is critical for our analyses in two different ways. First, in holding off his father from the family, and intervening in his sister's parenting of her young child, Lewis is actively involved in shaping family arrangements, connections, and disconnections. In effect, his interventions serve to reorder his broader family relationships. Second, and relatedly, Lewis's case emblematises how men sustain families over time, to the extent that such ordering is not just temporary but must be observed longitudinally. This has implications for our language of family participation, whereby participation is not reducible to presence in households and relationships and/or single acts or individual sets of actions. Instead, it refers to much longer, multiple, sustained, and engaged endeavours in and on behalf of families, which Roy et al. (2014) conceptualise as kinkeeping.

Furthermore, Josie's narrative about Lewis was crucially important in that it prompted us to explore whether these kinds of family participation by women's sons could be observed more broadly across the cases, and in this way we became analytically attuned to numerous accounts of sons behaving in ways that are vital for securing and sustaining families. Susan, for example, similarly describes her eldest son, Ethan over the course of her interviews as increasingly taking on caring roles towards his nephews and nieces, Nicky's children, to support Susan. He also intervenes between Susan and Nicky in fraught situations, addressing his sister's violent behaviour towards her mother, again to protect Susan. Sheila, discussed again in Chap. 7, is protected from her partner, Ben, by her eldest sons, who are instrumental in gatekeeping Ben's access to the residential family home when Sheila has finally 'kicked him out'.

Moving from seeing Lewis and Ethan as *sons*, to seeing them both as *uncles*, through intragenerational comparison, we also became alerted to the women's brothers in the cases we discuss in this chapter, acting intergenerationally as uncles in important ways. Sheila and Susan detail how their brothers intervene in the lives of their children and families. Sheila described a period during which her brother Michael lived with her, Ben and the children. As an uncle, Michael contributed food, to support her children alongside Ben.

Sheila: Well Michael lived with me then. Erm, four-bedroom house, my eight kids, Ben, me brother Michael. Erm, but, er, yeah, Michael lived with me then and what Michael would do was go out and do some shopping and bring it back to feed the kids.
          Sheila, Midlife Grandparents Study, Round One

Susan also describes her brother, in his role as an uncle, when he encourages his niece to go to school when the grandparents are unwell and unable to enforce this:

Susan: Nicky stayed with Mum and Dad for a while. And she refused to go to school. And they lived in a bungalow, and Dad was, by this time, on oxygen, quite a poorly man. Erm, and so, and Nicky was 15. Erm, and they couldn't cope. And my brother went along and said, "Look, you, you know, you're either gonna have to tow the line, go to school, and I will take you every morning. Or you can't stay here with your grandma and granddad, because you're making your granddad, you know, really ill with all of this."

            Susan, Midlife Grandparents Study, Round One

The analyses we present here begin to elucidate broader, more complex family arrangements and involvements, highlighting where and when men's family participation becomes instrumental in supporting and sustaining families and the women within them. The women develop narratives of 'good' and 'bad' men, where these might refer to the same man but at different points in the lifecourse of a family or a partnership history. These examples demonstrate the broader gamut of intergenerational activities in which men become engaged, and that can be described as different forms of caregiving and the 'doing of kinship' (Comas d'Argemir & Soronellas, 2019) that constitute their family participation. These cases therefore both illustrate and support the importance of multigenerational perspectives in understanding men's family participation longitudinally. Additionally, in the accounts presented in this chapter we also begin to see the complex intersection of broader health and social care contexts, needs and deprivations experienced by families living through circumstances of poverty (Rauh et al., 2008). Other examples include Lewis's parental custody of his younger siblings, Victor's cofostering of children with Carolyn, Naomi's injunctions against her abusive father. These experiences gesture towards a much broader landscape of formal services involvement and intervention shaping family relationships in particular ways. We explore this in more detail in Chap. 6.

Finally, the analytic framework outlined in Chap. 3 not only focuses on multigenerational identities at given time points, but also seeks to capture the longitudinal dynamics of families and the diverse character of intergenerational ties and responsibilities of men that comprise family configurations. In the next chapter, therefore, we focus specifically on men's accounts of their own family participation across the lifecourse. We include cases from men whose life stages mirror those of the women in this chapter, living in similar localities, thus sharing distinctive experiences of place-based poverty.

CONCLUSION

In this chapter, using a multigenerational approach, we analyse how men appear in women's accounts of low-income family life. The life history cases of the women analysed for this chapter, describe a myriad of forms and instances of men's participation in the context of often ruptured and discontinuous intergenerational family networks in which parent and grandparent generations are lost. Intergenerational ruptures, parents repartnering with people who do not take on parental roles towards existing children, moving in and out of care settings when young, all combine to produce difficult family situations from which the women consider they have been 'rescued' by their partner. In turn, the marital/partnership trajectories of the four women we discuss include violence, abuse, separation, and divorce. Essentially, what we observe are longitudinal patterns in which women are rescued from the very men that they have been rescued by. In these and other often difficult family situations, the women recount the involvement of other men, whose family participation emerges as a crucial component in the provision and securing of opportunities and resources, including the services the women require to leave violent partners.

Feminist perspectives, both in history and sociology, have understandably focused predominantly on what Strange (2012) calls the 'dark side' of breadwinning and its repressive effects for children and women, thus privileging women's accounts as wives and mothers. Our analyses are somewhat different in that while we remain able to consider how women describe their partners as failed providers and fathers, our analytic focus also extends to and includes men's lives in broader family contexts, and from a range of generational positions. Extending our analyses in this way, therefore, begins to afford analytical insight into a core question of this book, namely what might be the broader contextual longitudinal dynamics shaping men's family participation through poverty.

However, a second question for this book is, what are the distinctive challenges of persistent poverty for the possibilities of family participation for men? It is here that the limitations of drawing solely on women's accounts, which include the fragmentary and partial recalling of men in interviews orientated towards women's own experiences, become significant for our analytic purposes. The men recalled are framed through women's own relationships with them (e.g. abused wives, mothers, sisters, grandmothers, and so on) and so the men that emerge through these narratives, and which we take as our analytical foci, must be understood to be framed in distinctive ways. Because of these limitations, although our analyses here have supported an argument for a more interrogative approach towards investigating men's family participation, alongside a more critical stance on the 'absenting' of such men both through empirical and policy foci, we are unable so far to lay claims to any insights into men's own perceptions of their experiences of family.

Our discussions build on a long history of social sciences research which has sought to develop intellectual agendas through engaging with people and interrogating how they reframed the concerns and questions of sociology, such as in the seminal work on women by Ann Oakley. The next two chapters consider how men reframe the concerns of the sociology of the family and the sociology of poverty, where neither themes are lost or excluded. In this way, we seek to rewrite particular accounts *from men* into sociological debates and priorities that consider men, but perhaps not in the ways men consider themselves. To do so, we turn to interviews with the men themselves.

REFERENCES

Bailey, J. (2010). 'A Very Sensible Man': Imagining Fatherhood in England c. 1750–1830. *History, 95*(319), 267–292.

Bastos, A., Casaca, S. F., Nunes, F., & Pereirinha, J. (2009). Women and Poverty: A Gender-Sensitive Approach. *The Journal of Socio-Economics, 38*(5), 764–778.

Bennett, F., & Daly, M. (2014). *Poverty Through a Gender Lens: Evidence and Policy Review on Gender and Poverty.* Joseph Rowntree Foundation Report.

Bjørnholt, M. (2014). Changing Men, Changing Times – Fathers and Sons from an Experimental Gender Equality Study. *The Sociological Review, 62*(2), 295–315.

Brannen, J. (2015). Fathers and Sons: Generations, Families and Migration. Basingstoke: Palgrave Macmillan.

Chant, S. (2006). Re-thinking the "Feminization of Poverty" in Relation to Aggregate Gender Indices. *Journal of Human Development, 7*(2), 201–220.

Comas-d'Argemir, D., & Soronellas, M. (2019). Men as Carers in Long-Term Caring: Doing Gender and Doing Kinship. *Journal of Family Issues,* 40(3), 315–339.

Corlyon, J., Gieve, M., Stock, L., & Sandamas, C. (2009). *Separated Families: How Mainstream Services Support Disadvantaged Children & Their Non-Resident Parents.* Tavistock Institute of Human Relations for Fatherhood Institute & Big Lottery Fund.

Crutchfield, R. D., & Wadsworth, T. (2003). Poverty and Violence. In W. Heitmeyer & J. Hagan (Eds.), *International Handbook of Violence Research.* Springer.

Daly, M., & Kelly, G. (2015). *Families and Poverty: Everyday Life on a Low-Income.* Policy Press.

Dermott, E., & Pantazis, C. (2014). Gender and Poverty in Britain: Changes and Continuities Between 1999 and 2012. *Journal of Poverty and Social Justice,* 22(3), 253–269.

Dobash, R. P., & Dobash, R. E. (2004). Women's Violence to Men in Intimate Relationships: Working on a Puzzle. *The British Journal of Criminology, 44*(3), 324–349. https://doi.org/10.1093/bjc/azh026

Dorey, P. (2010). A Poverty of Imagination: Blaming the Poor for Inequality. *The Political Quarterly, 81*(3), 333–343.

Edin, K., & Lein, L. (1997). Work, Welfare, and Single Mothers' Economic Survival Strategies. *American Sociological Review, 62*(2), 253–266.

Emmel, N., & Hughes, K. (2010). 'Recession, It's All the Same to Us Son': The Longitudinal Experience (1999-2010) of Deprivation. *Twenty-First Century Society, 5*(2), 171–181.

Featherstone, B. (2009). *Contemporary Fathering: Theory, Policy and Practice.* Policy Press.

Gillies, V. (2006). Working Class Mothers and School Life: Exploring the Role of Emotional Capital. *Gender and Education, 18*(3), 281–293.

Golin, C. E., Haley, D. F., Wang, J., Hughes, J. P., Kuo, I., Justman, J., Adimona, A. A., Soto-Torres, L., O'Leary, A., & Hodder, S. (2016). Post-traumatic Stress Disorder Symptoms and Mental Health over Time Among Low-Income Women Are Increased Risk of HIV in the US. *Journal of Health Care Poor Underserved, 27*(2), 891–910.

Harding, D. J. (2009). Violence, Older Peers, and the Socialization of Adolescent Boys in Disadvantaged Neighborhoods. *American Sociological Review, 1, 74, 3,* 445–464. https://doi.org/10.1177/000312240907400306. PMID: 20161350; PMCID: PMC2776742.

Harman, D. (2001). Aging: Overview. *Annals of the New York Academy of Science, 928*(1), 1–21.

Hofferth, S. L., Pleck, J. H., & Vesley, C. K. (2012). The Transmission of Parenting from Fathers to Sons. *Parenting, Science and Practice, 12*(4), 282–305.

Hughes, K., & Emmel, N. (2012). *Analysing Time: Times and Timing in the Lives of Low-Income Grandparents*. Timescapes Methods Guides Series 2012 Guide No. 9. https://timescapes-archive.leeds.ac.uk/wp-content/uploads/sites/47/2020/07/timescapes-emmel-analysing-time.pdf

Hughes, K., & Tarrant, A. (2020). *Qualitative Secondary Analysis*. Sage.

Jensen, T. (2018). *Parenting the Crisis: The Cultural Politics of Parent-Blame*. Policy Press.

Klein, R. (2012). Collusion with Perpetrators. In *Responding to Intimate Violence Against Women: The Role of Informal Networks* (Advances in Personal Relationships) (pp. 100–114). Cambridge University Press. 10.1017/CBO9781113910.1016/j.016483.006

Liebow, E. (1967). *Tally's Corner: A Study of Negro Streetcorner Men*. Rowman & Littlefield.

Lister, R. (2005). *Poverty*. Polity Press.

Manhica, H., Straatmann, V. S., Lundin, A., Agardh, E., & Danielsson, A. (2021). Association Between Poverty Exposure During Childhood and Adolescence, and Drug Use Disorders and Drug-Related Crimes Later in Life. *Addiction, 116*(7), 1747–1756.

Maycock, P., Sheridan, S., & Parker, S. (2012). Migrant Women and Homelessness: The Role of Gender-based Violence. *European Journal of Homelessness, 6*(1), 59–82.

McDowell, L. (2000). The Trouble with Men? Young People, Gender Transformations and the Crisis of Masculinity. *International Journal of Urban and Regional Research, 24*(1), 201–209.

Milardo, R. M. (2005). Generative Uncle and Nephew Relationships. *Journal of Marriage and Family, 67*(5), 1226–1236.

Milardo, R. M. (2010). *The Forgotten Kin: Aunts and Uncles*. Cambridge University Press.

Neale, B., Lau Clayton, C., Davies, L., & Ladlow, L. (2015) Researching the Lives of Young Fathers: The Following Young Fathers Study and Dataset, Briefing Paper no. 8. https://followingfathers.leeds.ac.uk/wp-content/uploads/sites/79/2015/10/Researching-the-Lives-of-Young-Fathers-updated-Oct-22.pdf

Nelson, T. J. (2004). Low-Income Fathers. *Annual Review of Sociology, 30*, 427–451. https://doi.org/10.1146/annurev.soc.29.010202.09594

Newman, K. S., & Peeples Massengill, R. (2006). The Texture of Hardship: Qualitative Sociology of Poverty. *Annual Review of Sociology, 32*(1), 423–446.

Rauh, V., Landrigan, P. J., & Claudio, L. (2008). Housing and Health: Intersection of Poverty and Environmental Exposures. *Annals of New York Academy of Science, 1136*, 276–288. https://doi.org/10.1196/annals.1425.032

Ridge, T. (2009). *Living with Poverty: A Review of the Literature on Children's and Families' Experiences of Poverty,* Department for Work and Pensions Research Report No 594. http://www.bris.ac.uk/poverty/downloads/keyofficialdocuments/Child%20Poverty%20lit%20review%20DWP.pdf

Roy, K., Messina, L., Smith, J., & Waters, D. (2014). Growing Up as "Man of the House": Adultification and Transition into Adulthood for Young Men in Economically Disadvantaged Families. In K. Roy & N. Jones (Eds.), *Pathways to Adulthood for Disconnected Young Men in Low-Income Communities. New Directions in Child and Adolescent Development,* 143 (pp. 55–72). Jossey-Bass.

Shildrick, T., MacDonald, R., Webster, C., & Garthwaite, K. (2012). *Poverty and Insecurity: Life in Low Pay, No Pay Britain.* Policy Press.

Stack, C. B. (1974). *All Our Kin: Strategies for Survival in a Black Community.* Harper & Row.

Staley, S. (1992). *Drug Policy and the Decline of American Cities.* Transaction Publishers.

Strange, J.-M. (2012). Fatherhood, Providing, and attachment in Late Victorian and Edwardian Working-class Families. *The Historical Journal,* 55(4), 1007–1027.

Tarrant, A. (2021). *Fathering and Poverty: Uncovering Men's Participation in Low-Income Family Life.* Policy Press.

Wacquant, L. (1995). Pugs at Work: Bodily Capital and Bodily Labour among Professional Boxers. *Body & Society, 1*(1), 65–93.

Wikström, P.-O. H., & Treiber, K. (2016). Social Disadvantage and Crime: A Criminological Puzzle. *American Behavioral Scientist, 60*(10), 1232–1259.

Women's Budget Group. (2018). The Female Face of Poverty. https://wbg.org.uk/analysis/the-female-face-of-poverty/

CHAPTER 5

Men as Fathers and Providers

Introduction

Whereas in Chap. 4, we sought to retrieve and recover accounts of men's family participation through the narratives of women, in the remaining empirical chapters of the book we explore *men's* accounts of their family participation, through their narratives as partners and providers (this chapter), as grandparent kinship carers (Chap. 6) and men's experiences of being *absented* and excluded from low-income families (Chap. 7). Here, we begin with an analytic focus on how men describe themselves as husbands, partners, and fathers, building on the insights provided by women in the previous chapter and advancing their necessarily partial accounts by interrogating evidence of men's family participation from men's own perspectives. In our attention to men's family participation as husbands, partners, and fathers, we draw on and contribute to a rich body of interdisciplinary scholarship concerning fatherhood (e.g. Bosoni, 2014; Dermott & Miller, 2015), including in low-income families and localities (Edin & Nelson, 2013; Roy, 2014; Tarrant, 2021) but redress what is elsewhere identified as the empirical absence of low-income fathers in qualitative research (Tarrant, 2021), by examining experiences of partnering and parenting for men across the lifecourse.

To accomplish this, we analyse the cases of Bob and Victor who were interviewed for the linked *Accessing Socially Excluded* and *Midlife*

K. Hughes, A. Tarrant, *Men, Families, and Poverty*, Palgrave Macmillan Studies in Family and Intimate Life, https://doi.org/10.1007/978-3-031-24922-8_5

Grandparents studies (see Chap. 3). Bob and Victor are older men, and their cases were seminal in previous research as well as prompting the questions that have led to this book. Both cases challenge the invisibility of older men in relation to their family participation in low-income family contexts and alerted us to the inadequacy of existing policy and academic framings of men as absent as fathers and providers. Indeed, these cases prompted further and extensive research with men in these localities in the new empirical phase of Anna's Men, Poverty and Care study, shaping her recruitment and access pathways and the final empirical sample. While there have been modest attempts to establish a sociology of adulthood (e.g. Pilcher et al., 2003; Shefer & Hearn, 2022), middle-aged and older men receive relatively less empirical attention than younger men in research, especially in relation to their family contexts. However, we do acknowledge distinctive literatures on older men as caregivers (e.g. Russell, 2007; Milligan & Morbey, 2016), service and support recipients (Ruxton, 2002; Milligan, 2016; Fee et al., 2020), grandfatherhood (Cunningham-Burley, 1984; Mann et al., 2016; Tarrant, 2014), and more limited sustained sociological engagement with grandfather kinship carers (Tarrant, 2018).

Following the trend in existing literature, we investigated how men's family participation relates to and articulates with definitions of work and provisioning as partners/husbands and fathers, in context of the broader family, economic, legislative, and policy terrains they navigate. We use these cases critically to interrogate the assumptions underscoring policy representations of men's relationships to, and within, their families in low-income localities (Donald et al., 2021; Halpern et al., 2021). In so doing, we identify the importance and limits of the breadwinner model through longitudinal circumstances of poverty, and the associated challenges for people to secure work and sustain family navigating such conditions. Second, reflecting the concerns of policy and literature more generally, we consider the diversity and dynamics of their family participation in relation to their roles as partners/husbands and fathers. To do this, we draw on and advance our multigenerational analytic framework and develop longitudinal cases of these men's family experiences from their own perspectives. This enables us to capture the diversity and range of their participation in families from different generational positions, in and through low-income circumstances. First, however, we introduce the cases of Bob and Victor.

A Brief Overview of the Cases

Bob: Bob is in his mid-fifties and was first interviewed under the Accessing Socially Excluded study about the 'good and bad times' in his life, especially as they related to his health and locality. Bob has been married to Dianne for 35 years. Bob and Dianne are both long-term unemployed due to ill health, and Bob has not worked since he was made redundant in 1996, and is on depression tablets. Bob lost his parents 'young' at the age of 18. He was one of the younger children and his mother had him 'late on in life'. The couple are parents to five children and, through these, grandparents to 16 grandchildren. They see their children and grandchildren regularly. Most of them live nearby and visit Bob and Dianne at regular intervals. The key grandparenting relationship discussed in their interviews is that with Josh, eldest son of Jessica, to whom Dianne gave birth when she was 18. Bob and Dianne were informal kinship carers for Josh for twelve and a half years until Jessica wanted him back. Their eldest son has a child of 16 who began parenting at the age of 15. Bob also provides extensive support to his disabled sister, and then goes over to his Dad's house to help out. From across the interviews, it emerges that Bob found family stability with Dianne's parents, and when he was first made redundant had depression and a drinking problem that he subsequently resolved within his family. Bob and Dianne continue to express affection towards each other across the ten years of our fieldwork engagement with them.

Victor: Victor is in his early forties and is the partner of Carolyn, one of the four cases presented in Chap. 4. Victor is a step-father to Carolyn's four children and grandfather to one of Carolyn's grandchildren, two-year-old Richie. The most complicated relationship Victor experiences is as a step-father to Carolyn's oldest daughter Lorna, mother to Richie. Lorna's partner would trash her house with parties when she was gone and when they broke up and he left to join the army, his family took all the valuables from the house. She loses new private accommodation due to flooding, and a loses baby which sees her struggle to cope. For periods of time, Richie is cared for in an informal kinship care arrangement by Carolyn and Victor. He also has one biological son from a previous relationship whom he continues to see on an irregular basis. His relationship with his ex-partner is fraught, linked to finances and child maintenance. His decision to become a house husband and a foster carer is linked to these troubles. Victor comes from a family that they describe as traditional. As grandparents, his parents have informal involvement with both his son from his previous and current relationship, such as baking with the children. They are described as having an old fashioned and quite strict approach to parenting.

In reporting on these cases throughout the chapter, although we draw on historical data, we retain the present tense used by the men in their interviews, as it reflects the presents they were describing. We also found this useful in our reporting as a means of distinguishing between the presents they described, and their past histories. By using changing tenses, we have been better able to articulate the temporality, particularly the longitudinal dynamics, of the relationships and family circumstances the men described, as well as the broader socio-economic histories of the localities in which they live.

Bob's Case: Partnering, (Un)employment and Provisioning

In our QSA work, we first encounter Bob through data from the Accessing Socially Excluded study. While his wife, Dianne, is being interviewed, Bob arrives home and joins a discussion that has already begun. In response to the interviewer's explanation that the interview is about 'good' and 'bad' times in people's lives, especially in relation to their health, Bob launches into a detailed account of his employment history, that over the course of the longer interview develops into a discussion of the complex entanglements of his work history with his family responsibilities, and how these have impacted on his physical and emotional health.

As soon as he begins talking, Bob describes his commitment to a manufacturing job, illustrated through his account of working extended full-time hours even though he only had a part-time contract: 'I just worked and slept..... I used to work, 12, 14, 16 hours a night'. Bob uses the language of redundancy to explain how he lost his job, but also ascribes his job to another man at the factory, who 'got a load of us the sack because we wouldn't be yes men'. Bob went to a tribunal for unfair dismissal where he was offered and accepted a £17,050 settlement, following the solicitor's advice that:

Bob: 'owt over that I'll have to, you see, I was signing on me, you know on't dole, so he said owt over that and you'll have to declare it'.

The loss of his job led to depression:

> I'll tell you straight, I lost the plot. Because I looked forward to going...
> Like I said, cos I spent more time at work because I liked going. I did, I
> loved it....sometimes I say to Dianne, I'm sat here and I say, I should be up
> there do you know what I mean? And then I started getting depressed and
> I started getting down because I wasn't going … it just really threw me out
> of kilter …. I was just moping about the house. I didn't want to get shaved.
> I just didn't want to do owt.

It is well established in existing research that employment and work
remain central pillars of male identity and are foundational to how men
achieve their status (Hearn, 2004; Connell, 1995; McDowell, 2000).
Fodor (2006) attributes men's experience of a gender role crisis in low-
income households in Hungary to their inability to fulfil expectations of
breadwinning. For Bob, the sense of loss linked to his dismissal and his
continued inability to find new employment constitutes a 'social death',
wherein he 'just didn't know what to do'. He further elaborates:

Bob: I had my heart set on stopping there until I was 65 because I liked
       it that much. And I think half of it is, if you like your job, it doesn't
       matter what it pays. But as I say, the money were good as well, do
       you know what I mean? So I not only liked the job, and I liked to
       go, I were getting a decent wage out of it as well. As I say, when I
       got finished there, I just didn't know what to do. Bob and Dianne,
       Accessing Socially Excluded Study

We note that Bob does not use the language of breadwinning in his
accounts and although he describes his wage as 'good money', Bob and
Dianne live in social housing, are in receipt of welfare benefits, and are
managing a complex range of resources in order to 'get by' (see also
McKenzie, 2015). In contrast to the 'work shy' narratives of contemporary discourses of people residing in poverty and in low-income localities
and family contexts (MacDonald et al., 2020), Bob valued his work and
when he lost it, felt that he had lost out on a secure, long-term job that he
enjoyed and was fulfilling for him. Instead, Bob's case supports the use of
the language of 'provision' rather than 'breadwinning' when used about
men in low-income contexts, where work is characterised as a low pay, no
pay cycle (Shildrick et al., 2010), and where 'provisioning' captures the

complex blend and range of support—financial, emotional, practical, physical—that we learn Bob provides to sustain his family over time, across households, and through different employment and welfare circumstances.

As Bob's narrative about his work history unfolds, for example, an ostensibly simplistic account of unemployment due to unfair dismissal becomes much more complicated. In explaining why he was unable to achieve the stable, long-term, and rewarding career he had hoped for, he begins to interweaves examples of changing family commitments and the challenges these presented for him in his employment and subsequently. An especially difficult situation arose when Bob's eldest daughter began to have difficulties in looking after her child. Bob and Dianne assumed parental care of their grandson, this coinciding with a period of illness for Dianne, who began to need additional care from Bob to the extent that when he was interviewed he was her carer:

Bob: I were having some time off because of Dianne and then my daughter had gone through a bad patch with our Josh hadn't she?

Dianne: Yeah

Bob: And she'd, it were her first child and she'd gone through a bad patch with him and (Dianne: he were poorly) and I couldn't, I mean, I had to check. I wasn't only in charge of, well, supervisor of cold store, I had to sort all the orders out and then I had to check them out. To make sure that all the pallets had all the right stuff on. And sometimes I were thinking of her and the grandkid and not only that, summat else had happened, and sometimes I just couldn't concentrate. If you know what I mean, I just couldn't concentrate because I was either thinking of her, are they all right? And when I tried to explain that to them when we went to see the manager…. they called him but I don't know why he were there because he were transport manager. But I tried to explain to him. I missed a couple of things over the pallets, but I'd put some stuff on a pallet that had been on hold. If it's on hold it can't go out. But it had hold stickers on it. If you see a hold sticker, that stays where it is, and you go ta next pile, but it didn't have any hold stickers on it. So of course, I sent it out….I ended up on depression tablets. I'm still on them aren't I? Yeah, I got right down because I missed

it, I missed the job. I did. I got right down, I didn't want to know.
Bob and Dianne, Accessing Socially Excluded Study

Bob's contributions to the interview describe the challenging dynamics involved in sustaining work and family lives and relationships. At this stage of his life Bob's has intensive fathering responsibility for his daughter and simultaneously for his grandson (who later comes to call Bob and Dianne 'mum and dad'). Age-differentiated generational identities are seen to collapse at this juncture in Bob's life, constraining his ability to do his job. His employer's inability to accommodate the complexities of his family life lead to Bob losing his job, with catastrophic and long-lasting effects. Bob's narrative demonstrates the limitations for research engagement with men that seeks to separate men's identities as *either* workers, *or* fathers, *or* grandfathers by disrupting simplistic generational, caring and employment identities and boundaries. Bob's case provides additional insight into how lack of resources across families intensifies family responsibility for some members rather than others and shapes the possibility for paid work, especially as the physical and emotional health of other family members declines. The shifting emphases and intensification of family responsibility both articulate and characterise what we describe as the 'dynamics' of poverty. Bob's account is less one involving an emotional struggle around identity work between worker and carer, as has been observed elsewhere with more resourced men (Elliott et al., 2017), and more that of managing the continuing consequences of these combined responsibilities in his working life.

Bob's wider narrative across both the 'Accessing Socially Excluded' and 'Midlife Grandparents' studies, also describes a *diversity* of caring responsibilities that involve supporting and sustaining family members across households. For example, when interviewed in the 'Midlife Grandparents' study, Bob and Dianne talk about how he visits his elderly, 72-year-old sister to give her dinner, and do domestic chores for her, something he also did for his own father when he was alive:

Bob: If she [Bob's sister] can't do it, she'll phone Dianne up. And either I'll do it, or Dianne'll do it. I tidy up for her at least once a week. Give the house a good clean, kitchen, toilet room. A good vac and a good clean. Dust the cooker down and everything, so it's all tidy for her.... We used to do it when (inaudible) dad were alive. I used to go down half past 2 in the morning, haven't I, love? As long as (inaudible) we're all right, and they were all right, then that's the main thing....I mean

I'm, often I'm taking her out in a wheelchair to the lane and to the park.

Bob, Midlife Grandparents Study, Round One

Bob's narrative illustrates the diversity of care and support provided by men to sustain families, what can be conceptualised as the doing of kinship (Comas d'Argemir & Soronellas, 2019). Despite his lack of paid income, through the 'work of poverty' (Ridge, 2009) involved in securing welfare payments and other resources, caring activities, housework and domestic labour, Bob centrally positions himself as a 'provider' in his family setting, albeit using a different language. In this way, his case encourages a shift from the language of breadwinning to that of 'provisioning'. This shift was evident in women's accounts, which were not typically orientated towards male partners and ex-partners as good or bad 'providers', where 'provision' relates to men's paid work (Neysmith et al., 2010; Doucet, 2020). Instead, the women developed nuanced accounts of how difficult secure, stable paid work was to sustain in localities where the history of industry, labour, and employment is one of decline, where work is increasingly harder to come by, exploitative, and low paid, and where the localities themselves are highly stigmatised within and across the city, creating additional problems for accessing work in the broader region (Emmel & Hughes, 2010, Shildrick & MacDonald, 2013; see also Chap. 6). Distinctive to low-income family contexts, is that the language of 'provision' is additionally associated with peoples' accounts of the persistent and stigmatised challenges of accessing, securing, and managing social welfare payments. The UK welfare system has become increasingly precarious, punitive, and conditional over the course of the linked studies (Dwyer et al., 2020; Wright & Patrick, 2020; MacDonald et al., 2020), making it much more difficult to sustain familial and care responsibilities as a form of unpaid labour.

Bob's narrative also articulates experiences relating to a broader national trend in the UK of the intensification of caring by people as they age (Yeandle & Buckner, 2017) with a sharp increase in caring by people between the ages of 60 and 64 years, especially by men. His interview articulates precisely this trend, although he does not fall within this older age group. This corresponds with the broader findings by the original 'Accessing Socially Excluded' and 'Midlife Grandparents' research teams, who used local health ward data from these research localities to demonstrate how people living in low-income contexts were more likely to experience midlife morbidity—chronic illness early in their lives—coupled with significantly shorter life expectancy than those in adjacent, more affluent, neighbourhoods in the same city. Bob's experiences of an intensification of caring responsibilities alongside ill health himself—albeit at a younger age than that of his national counterparts—reflects the poorer health chances and outcomes of people in his neighbourhood (Emmel & Hughes, 2010; also Atkinson & Kintrea, 2000; Lupton, 2003; see Cummins et al., 2007 for a critical view; Hagedoorn & Helbich, 2021). Bob's wider case demonstrates that his ill health is not confined only to himself and Dianne, when he enumerates all the immediate relatives (siblings and parents) that have died:

Bob: Yeah. I don't know what that mean, well as I say, like I said I lost me mam and dear dad when I were eighteen, I were only one n' I lost them in six month, then two uncles died straight after. An' then I lost me sister, then me brother, then me brother-in-law, then another brother-in-law, you know what I mean, it don't help…And then when Frank died, cos our Anne got worried, she's 72 now is our Anne, and when me mam passed away 59 and me dad were 63, n' me sister were 63 and that really frightened 'er, you know what I mean? Thinking that she were gonna' die at an early age…but touch wood. And then when Frank died at 51. And er, her husband died of cancer. And er, our Anne don't smoke, but with 'em all at an early age it's scared her, you know what I mean, thinking that we're all gonna die at an early age… I got worried then, thinking, bloody 'ell, 51, 59, 60, no 63, I ain't got a lot in me now. But as I say, as all luck or whatever, I'm still going.
Bob, Midlife Grandparents Study, Round One

By the conclusion of the 'Midlife Grandparents' study some eight years after he was first interviewed, Dianne's father and Bob's older sister, Anne, had also died. Bob's experiences additionally mirror other national trends, such as in the intergenerational patterning of care within families, whereby formal or informal care for grandchildren by grandparents is characteristic of low-income families (Nandy & Selwyn, 2013; Hunt, 2018). In this respect, the cases developed across each of the linked studies evidence how longitudinal experiences of poverty are articulated through unequal health outcomes for those in these localities. Our QSA thus demonstrates the importance of interrogating generational and familial identities alongside longer-term income or working experiences to support empirically grounded and depth understanding of how poverty processes shape families over time, and thereby the futility of seeking to individualise behaviours or families in policy approaches or sociological explanation (see also, Edwards & Gillies, 2012; Tyler, 2013).

Bob's account is useful for troubling a generalised orthodoxy concerning the gendered character of care, whereby men are believed to be more likely to assume breadwinning roles and women caring roles (e.g. Macdonald, 1997) as 'gender-bound' responses to hardship. The gendered dynamics of caring, provisioning, and other sorts of family support emerge as more complex in the lives and narratives of Bob and Dianne. Together, they reflect below on the interplay of work and family for women in the lives of their adult children, for example, where women take on breadwinning responsibilities in low pay, no pay employment contexts:

Dianne:	Tracy [one of their daughters] likes working down there and like I said, Tracy likes working.
Bob:	She loves it.
Dianne:	She loves it, she loves her job in [local hospital] …. She's a porter, she come from a cleaner to a porter.
Bob:	I've got a mate down there and she says the only way they'll get him out is in a box, she loves the place.
Dianne:	Yeah, she loves it. Yeah, she's on about doing a nursing course isn't she?
Interviewer:	Is she?
Dianne:	Mmmm.
Interviewer:	Right. Good for her.
Bob:	Well it's the first job she's ever had you see.
Dianne:	She looks after the kids, she had the kids. And he [Tracy's partner] went to work and then he got laid off cause he worked for cable and that, so he got laid off. And she went to work, and he's looked after kids, she's been working.
Interviewer:	Right, so they've sort of switched round.
Dianne:	And then when he said when the youngest went into full-time school, he would go back to work which he starts back a week on Monday, so it's not bad for him.

Bob and Dianne, Midlife Grandparents Study, Round One

These shifting patterns of working and caring for men and women in low-income contexts, the exchange of childcare and breadwinning roles, the challenges of these through precarious economic periods, retreating industry, and a diminishing welfare state, demonstrate how families, within and across generations and different family configurations, collectively and flexibly respond to their economic contexts to secure the work and resources they need to survive. The language of 'earning' or 'breadwinning' is not only inadequate for describing what individuals do, but also for how these families through these circumstances provide for their everyday family sustenance. Again, the language of provision becomes essential as a means of capturing this rich complex of participation.

In these multiple ways, Bob's case serves to inform on the complexities of how shifts in men's roles and identities in family life are consequent on macro-level and socio- historical processes. For Bob these include a decline in men's wages, and a shift in the UK's economy from manufacturing industry to service work (McDowell, 2009; Yeandle & Cass, 2013), affecting not only himself but also his wife and adult children. These processes are also localised, offering insight into the cumulative build of place-based hardship. Bob's unfair dismissal and inability to find more work are not only linked to the 'fortunes' of his family, but importantly and closely associated with the broader economic fortunes of the estate on which he lives. Over the various interviews in which he participates, Bob provides a detailed generational account of the microdynamics of macro-level economic downturn, increasing locality-based deprivation, the rise of family poverty and associated health inequalities, alongside the rolling back of the welfare state (see also Emmel & Hughes, 2010). Finally, the consequences of longitudinal and intergenerational hardship are expressed through the worsening health and declining abilities of both Bob and Dianne, already apparent from his first interview, and continuous throughout the long period of research contact with them both.

This section began with a consideration of men as breadwinners. As Bob's case demonstrates neither the language of, nor focus on, breadwinning is adequate to understand men's family participation through circumstances of poverty, throughout their lives and the lives of their families. However, we do not want to overstate Bob's self-identification as a carer either, or over-state his own emphasis on his family roles. Over the course of the Midlife Grandparents' study, Bob gradually disengaged from the interviews because of the shift in analytic focus to family and grandparenting, rather than on 'good' and 'bad' times in his life. He no longer considered the study to be 'about him'. One of the original team members reflected on this in their field diary:

Was enormously relieved that he [Bob] had agreed to be interviewed as I knew from previous interviews he's rather disaffected from this particular study because of its focus on grandparenting. (Lou Hemmerman, From fieldnotes, November 2011)

In this regard, Bob's case is very different to Victor's, whom we now move on to discuss, and who presents a much more cogent and rehearsed narrative around his identity as father, step-father, foster-father, and grandfather in relation to practices of provisioning. Victor's case is one which describes how he has been either actively forced or encouraged to identify himself in relation to his paternal roles, by different welfare support and provision agencies, both in terms of money he is required to pay for his previous family, and money that he receives for fostering in his current step-family. Indeed, Victor's case is also an exemplar for elaborating our orientation towards the language of provision in low-income family contexts rather than the language of 'breadwinning', although with significantly different emphasis made by Victor himself. Whilst Bob's case is important for gaining insight into the complex interplay between work and family life for men over their lifecourse, Victor's is important in supporting analyses of the changing contexts of partner separation and consequent strategic decision-making around provisioning across multiple family contexts. In this respect, Victor's case provides insight into the longitudinal interplay between family and policy through changing family contexts.

Victor's Case: Repartnering, Resourcing, and Moral Guardianship

Victor develops an account of his marital and fathering history that both acknowledges and resists policy representations of 'absent dads'.[1] Victor is the current partner of Carolyn, whose case is presented in Chap. 4, and begins by discussing the history of his relationship with Carolyn and his role as a step-father and grandfather. This is no coincidence as the study was focused on the experiences and circumstances of Carolyn and, by marriage, Victor as midlife grandparents. Through these interviews it becomes clear that this is not the first family for which Victor has

---

[1] In the QSA stage of her Men, Poverty and Care study, Victor's interviews confirmed and supported the new questions Anna was bringing to the existing data, and additionally served as a catalyst for a new range of questions. It was precisely these policy framings that the Men, Poverty and Care study sought to address empirically as a distinctive analytical departure from the concerns of the original Midlife Grandparents study team. Victor's case has also been analysed and noted in several publications already, albeit for different purposes and to make different theoretical and methodological arguments (Tarrant, 2017; Tarrant & Hughes, 2020; Tarrant, 2021).

fathering responsibilities. He describes his past and present relationship with his ex-partner and their son, with whom he no longer lives. What becomes evident is how and why he makes decisions about his employment and finances based on the needs of his current family with Carolyn. As described in Chap. 4, from Carolyn's perspective, Victor occupies a 'saviour' role, having rescued her from an abusive marriage, taken on a step-father role to her children, a grandfather role to her grandson, and is now her partner in fostering children, for which they receive an income as a couple.

In contrast, from the reported perspective of his former partner, and in relation to the biological son still living with her, Victor knows himself to be stigmatised as a 'crap dad'. Additionally, from the perspective of the Child Support Agency (CSA),[2] he is an 'absent father' who has abandoned his son and ex-partner leaving them financially to fend for themselves. Importantly, this is not solely a reputational matter for Victor. In the extract below, he describes how making choices about where and with whom he invests financially has implications for how and even whether he is able to parent his biological son:

> … from when I left my ex, I was paying her maintenance, but she was refusing to let me see [biological son from previous relationship] … my ex-partner, she's never worked and she's always sat on benefits, which then affected what happened to me, then, with the Child Support Agency... What she did was, she took two part time jobs, the emphasis then was on me...They weren't legal jobs. The emphasis was then on me to grass her up for working on the side whilst at the same time being pursued for maintenance by the Child Support Agency. I couldn't convince them, because they saw me just as an absent father, who was disgruntled and would say anything, and, erm, they, the Child Support Agency, although I had four step-children, dismissed [*names step-children with Carolyn*] and said that they, and they actually wrote to us...They said, "They do not count, you are an absent parent. It meant Carolyn was worse off and her children were worse off than before I moved in, and I thought that was intolerable." *Victor, age 44, re-partnered father*

In this extract, Victor's narrative navigates a complex set of concerns. He begins by expressing a morally driven rationale about not 'grassing up' his ex-wife. He distances himself from exposing her to the punitive actions

---

[2] This is now known as the Child Maintenance Service.

of other government agencies connected with the provision or—if he reported her—the withdrawal of welfare benefits, housing, and other resources essential to the survival of her and their son. He also observes that his current investments in his role as a step-father to Carolyn's children are 'dismissed' by the CSA. Victor's account describes two overlapping assumptions built into the CSA's orientations towards him as a father. First, is the primacy of his relationship to his biological child over those of step-children and similar fathering roles, and second, that a 'good' father, first and foremost, is able to provide financially. As Doucet (2020) observes, and as we discuss above, there has been a tendency to separate out provisioning, working, and caring by men whereby investment in one sphere is considered a form of neglect from another. Working is seen to preclude caring, caring to preclude breadwinning, and so on. This production of oppositional binaries through the gendering of care, breadwinning, and provisioning is problematic (Doucet, 2020), and Victor's case challenges some of these existing assumptions.

The foregrounding of the primacy of his relationship with his biological child by the CSA ties in with Victor's assertion that the CSA ultimately fails to take into account his ongoing fathering of his step-children. In our QSA of the linked datasets, we have observed how children become increasingly vulnerable to violence and neglect the more 'removed' biologically, and through successive repartnerings, their relationship with the resident male becomes.[3] Victor's account demonstrates the problematic nature of policy orientations that conflate 'families' with biological relations, and that consequently problematise men's strategic investments in new families. Such policy orientation, in privileging the needs of some children, may render those without a biological relationship to the resident male increasingly vulnerable through repartnering and the formation of new families. This is present in Victor's account of his strategic provisioning. Neysmith et al. (2010) use the concept of 'provisioning' to reclaim what women in low-income contexts do for their families as a form of *work*, demonstrating the complex interplay of various relationship-based and caring orientated responsibilities women have. In their paper, the authors—albeit briefly—indicate the challenges men experienced in describing the 'invisible work' they do in providing for their families when lacking a 'breadwinner' identity. Key here is the conflation for men, and women, of provisioning and caring. For men in

---

[3] These findings build out of analyses by the original Accessing Socially Excluded and Midlife Grandparents study teams.

Neysmith et al.'s work (2010), this was especially important in securing welfare for their non-resident children, and has resonance for our findings here. In contrast, Doucet (2020) uses the language of provisioning to reframe men's *breadwinning* as interconnected with care, and therefore to be treated as part of the broader repertoire of men's caring, specifically in relation to 'father involvement'. While our arguments here align more with Neysmith et al. (2010) in seeking to elucidate often 'invisible' practices of family participation by men, Doucet's work is important in articulating the often-challenging conflation for men of how they treat and align the provisioning of families more closely with 'breadwinning', financial support and caring. Victor's case is an exemplar here, not least because he 'earns' through foster caring. Not only are Victor's previous partner and biological child financially affected when he prioritises investments towards Carolyn's children and grandchild, but when Carolyn's are not accepted as 'his' financial responsibility by the CSA and other welfare departments, they too become worse off financially.

Through this extract, we are therefore afforded insight into how family relationships are shaped through and explicitly impacted by broader policy, institutional and welfare relationships. In Victor's case, this is first, through his exclusion from seeing his biological son by his former partner because of his withdrawal of financial support. Second, to ameliorate the significant penalties Victor and Carolyn incur from the CSA because he is not providing for his first family, he and Carolyn become involved in fostering as a new form of 'provisioning' for their family. Victor's narrative therefore demonstrates how, in low-income contexts, 'provision' does not necessarily always refer to paid work. Instead, Victor and Carolyn choose to secure certain sorts of resources (for fostering) rather than others (through taxi driving, his previous employment) in the provision for Carolyn's children, her grandchild, and (via) the children that they foster.

Importantly, Victor's account demonstrates how men might make strategic investments where they have limited financial resources. Observing how he does so through the broader context of the complex nexus of his changing family and policy-driven responsibilities begins to highlight how low-income circumstances may shape the character, and indeed perceptions, of men's family participation. Victor's choices traverse complex welfare services and benefits, linking both policy-driven and personal narratives of 'who' constitutes 'family' through processes of repartnering. Victor is excluded from one family through one government agency, the CSA, for example, but secures resources for his new family with Carolyn through a different government agency, namely children's services.

Illustrated here are examples of the collective careful and strategic decisions that families in low-income contexts may make to navigate through these complex policy landscapes and to secure even modest resources for sustaining family life. This decision-making and securing of resources are otherwise invisible forms of 'doing kinship', often obscured by dismissive tropes that are assigned to individual family members, specifically men as fathers, that designate them as 'absent'. These insights therefore support an analytic shift from questions concerning *why* men are 'absent' from families, shaped through policy rhetoric that foregrounds normative, voluntaristic explanations of men's family participation. Thus they are often assumed to be failing at providing or participating, as a consequence of poor choices and a lack of responsibility as a father. It is to this rhetoric that Victor deliberately speaks and resists, and which he and Carolyn are forced to confront in managing their family.

Such resistance is present in how Victor develops accounts of his endeavours for Carolyn's family, such as becoming a 'step-father' and a foster carer, by using policy-based language based on his growing expertise in these relationships. How he articulates the character of his family participation and responsibilities in this new family configuration draws directly *on* the normative framing and discourses of the social care professionals with whom he engages. Furthermore, he actively frames what he does in ways which address the *requirements* underpinning the codes of professional practice through which he is assessed. More than that, Victor arranges his time, his professional occupation and familial identity in Carolyn's family in ways which explicitly meet such criteria. In this process of identity, responsibility and relational activities and language, including his ongoing estrangement from his first partner and his biological son, Victor is actively engaged in an ongoing process of 'civic' ordering wherein his new family relationships are reconfigured through governmental engagements, language, and requirements.

In the extended narrative of his interview, and in constructing their accounts of their relationship and familial circumstances, both Victor and Carolyn place significant emphasis on (re)positioning Victor as a 'good' dad who is making careful yet constrained financial choices across households and sometimes fraught familial and intergenerational interdependencies. However, as in Bob's case, generational positioning is not necessarily straightforward. Carolyn's eldest daughter, Lizzie, has a young child, Richie, for whom Carolyn and Victor periodically assume parental care for days or sometimes even weeks. In this way, they act as both parents and grandparents simultaneously:

Carolyn: ... I were going up to see Lizzie every week, you know, helping her out, tidying up and stuff like that. And, erm, and then Richie were getting more and more upset because he wanted to be here, because I had to leave him there, and I could see that he, he were... erm, not being neglected, but he was having to be part of her friend's circle.

Victor: Well, he was neglected in a way... She'd left him in his bedroom and he's only two, and she put, left him there while she entertained her friends downstairs, day or night. [...] we're still trying to get him back to a normal child routine. He's got used to getting, snatching, sort of, eight hours sleep, and that is terrible for a child of that age. [...] So he might be going to bed 10, 11, midnight, whatever, that means he's sleeping till midday the following day. So, we're having to break him out of that and it's very difficult.

Victor and Carolyn, Midlife Grandparents Study, Round One

Across the 'Midlife Grandparents' study, the grandparents described aspects of their grandparenting in terms of norms of 'non-interference', a characteristic of a 'leisure/pleasure' approach where grandparents provide occasional care and are reluctant to interfere in the disciplining of their grandchildren, identifying these as more properly within the province of parenting (Douglas & Ferguson, 2003; Mason et al., 2007; Bengston et al., 2008). Yet, these came into conflict with what they also describe as the responsibility, or 'obligation' (Mason et al., 2007), to pass on advice about good parenting to their adult children, as well as anticipating and dealing with what they considered to be risks to their grandchildren. Rather than these conflicting feelings being managed through a disposition of ambivalence, described elsewhere (e.g. Mason et al., 2007), these grandparents, including Carolyn and Victor, reframed their experiences of grandparenting in a broader narrative of what they described as 'rescue and repair' (Hughes & Emmel, 2012).

'Rescue and repair' grandparenting involves 'parachuting in' to a difficult situation and either rescuing and repairing the *situation* for their grandchildren and their adult child, or rescuing the *grandchildren* from the situation, taking them into their home and repairing the damage that has been done. While not exclusive to low-income families, rescue/repair grandparenting is connected to the need for families with high formal health and social care involvement to avoid potentially punitive service interventions, including 'the social taking the children away' (Hughes &

Emmel, 2012). In the 'Midlife Grandparents' study, many grandparents lacked the luxury of ambivalence, needing to react to situations and override the parent's authority. This narrative was juxtaposed with 'leisure and pleasure' grandparenting where grandparents have regular access to their grandchildren, perhaps take part in their leisure activities, or even provide a supplementary support role where both parents are working on a stable, routinised basis (see also Sudbury & Simcock, 2007).

Across his interviews, Victor's narrative describes a shuttling process between supplementary and parental care for Richie, through which he and Carolyn additionally support his identity as a 'moral guardian' in his new family. Together, they describe ongoing process of 'rescue and repair' for Richie, whereby they *rescue* him from a difficult situation—such as from Lizzie who secures protected housing but then experiences an influx of drug-users and dealers led by her boyfriend—and *repairing* the damage that has been done, such as reintegrating him into waking/sleeping routines. We explore the dynamics of rescue/repair grandparenting further in the next chapter, but conclude here that Victor's relationship with his grandson and step-daughter may be described as a type of informal kinship care, wherein Victor is *doing* kin, although lacking biological connections to Carolyn's children. Nevertheless, his experience as an informal kinship carer exemplifies the often-invisible ways in which men engage in provisioning for their family members within and across households, identified in Chap. 4, and illustrated through Bob's case above. Through analytic engagement with men's diverse generational positions and responsibilities, which they enact simultaneously, we become able to develop a more complex reading of provisioning as a key aspect of men's family participation that resists a unilinear reading of them.

Men, Family Participation, and Provisioning

The cases of Bob and Victor provide important insights into their multiple generational identities; Bob, as brother, father, and grandfather; and Victor, as father, step-father, and step-grandfather. For both of these men, these roles are 'within the scope' of what is to be expected from them despite changing family configurations and circumstances. In other words, what they do emerges as congruent with normative framing of family responsibilities and 'doing kin' for men (Roy, 2014). These two cases demonstrate how men engage in vital but often obscured roles, responsibilities, and practices in the ongoing formation and sustaining of families (see also Comas d'Argemir & Soronellas, 2019), including roles that are normatively presumed to be the preserve of women. They additionally provide unique and often overlooked insights into how persistent poverty shapes their experiences in this regard and produces distinctive challenges for, and patterns of, family participation specifically for men.

We began with Bob's case to account for why we need to research men's accounts of their participation in low-income family contexts as partners and ex-partners, which resists or at least troubles the discourse of men's 'absence' from their families. Bob's narrative describes how he becomes progressively involved with caring responsibilities as a two-fold consequence of the loss of his job and the onset of age-related morbidities experienced by his wife, Dianne, and his ageing sister. Nevertheless, Bob continues to foreground his identity as a worker, a colleague, and bread-winner, while downplaying his role as carer. His case is an exemplar of how men recount intertwined and often fraught histories of work and family responsibilities and participation through low-income contexts. Bob presents a narrative of himself emphasising his experiences of employment, unfair dismissal, and unemployment, themes foregrounded by the originating research team in some of their analyses (Emmel & Hughes, 2010). Our QSA demonstrates that to understand and account for Bob's family participation over time, we need to move beyond a sole reading of his identity as a breadwinner and to one of provisioning. This enables us to account for how men understand what it is they do in and for their families more generally (see also Neysmith et al., 2010; Strange, 2012; Tarrant, 2021) and how they may view themselves.

It is this language of *provisioning* that Victor's narrative takes forward, highlighting as it does the longitudinal processes of care and resource distribution over time within families. The nuances and complexities of Victor's case allow us to extend the arguments we develop in Chap. 4, about the need to move away from categorical and binary angel/demon narratives characteristic of many women's accounts of previous and past partners. By eschewing normative, voluntaristic explanations of men's family participation in our analyses of Victor's account of himself, we thus further our case for avoiding questions of whether he is a 'good' or 'bad' dad and, instead, seek to elaborate the circumstances through which Victor comes to define and deploy definitions of 'provision', 'fathering', and 'absence', and consider how these terms are shaped through the broader policy and welfare processes in which he is so intimately enmeshed. Considering the financial dependency of low-income people on different welfare sources and therefore the broader health and social care relationships through which they secure income and resource, we are better able analytically to engage with the circumstances through which men's strategic choices and investments are shaped and made. Furthermore, this shift allows us to comprehend the multiple place-based 'economies' of work, welfare, informal exchange, and health and social care through which these families navigate in the 'making-do and getting by' of low-income life. Doucet's work is useful here in cautioning against unintentionally letting fathers 'off the hook' in terms of caregiving, which may serve to reverse hard-won recognition in feminist research of the value of men's engagements in caregiving both for women and for men. Like Doucet, however, the conceptual distinction between breadwinning as a broad earning practice and provisioning work directed towards supporting children and family life is useful.

In policy, men in low-income contexts tend to be painted as dangerous or risky, yet qualitative data demonstrate that they play active *caregiving roles* in their families and over time, continue to invest in caregiving. Men do not just become 'bad dads' over time and abandon their children, as broader stereotypes such as the 'absent' and 'feckless' father would suggest (see Chap. 2). They have strong aspirations to be involved in their children's lives from a young age and when they look back as grandfathers, they relish the opportunity of a second chance to learn from their mistakes. Additionally, their care responsibilities are not limited to fathering and grandfathering. Men actively engage in 'doing kinship' (Comas d'Argemir & Soronellas, 2019) for family members in their personal networks of care and try to protect them from the trappings of their locality. Nevertheless, they face constraints over time that impact upon the extent to which they can fulfil their care responsibilities. These include negotiating sometimes difficult relationships with the mothers of their children, balancing multiple responsibilities; and trying to manage the emotional consequences of negotiating care responsibilities in constrained circumstances (as separated or non-resident dads or as kinship carers). Our analyses of Bob and Victor—even through a concerted examination of their identities as fathers and providers—demonstrate the multilinear, multigenerational involvements of men in families, to the extent that it has been impossible to develop discrete accounts of their identities *solely* as biological fathers. Instead, these cases demonstrate the generationally interlayered character of families in these localities, and that are distinctive to these, whereby different 'generations', for example, children and grandchildren, may share similar ages and require similar parental care and support. Further, we identify a continuity in men's experiences both of work and worklessness in low-income localities, as well as through different family configurations, involvements, responsibilities, and relationships. Our analyses in this chapter link closely with those of Chaps. 6 and 7, and articulate the close parallels of these cases with other men across the broader datasets living in similar localities, through circumstances of poverty (see also, for example, Tarrant & Hughes, 2019).

We suggest that the longitudinal character of life history methodology adopted across the studies, as well as the intergenerational analytic framework we employ for our QSA, allows us to observe and explain, through accounts of low-income life, how place-based poverty is shaped through longer socio-economic processes; is stubborn, continuous, and unremitting (Emmel & Hughes, 2010, 2012), and integral to the longitudinal dynamics and character of men's family participation. For example, Bob's case provides insight into shifting patterns of working for men and women in low-income localities and how these produce an exchange of childcare and breadwinning roles for men and women through precarious economic periods, retreating industry, and a diminishing welfare state, and how families and the individuals within them respond flexibly to secure the work and resources they need to survive. Bob's case also exposes the limitations of the language of 'earning' or 'breadwinning' for these families through these circumstances, especially in its ability to describe what it is people provide for the everyday sustenance of their families. Instead, the language of provision becomes essential as a means of capturing this rich complex of practices of participation.

However, these men's family relationships are not unproblematic. Longitudinal analyses reveal histories of violence either as victim or perpetrator, anger, work insecurity, substance addiction, poor physical and mental health, and family estrangement. When intimate relationships end, women's accounts, such as those analysed in Chap. 4, often describe how their relationships with men require additional mediation, say by other family members. By working across four datasets gathered at different times, we can observe a continuity of constraints in the resourcing, working, living, and caring that is consequent on poverty, over a period of two decades. Poverty is stubborn, continuous, and unremitting and so too are men's efforts to sustain their families. Their accounts of seeking access to resources—work, benefits, legal recognition, housing—in and on behalf of their families, and where men describe persistent challenges to these efforts, they also describe episodes of mental ill health, and relationship breakdown.

Conclusion

Our examination of the cases of Bob and Victor in this chapter has enabled us to develop a more complex understanding of processes of strategic decision-making in family contexts, including how men make constrained choices about their financial and emotional resources, often with limited knowledge about their rights and in a context of dwindling financial and legal support. Such analytic attention moves us away from considering men as 'absent', and engages us in more fruitful engagement with the dynamic interplay of men's absence and presence in changing family configurations. We can also observe what formal and informal services landscapes these men are navigating and the choices that they have to make.

In the next chapter, 'Men in the system', we explore men's family participation in two additional cases; Geoff and Sam, men who, like Bob and Victor, are confronted with a complex of circumstances requiring them to assume parental or kinship care of grandchildren. Rather than the somewhat voluntaristic approach to taking on such parental responsibility, Geoff and Sam consider themselves—for different reasons—to lack any real choice in that the alternative care arrangements for their grandchild/ren are not acceptable to them. We examine the relationships and services they are required to navigate both to secure rights to kinship care, as well as the resources and support they need in these endeavours. These include extended family relationships, but also formal and informal health and social care, community services, educational institutions, courts and legal professionals, policing and probation services, housing, as well as relationships and resources contingent on unemployment and welfare. Distinctive in their accounts are how men are erased, marginalised, and recovered in becoming kinship carers and continue in such relationships.

References

Atkinson, R., & Kintrea, K. (2000). Owner Occupation, Social Mix and Neighbourhood Impacts. *Policy and Politics, 28*, 93–108.

Bengston, V., Copen, C. E., Putney, N. M., & Silverstein, M. (2008). Religion and Intergenerational Transmission Over Time. In K. W. Shale & R. P. Abeles (Eds.), *Social Structures and Aging Individuals: Continuing Challenges.* Springer Publishing.

Bosoni, M. L. (2014). "Breadwinners" or "Involved Fathers?" Men, Fathers and Work in Italy. *Journal of Comparative Family Studies, 45*(2), 293–315.

Comas-d'Argemir, D., & Soronellas, M. (2019). Men as Carers in Long-Term Caring: Doing Gender and Doing Kinship. *Journal of Family Issues, 40*(3), 315–339.

Connell, R. (1995). *Masculinities*. California University Press.

Cummins, S., Curtis, S. V., Diez-Roux, A., & Macintyre, S. (2007). Understanding and Representing 'Place' in Health Research: A Relational Approach. *Social Science & Medicine, 65*(9), 1825–1838.

Cunningham-Burley, S. (1984). 'We Don't Talk About it…': Issues of Gender and Method in the Portrayal of Grandfatherhood. *Sociology, 18*(3), 325–338.

Dermott, E., & Miller, T. (2015). More Than the Sum of its Parts? Contemporary Fatherhood Policy, Practice and Discourse. *Families, Relationships and Societies, 4*(2), 183–195.

Donald, L., Davidson, R., Murphy, S., Hadley, A., Puthussery, S., & Randhawa, G. (2021). How Young, Disadvantaged Fathers Are Affected by Socioeconomic and Relational Barriers: A UK-Based Qualitative Study, *Families, Relationships and Societies* (published online ahead of print 2021). Retrieved July 3, 2022, from https://bristoluniversitypressdigital.com/view/journals/frs/aop/article-10.1332-204674321X16321468785082/article-10.1332-204674321X163 21468785082.xml

Doucet, A. (2020). Father Involvement, Care and Breadwinning: Genealogies of Concepts and Revisioned Conceptual Narratives. *Genealogy, 4*(1), 14.

Douglas, G., & Ferguson, N. (2003). The Role of Grandparents in Divorced Families. *International Journal of Law, Policy & Family, 41*, 41–67.

Dwyer, P., Scullion, L., Jones, K., McNeill, J., & Stewart, A. B. R. (2020). Work, Welfare, and Wellbeing: The Impacts of Welfare Conditionality on People with Mental Health Impairments in the UK. *Social Policy & Administration, 54*(2), 0144–5596. https://doi.org/10.1111/spol.12560

Edin, K., & Nelson, T. J. (2013). *Doing the Best I Can: Fatherhood in the Inner City*. University of California Press.

Edwards, R., & Gillies, V. (2012). Farewell to Family? Notes on an Argument for Retaining the Concept. *Families, Relationships and Societies, 1*(1), 63–69.

Elliott, S., McKelvy, J. N., & Bowen, S. (2017). Marking Time in Ethnography: Uncovering Temporal Dispositions. *Ethnography, 18*(4), 556–576. https://doi.org/10.1177/1466138116655360

Emmel, N., & Hughes, K. (2010). 'Recession, It's All the Same to Us Son': The Longitudinal Experience (1999-2010) of Deprivation. *Twenty-First Century Society, 5*(2), 171–181.

Fee, A., McIlfatrick, S., & Ryan, A. (2020). Examining the Support Needs of Older Male Spousal Caregivers of People with a Long-term Condition: A Systematic Review of the Literature. *International Journal of Older People Nursing, 15*, e12318.

Fodor, E. (2006). A Different Type of Gender Gap: How Women and Men Experience Poverty. *East European Politics and Societies, 20*(1), 14–39.

Hagedoorn, P., & Helbich, M. (2021). Longitudinal Exposure Assessments of Neighbourhood Effects in Health Research: What Can be Learned from People's Residential Histories? *Health & Place, 68*, 1–7.

Halpern, A., Perez-Vaisvidovsky, N., & Mizrahi, R. (2021). Involving Fathers in Family Social Services in Israel: In the Shadow of a Conflicted Policy. *Families, Relationships and Societies*. https://bristoluniversitypressdigital.com/view/journals/frs/aop/article-10.1332-204674321X16297306778771/article-10.1332-204674321X16297306778771.xml

Hearn, J. (2004). From Hegemonic Masculinity to the Hegemony of Men. *Feminist Theory, 5*(1), 49–72.

Hughes, K., & Emmel, N. (2012). *Analysing Time: Times and Timing in the Lives of Low-Income Grandparents*, Timescapes Methods Guides Series 2012 Guide No. 9. file:///Users/anna/Downloads/analysingtimeandtimingshughesandemmel.pdf

Hunt, J. (2018). Grandparents as Substitute Parents in the UK. *Contemporary Social Science, 13*(2), 175–186.

Lupton, R. (2003). *Poverty Street: The Dynamics of Neighbourhood Decline and Renewal*. Policy Press.

MacDonald, R. (1997). *Youth, the 'Underclass' and Social Exclusion*. Routledge.

MacDonald, R., Shildrick, T., & Furlong, A. (2020). 'Cycles of Disadvantage' Revisited: Young People, Families and Poverty Across Generations. *Journal of Youth Studies, 23*(1), 12–27.

Mann, R., Tarrant, A., & Leeson, G. (2016). Grandfatherhood: Shifting Masculinities in Later Life. *Sociology, 50*(3), 594–610.

Mason, J., May, V., & Clarke, L. (2007). Ambivalence and the Paradoxes of Grandparenting. *The Sociological Review, 55*(4), 687–706.

McDowell, L. (2000). The Trouble with Men? Young People, Gender Transformations and the Crisis of Masculinity. *International Journal of Urban and Regional Research, 24*(1), 201–209.

McDowell, L. (2009). *Working Bodies: Interactive Service Employment and Workplace Identities*. Chichester: Wiley-Blackwell.

McKenzie, L. (2015). *Getting By: Estates, Class and Culture in Austerity Britain*. Policy Press.

Milligan, C., & Morbey, H. (2016). Care, coping and identity: Older men's experiences of spousal care-giving. *Journal of Aging Studies, 38*, 105–114. https://doi.org/10.1016/j.jaging.2016.05.002

Nandy, S., & Selwyn, J. (2013). Kinship Care and Poverty: Using Census Data to Examine the Extent and Nature of Kinship Care in the UK. *The British Journal of Social Work, 43*(8), 1649–1666.

Neysmith, S. M., Reitsma-Street, M., Baker-Collins, S., Porter, E., & Tam, S. (2010). Provisioning Responsibilities: How Relationships Shape the Work That Women Do. *Canadian Review of Sociology, 47*(2), 149–170.

Pilcher, J., Williams, J., & Pole, C. (2003). Rethinking Adulthood: Families, Transitions, and Social Change. *Sociological Research Online, 8*(4), 181–185.

Ridge, T. (2009). *Living with Poverty: A Review of the Literature on Children's and Families' Experiences of Poverty,* Department for Work and Pensions Research Report No 594. http://www.bris.ac.uk/poverty/downloads/keyofficialdocuments/Child%20Poverty%20lit%20review%20DWP.pdf

Roy, K. (2014). Fathering from the Long View: Framing Personal and Social Change Through Life Course Theory. *Journal of Family Theory and Review, 6,* 319–335.

Russell, R. (2007). The Work of Elderly Men Caregivers: From Public Careers to an Unseen World. *Men and Masculinities, 9*(3), 298–314. https://doi.org/10.1177/1097184X05277712

Ruxton, S. (2002). *Men, Masculinities and Poverty in the UK.* Oxfam.

Shefer, T., & Hearn, J. (2022). *Knowledge, Power and Young Sexualities: A Transnational Feminist Engagement. Routledge.*

Shildrick, T., & MacDonald, R. (2013). Poverty Talk: How People Experiencing Poverty Deny Their Poverty and Why They Blame 'The Poor'. *The Sociological Review, 61*(2), 285–303.

Shildrick, T., MacDonald, R., Webster, C., & Garthwaite, K. (2010). *The Low-Pay, No-Pay Cycle: Understanding Recurrent Poverty.* Joseph Rowntree Report: York.

Strange, J.-M. (2012). Fatherhood, Providing, and attachment in Late Victorian and Edwardian Working-class Families. *The Historical Journal, 55*(4), 1007–1027.

Sudbury, L., & Simcock, P. (2007). Grandparenthood and Cognitive Age: Key Variables for Targeting the Over-50 Market, *Micro and Macro Marketing, 3.* https://papers.ssrn.com/sol3/papers.cfm?abstract_id=2362835

Tarrant, A. (2014). Negotiating Multiple Positionalities in the Interview Setting; Researching Across Gender and Generational Boundaries. *The Professional Geographer, 66*(3), 493–500.

Tarrant, A. (2017). Getting Out of the Swamp? Methodological Reflections on Using Qualitative Secondary Analysis to Develop Research Design. *International Journal of Social Research Methodology, 20*(6), 599–611.

Tarrant, A. (2018). Care in an Age of Austerity: Men's Care Responsibilities in Low-income. *Families, Ethics and Social Welfare, 12*(1), 34–48.

Tarrant, A. (2021). *Fathering and Poverty: Uncovering Men's Participation in Low-Income Family Life.* Policy Press.

Tarrant, A., & Hughes, K. (2019). Qualitative Secondary Analysis: Building Longitudinal Samples to Understand Men's Generational Identities in Low Income Contexts. *Sociology, 53*(3), 538–553.

Tarrant, A., & Hughes, K. (2020). Collective Qualitative Secondary Analysis and Data-Sharing: Strategies, Insights and Challenges. In K. Hughes & A. Tarrant (Eds.), *Qualitative Secondary Analysis* (pp. 101–118). Sage, London.

Tyler, I. (2013). The Riots of the Underclass?: Stigmatisation, Mediation and the Government of Poverty and Disadvantage in Neoliberal Britain. *Sociological Research Online, 18*(4), 6.

Wright, S., & Patrick, R. (2020). Welfare Conditionality in Lived Experience: Aggregating Qualitative Longitudinal Research. *Social Policy and Society, 18*(4), 597–613.

Yeandle, S., & Buckner, L. J. (2017). Older Workers and Care-giving in England: The Policy Context for Older Workers' Employment Patterns. Journal of Cross-Cultural Gerontology, 32, 303–321.

Yeandle, S., & Cass, B. (2013). Working Carers of Older People: Steps Towards Securing Adequate Support in Australia and England? In T. Kroger & S. Yeandle (Eds.), *Combining Paid Work and Family Care*. Bristol University Press.

CHAPTER 6

Men in the System: 'Rescue and Repair' Through Kinship Caring

A significant context in which men in low-income families negotiate their identities as 'present' fathers is in encounters with health and social care services.
—(Tarrant, 2021, *Fathering and Poverty: Uncovering Men's Participation in Low-Income Family Life*. Policy Press, p. 79)

Introduction

In this chapter we examine men as grandparent kinship carers, an often over-looked experience for men in low-income family circumstances in which they become critical to sustaining families over time. In so doing, we advance our discussion of older men's 'rescue and repair' grandparenting, introduced in Chap. 5. Using the cases of Sam and Geoff, we consider how, through specific selections, choices, and interventions by health and social care services, men may or may not be involved or marginalised in decisions concerning becoming grandparent kinship carers, as well as whether and how they are supported, resourced, or recognised in these roles. These interactions with health and social care services offer detailed insight into circumstances of poverty, including how they may produce additional challenges for men and families across the lifecourse and intergenerationally.

To support our analyses of Sam and Geoff as grandparent kinship carers, we provide an overview of definitions of kinship care and kinship care

K. Hughes, A. Tarrant, *Men, Families, and Poverty*, Palgrave Macmillan Studies in Family and Intimate Life, https://doi.org/10.1007/978-3-031-24922-8_6

141

arrangements, reviewing existing academic literatures that evidence the relationship between low-income family life and interventions into parenting both by the state and other family members (Farmer & Moyers, 2008; Hunt et al., 2008; Tarrant et al., 2017; Smethers, 2015; Hunt, 2018). Few sociological studies have adopted a gendered lens or explored kinship care from the perspectives of men (although see Tarrant, 2021) and our analyses of Sam and Geoff as well as Bob and Victor in the previous chapter, address these lacunae. The motivations, gendered meanings, lived experiences, and relational dynamics of the lives of male kinship carers are examined here, alongside a broader consideration of the economic hardships that kinship care may produce. Our intergenerational, lifecourse framework permits an investigation into the long-term formal kinship care arrangements of Sam and Geoff, and supports new and novel insights into the diversity of men's care responsibilities in low-income families. It is in this regard that these men's experiences demonstrate the importance and centrality of long-term relationships with formal and informal health and social care service providers. This is not only for the sustaining (Chap. 4) and resourcing (Chap. 5) of the everyday lives of low-income families (see also Emmel et al., 2007; Neale & Lau Clayton, 2014) but also their ability to *be* families through gaining formalised recognition of certain forms of 'relating' and kinship (see also Tarrant & Hughes, 2019). Finally, we observe how the men's own family histories are 'brought forward' and serve as narrative resources on which they draw to explain their approaches to grandparent kinship care. These provide useful biographical settings through which to understand intergenerational trajectories and perspectives of family participation. Significantly, understanding these people's conceptions of, and engagement in, these wider place-based relationships is crucial to developing a fuller understanding of how such caring orientations are integral to sustaining families through poverty.

Kinship Care

Our analyses of men's provisioning of low-income families in Chap. 5 signify how men, and particularly older men, may become grandparent kinship carers at various points over time. Kinship care, sometimes also known as friends or family care, is a relatively invisible yet deeply significant placement option, that supports children to remain with family members in contexts where parents are no longer able, or deemed incapable of, providing care. Up to 180,000 children in the UK are being raised by a family member under formal kinship care arrangements (Wijedasa, 2017).

Anna's 'Men, Poverty and Care' study sought to access men providing kinship care as part of a purposive sampling strategy that built out of her secondary analysis of data from the 'Midlife Grandparents' and 'Young Fathers' studies (see Chap. 1, Tarrant, 2017; Tarrant & Hughes, 2019). Illustrating the connections between young parenthood and kinship care, across both samples, we have also observed high levels of grandparent care for grandchildren, especially among families in low-income localities. This includes in all of the eight cases of grandparents (aged 35–55) in the 'Midlife Grandparents' study (Emmel & Hughes, 2010; Hughes & Emmel, 2007–2012), in 15 of 31 cases of young fathers in the Young Fathers Study, and 6 of 26 cases in the 'Men, Poverty and Care' study. All three studies confirm the close layering of generations, strong, locally based kin ties, and enduring, if volatile, relationships with families, as a relatively common feature of family life in disadvantaged communities (Hughes & Emmel, 2012; Emmel & Hughes, 2014; Neale & Lau Clayton, 2014; Wijedasa, 2017; Tarrant, 2021).

Not all the arrangements across these studies are formally regulated or ratified by the state. For example, across the studies, participants describe a continuum of supplementary to parental care, wherein informal kinship arrangements are managed and negotiated within family contexts with no state or financial entitlements. Alternatively, they may have formal kinship arrangements where state involvement facilitates greater recognition via legal orders and some, albeit limited, access to financial and material resources (see also Hughes & Emmel, 2012; Skoglund & Thørnblad, 2019). Given the variety of care arrangements, the term 'kinship care' sometimes has little resonance within the families themselves. It is only in encounters with formal health and social care providers that grandparents or other family members come to be defined this way, or come to describe themselves as such as part of a broader array of purposeful health and social care engagements in the pursuit of resource or financial support necessary for everyday living. For example, participants in the 'Midlife Grandparents' and 'Men, Poverty and Care' studies described pursuing social services contacts for items such as nappies, milk formula, feeding bottles, towels, bedding, beds, emergency clothes, and so on for their grandchildren when unexpectedly confronted with their long-term parental care.

Sociological attention to kinship care in families living through poverty is much needed in any consideration of how poverty may shape the longitudinal and intergenerational dynamics of families. A systematic, nationally representative review established a significant relationship between poverty and children in kinship care (Nandy & Selwyn, 2013) with children in families in poverty being 'more likely to be looked after' (Nandy & Selwyn, 2013; see also Bywaters et al., 2020). However, the directional character of this relationship is complex and there is a need for detailed processual accounts of such arrangements and their familial configurations. The increase in grandparent-carers has been attributed to a range of causes typically experienced by the middle generation including drug and alcohol abuse, mental illness, death, the inability to parent, domestic violence in the home of the grandchild/ren, divorce, and increasing participation in full-time working for parents (Newsome & Kelly, 2004; Kinship, 2017). Each of the above causes, such as mental illness, drug abuse, and death of the adult child/parent of the grandchildren, were in evidence in the cases of the grandparents in the linked studies analysed for this book.

There has been a tendency for kinship care research to focus predominantly on the experiences of women, reflecting trends in broader evidence. Statistical data indicate that, as a population, the majority of kinship carers are women (Nandy et al., 2013). Women are more likely to be primary caregivers, for example, and as kinship carers are particularly vulnerable and at risk of impoverishment (see also Bennett & Daly, 2014), ill health, and poor housing conditions (Hunt, 2018). Yet kinship carers are far from a uniform, homogenous population, with great variation according to characteristics, roles, and statuses (MacDonald et al., 2018). Qualitative analyses of men's experiences as kinship carers rarely feature in existing sociological or policy research literatures (Neale & Patrick, 2016), and there is a lack of focused engagement with grandfather kinship carers (although see Tarrant, 2018, 2021). This is perhaps unsurprising as sociological research about grandparents often treats 'grandparent' as synonymous with 'grandmother'. Excepting an early contribution by Cunningham-Burley (1984), grandfathers have only been researched in piecemeal fashion, although there has been a burgeoning literature in recent years (Tarrant, 2013, 2014; Mann et al., 2016; Buchanen & Rotkirch, 2016; Jamieson et al., 2018). Men are therefore absent from accounts of grandparent kinship care in the broader literature, yet our four datasets are replete with examples of men in these roles.

Although indicative of some of the crisis circumstances in which government agencies and family members might intervene in the support of children, we also lack research into the particularities of circumstances through which people assume kinship care responsibilities, and how unanticipated care responsibilities are experienced and resourced longer term. This lack of longitudinal engagement in how families are reconfigured over time and intergenerationally in response to changing care responsibilities, means that research into the 'ripple' effects (Valentine & Hughes, 2010) of poverty across generations is less developed. Effectively, we lack insight into how intergenerational poverty shapes family interdependencies, through which circumstances and how, with whom and how, whether and by whom these are navigated and managed. Consequently, there is a need for more concerted sociological engagement with how changing welfare and policy contexts shape the experiences of kinship carers in low-income families as part of a broader project of understanding families through poverty. In this chapter, we address and advance these two strands of debate.

Sam and Geoff: Grandparent Kinship Carers

In terms of their grandparenting, Sam and Geoff's cases resemble Bob and Victor's in Chap. 5. All four men make huge, predominantly unanticipated, investments in the lives of their grandchildren, and sometimes their great-grandchildren, working alone or alongside their partners to support these younger relatives when their adult children are in crisis or no longer deemed capable to look after their own children. These cases provide insights into kinship care as a relatively common family occurrence, subject to particular forms of governance that affects how they sustain their families over time.

Although their interviews were separated by a gap of ten years there is significant continuity in Sam and Geoff's experiences, despite the somewhat different study foci. Sam took part in Anna's Men, Poverty and Care study, wherein men in different generational positions were interviewed about their family participation and processes of economic constraint on their fathering. Despite the ten-year gap between the two men's interviews, Sam's case articulates and extends the combined themes and experiences of the men across all four studies drawn on for this book (see Chap. 3). Geoff participated in the Midlife Grandparents study, where the focus was specifically on participants' experiences of being grandparented and being grandparents themselves. An unexpected finding of that study was the frequency and ordinariness of grandparenting kinship care of one form or another. Our selection of Sam and Geoff is theoretically driven. Despite expressing very different emotional orientations towards becoming kinship carers, they share distinctive experiences that facilitate insight into the microdynamics of managing and sustaining families through low-income circumstances.

A Brief Overview of the Cases

As with the previous empirical chapters, we begin with the men's pen portraits, highlighting any connections to cases discussed in Chaps. 4 or 5 to contextualise the analyses we present.

Sam: Sam was 52 years old when he was interviewed for the Men, Poverty and Care study in 2015. At the time of interview, he is an informal kinship carer for a neglected grandson, Leo, and was in the process of securing parental responsibility via a Special Guardianship Order. A second follow-up interview confirmed that he had acquired this status. To become a kinship carer, he was actively navigating the courts and social services, to challenge the decision that his grandson had been released to his maternal grandmother who has a history of her children being taken into care. Sam raises concerns with social services when he sees signs of abuse in his grandson. This results in a protracted process in which they need to determine that he is not responsible for the abuse. Sam has a widespread reputation in his job, and it is his community standing and connections that eventually persuade the courts to assign him this responsibility. He also describes a more distant relationship with his daughter who lives in a different part of the UK. He rarely sees the children of his daughter because of the long distance and because of an historic argument caused by the breakdown of the relationship of Sam and his daughter's mother. In this relationship he considers himself to be perceived as an 'absent' father and grandfather.

Geoff: Geoff was 59 years old when first interviewed for the Midlife Grandparents study in 2008. He is married to Margaret who was 49 years old. Geoff and Margaret have three adult daughters and have ten grandchildren, one of whom they have rarely seen. They have been grandparent carers for eight years to their two granddaughters from their middle daughter, aged 11 and 12 at the time of the first interview. Geoff describes a difficult childhood in which he was abandoned by his mother, and later by his father, had few family relationships, and close family members that he never knew. Geoff was abused by his alcoholic father and was sent to foster parents. He had been excited about being fostered, although the foster parents abused him, and when offered to return to his parents, Geoff chose to go into care. He describes being in care as the most stable period in his childhood, and his view of the families he experienced as a child is that they are not safe places. Geoff and Margaret both have extensive and ongoing health and mental health problems. Geoff has a history of depression and alcoholism, but currently is sober. The couple were receiving extensive support from a third sector worker who was supporting Geoff to manage his anger via an anger management group for men, and a group for grandparents who are kinship carers. They have a grandson who became a father at the age of 13, and they discuss the access barriers to his child, and how he is supported by social services in seeing his child.

Sam's Case: 'Rescue and Repair' Grandparent Kinship Care

In Chap. 5 we discussed categorisations of 'rescue' and 'repair' grandparenting, which conceptualise the practices of care kinship carers engage in to support their grandchildren. 'Rescuing' refers to when grandparents 'rescue' grandchildren from problematic situations by removing them temporarily or permanently from their parent's home. 'Repair' refers to situations in which the adult child is struggling that raises concern in the grandparent for their grandchild/ren. Here, grandparents 'pilot in' to repair these situations and ameliorate risks and impacts on the grandchildren. These terms are not mutually exclusive. 'Repair' often occurs in rescue situations, where grandparents describe repairing their children's mental and physical health, and rescue is often the reason for 'repair' involvement, where grandparents describe feeling an urgency to intervene in their adult child's family life, as a means of preventing a difficult situation becoming worse.

While not exclusive to low-income families, rescue/repair grandparenting is connected to the need for families with high formal health and social care involvement (Bywaters et al., 2020; McCartan et al., 2018) to avoid potentially punitive professional interventions, including 'the social taking the children away' (Hughes & Emmel, 2012). Both Sam and Geoff are involved in 'rescue' grandparenting, albeit in different ways. While Geoff's 'rescue' grandparenting has been really fraught, as we see below, Sam's narrative is valuable as it reflects the generality of experiences across the grandparent generations in the four studies. Sam describes how he actively identifies risk to his grandson, Leo, and engages in a protracted process to secure parental responsibility for him. Leo has a number of hospital visits and on release from one of these, during a visit with Sam and Mike, Leo's father, Sam raises concerns about his grandson's health. A medical examination identifies green stick fractures and brain bleeds in the young child. Despite Sam being visible to social services, raising concerns and identifying himself as his grandfather and a potential kinship carer, Leo is placed away from the family and spends 12 months with a foster family.

In tracing this history of becoming a grandparent and then a grandparent kinship carer, Sam describes his family circumstances as having distinctive features. His youngest son, Mike, who is Leo's father, has significant learning disabilities. Mike is 18 when he becomes a father, is living at home, dependent on Sam and likely to remain so throughout his life. The unexpected pregnancy, and birth of Leo, prompts Sam to investigate the maternal family to understand how and by whom parental responsibility for Leo would be taken:

> [Mike's] not a bad lad, you know. So when we found out Leo was on his way, the first thing I wanted to do was speak to the girl's parents. She wasn't a local girl, and after meeting her, we found out she was very, very streetwise. And the reason for having Leo was so that she could get a flat and money.

> I mean, then, at that point I found out, she was also a product of the care system. Her and all her siblings had been removed from her mother, all five of them had been removed for various mis-goings on of the very, very worst kind. When I raised these concerns with social services, they told me to go away and mind my own business. I was trying to raise concerns for three months, four months, on a daily basis, and all I got from them – they all pulled together, shut me out, shut everybody out and said, "Go and get some legal advice." Then they broke the golden rule. My lad was actually going to review meetings and, in the meantime, she'd had the baby, twelve weeks early. He was twenty-six weeks, wasn't he, when he was born? .... "We've got somebody lined up for him." I said, "You don't even know if he's going to survive or not." No, no, they were putting him up for adoption.

> Even though I'm saying I'll have him. Even when I found out she was pregnant, my lad's not capable, she's not capable. Then I found out that she was a product of the care system. *Sam, Men, Poverty and Care Study, Round One*

Here, Sam describes becoming a grandfather, but also becoming involved in multiple systems as a consequence of recognising and identifying risk to Leo, through which his capability as a potential carer to Leo is assessed. In turn, this involves Sam himself being treated as risky.

In accounting for getting involved in risk assessments and for the risks Leo's mother and her maternal grandparents pose to him, Sam describes Leo's mother as 'streetwise', drawing on a more general narrative that stigmatises young, single mothers. Above, Sam subscribes to a prevalent narrative trope, being 'streetwise', that describes them as becoming mothers to secure social housing and related financial benefits. In effect, these young women are stigmatised by their framing as 'career parents', where the careers involve securing welfare resources through maternal labour rather than paid labour (see also, Wenham, 2016). While we are not focused on these discursive tropes, Sam can be observed to be bringing his understanding of the mother's childhood into the present to evaluate her as a parent. Sam's treatment of the young mother's history of having been removed from the care of the grandmother is used by him to be both indicative of, and possibly productive of, her own inability to mother Leo, moving her from being 'at risk' as a child, to being 'a risk' as a parent (see also Blaxland et al., 2021 for a full discussion of this). This illustrates how the requirements of social care systems often position different individuals in opposition to each other (Sam vs the young mother) through processes in which each is required to demonstrate their own 'fitness' as a guardian to a young child, in preference to the other. Given the continued primacy of the mother-child dyad in legal and health and social care decision making, men are often less likely to be considered as potential carers than women (Neale & Davies, 2015; Tarrant, 2021) especially where they are non-resident (Sobo-Allen & Howarth, 2020; Halpern et al., 2021). Sam's evaluation of his grandson's mother, to some extent, is therefore reflective of these requirements and of the need to construct a narrative that asserts his 'rescue' of Leo, implying a need for men to *learn* how to position themselves and others in the competition for child custody. Such concerns are just one of several influences expressed as part of his own rationale for taking on parental care of his grandson.

As well as accounting for the maternal family, Sam brings his own childhood forward in his explanations for why he has 'rescued' his grandson:

I was brought up by my Gran, who had eight children of her own. So I'd have been the youngest of nine kids, if you like. I mean, I've never had anything at all to do with my mother, so it was uncles, aunties, cousins, that side of things. It was a very tight family. And, you know, I'm saying all this, that I was brought up by my Gran and not my parents, no offence whatsoever, I think it's actually been good. I think it's given me a better standing now as I've got older. There was nobody to lean on. There was nobody to rely on. I think what it does is it does build character and it does build strength....I think, in the sixties – I mean, we're talking about 1963 here – my mother lived in a student area of Leeds, if you like, took full advantage of it, to put it in a nice way. As did my old man. But to give him his due, he did try and get in touch and play his part. He did. He did want to do that. But an Irish Catholic family, you know, I think a lot of it, my Gran in particular who was staunch Irish, they weren't having any of that. So it just kind of fell apart and drifted apart and now we're here. *Sam, Men, Poverty and Care Study, Round One*

Sam's own upbringing by a grandmother underscores his confidence in being a grandparent carer himself. He elaborates his own history of being brought up in a family setting that was highly disciplined, safe, and with a strong moral narrative about the family and family responsibilities. Combined with the security of his family history, he explains that he is well respected by others locally, established through a history of community engagement, where he plays an active and visible role in supporting and training young people:

Bearing in mind I've been involved in amateur [sports] and, at the point this happened, I'd got myself a job. I've been a cab driver for a lot of years and what I was doing was transporting special needs kids and adults... I was also a member of the [UK wide community club]. I was the chairman for a lot of years. So they're not just talking to someone who's a good member of the public, you know. *Sam, Men, Poverty and Care Study, Round One*

Sam's experiences describe a broader locality where he is involved in a wide range of community-level roles, and he emphasises the professional character of these roles to invoke his externally validated moral standing, recognised by members of professional organisations. This status becomes crucial to gaining recognition of his capability to secure parental responsibility for Leo, and was asserted in situations where services and legal systems were required to determine if he could be a potential risk and threat to his grandson. He also describes an extensive family network of cousins and older relatives within travelling distance with whom he is in regular contact and who have become important family relationships for Leo. Sam thus mobilises his family experiences, skills, and expertise as well as a securely networked family in gaining professional support for becoming a grandfather kinship carer.

Gaining parental guardianship of Leo involves successfully 'fighting' social services. In this 'fight', despite his expertise as a parent of a son with a global developmental delay, his understanding of professional language and 'systems', and as a parent of two young men, securing parental responsibility is a protracted struggle for recognition:

> My lad had been to a meeting there and one social services staff had said … he was a reviewing officer who basically, when Mike told him, "I've got special needs. I think my dad should be here because I don't understand," he called him a liar. He did call him a liar. There was no way round it. "I think you're lying. Why haven't you got a job?" He said, "Because I'm not allowed to work." Again, "I think you're lying. I think you're just lazy." At that point, that really fired me up then and I've come home, picked the phone up and I said, "My house is now for sale. I'm raising money to bring us all together, and I will do it."… So it's kind of like a smack in the face. You put years and years into the community, into kids, special needs adults, and then you get told something like that. It's not good.

> They were backing me then and bent over backwards to help. They did keep a close eye on things, which I don't blame them. I'd rather that. I wished they'd done that from the start and he wouldn't have had these injuries and things. *Sam, Men, Poverty and Care Study, Round One*

This excerpt provides evidence of how professionals draw on blame rhetoric for poverty to justify exclusion of impoverished men from families. Sam is simultaneously managing intergenerational hardship through working to mitigate difficulties for both his son and grandson, with is responsibilities running across multiple family generations, whilst also needing to manage the stigma associated with poverty on behalf of his son, and himself, expressed through various professional interactions. In this case, these assumptions about poverty additionally express ableism, sexism, and ageism towards a young dad and an older grandfather kinship carer. This excerpt also exemplifies broader themes in Sam's interviews including experiences of multiple, interlacing, 'systems': family relationships, legal processes and involvements, health services, and social care services including social workers. Combined, these variously involve practices of monitoring and intervention that shape family relationships over time, rendering some members visible whilst simultaneously marginalising others, not necessarily via policies of 'best practice' (indeed, in placing Leo away from his family this contradicted policy), nor aligned with the available evidence in these decision-making processes (Gupta & Featherstone, 2016; Halpern et al., 2021).

For Sam, the stakes are high because these decision-making processes serve to exclude him from active caring and participation during Leo's early years, and constrain him from intervening in Leo's life. For Leo the stakes are high, because his risks of abuse were exacerbated by keeping him in a family context where his mother had been on an 'at risk' register, and his maternal grandmother had been identified as an unsuitable parent. Risks for Leo were also exacerbated when he was placed outside his family context as a direct consequence of a social care orientation towards Sam and Mike wherein they were not considered to be a potential family context for him (see also Sobo-Allen & Howarth, 2020).

Finally, Sam's case indicates that even once recognition and parental responsibility has been secured, this does not necessarily translate into securing adequate resources (financial/material). In his interview, Sam struggles to answer a question about his employment status and what finances he receives:

> Current employment status. Now, the thing is, with this, with social services, they've got me down as working. I suppose I'm self-employed, aren't I, really? I don't get a wage as such. What I get is a maintenance allowance. So you're actually not well off as a foster carer but eh. I make my own kind of luck, if you like…better put self-employed. *Sam, Men, Poverty and Care Study, Round One*

This lack of clarity around his relationship and status with the state continues when in later discussions he confirms that he has successfully secured a Special Guardianship Order (SGO). Having secured the SGO, Sam explains that this does not entitle him to welfare support in the long term. He articulates the challenges of this and his uncertain status as a kinship carer by asking; 'Am I a carer, a worker or a job-seeker?' This question about status arises in response to a requirement by social services early in the process of becoming a kinship carer that carers stop working in order to provide adequate care, such as is the case for Geoff, below. However, across the datasets we have observed how male kinship carers are then later asked to explain how they intend to secure financial stability, later in life through employment. As Tarrant (2021) notes, securing work around care responsibilities is problematic in a context where employment conditions do not provide opportunities for family/work flexibility or recognise men as carers, as for Bob in Chap. 5 (see also Tarrant, 2021).

Furthermore, where men have left employment to become kinship carers in localities experiencing a decline in work opportunities, securing a job following a period of leave is challenging (Tarrant, 2021). In this way, the role of kinship carer for men produces conflicts between their 'breadwinner' and 'carer' identities, that they subsequently have to confront in their interactions with professionals. This tension exposes the gendered character of health and social care decision making, based on normative practices that assume and situate women as carers and men as breadwinners, thereby gendering the organisation and resourcing of families. Sam's case demonstrates how these normative practices are embedded in, and foundational, to social care and legal systems involved in decision-making around the guardianship of children at risk. Combined, tensions and uncertainties introduced into kinship care decision making based on these gendered assumptions produces confusion and additional challenges that may involve risky negotiations with professionals about the relative importance of securing guardianship and demonstrating financial stability and security for doing so.

Sam's case permits engagement in two strands of enquiry. The first concerns gendered divisions of care—or how what men 'do', sustains family. There is evidence that these gendered ideologies shape men's experiences of securing primary care of children (Neale & Davies, 2015; Tarrant & Hughes, 2019), as well as their engagements and relationships with health and social care professionals. Recent research exploring men's experiences of the child protection system as *fathers* confirms that effective engagements with men are yet to be seen as part of the '"core business" of social work' (Brandon et al., 2017; Zanoni et al., 2013), raising considerable doubt around men's visibility as potential kinship carers as *grandfathers* (Tarrant, 2021). This lack of visibility is reinforced by a lack of research engagement with men as kinship carers, again predicated on gendered ideologies assuming women should be the primary carers of children (Neale & Patrick, 2016). Given this dearth of understanding, effective engagement with male kinship carers in a range of familial and generational positions (uncles, brothers, grandfathers), and recognition they can provide appropriate care, is only possible based on new evidence on how they engage in kinship care arrangements and responsibilities. Second, via a longitudinal family lifecourse framework, Sam's case illustrates how becoming kinship carers for people in low-income contexts serves to render them, whether male or female, additionally vulnerable to deprivation through the multiple, interlayered health, social care, legal and welfare 'systems'. While Sam is positive about his kinship carer role, describing it as 'keeping him young', and looking forward to seeing Leo grow up in his care, this is not a universal experience. We move on to Geoff's case to discuss how, when starting kinship care from an already vulnerable vantage point, the hardships and difficulties of new and unexpected responsibilities may combine to expose longer-term vulnerability (Emmel, 2017).

Geoff's Case: From Grandparent to Kinship Carer

In direct contrast to Sam's 'at all costs' narrative above, Geoff's account of being a grandparent kinship carer is fraught.[1] Far from the leisure/pleasure grandparenting of more resourced families described in existing research (Mason et al., 2007), or the non-negotiable attitude of grandparents and other relatives across the four datasets in relation to taking on the care of younger relatives in times of need, Geoff expresses a continuing unhappiness over the four years of the Midlife Grandparents study that he has had to take on kinship care of two of his granddaughters.

Geoff's perspective is shaped by his own family history and the challenging circumstances in which he and his wife Margaret become kinship carers to two of their granddaughters. They were removed by social services from their mother as they were considered 'at risk', and brought to their doorstep in crisis with little notice through what Geoff and Margaret describe as 'the midnight drop'.[2] Social services arrived with the girls, saying that either Geoff and Margaret take them in, or the girls would be placed in formal care. Across all four interviews, Geoff continues to express

---

[1] While we foreground Geoff's narrative in this section and the relevance of his experiences for our analyses and other men across the datasets, the joint character of their interview and profoundly interlayered negotiation around meanings of kinship care for Geoff, means we need to discuss Geoff *and* Margaret simultaneously.

[2] The term 'midnight drop' is also used to refer to the limited opportunities for grandparents to engage in considered decision-making around what might be best for their grandchildren, alongside a lack of rights to the necessary resources to care for additional children, in these family crisis situations where they already lack resource.

frustration at the constraints that becoming kinship carers places. This includes on their family resources and on his own expectations of how his later life with Margaret should have been. The social workers who brought the girls to Geoff and Margaret at midnight promised to provide more resources on the following day, but these failed to materialise, and this continues to be a source of frustration years later. While Geoff and Margaret's acceptance of the care of their granddaughters constitutes a form of 'rescue' grandparenting, as a couple, their interviews describe how kinship caring has intensified their own needs for additional support, both emotional and financial. Unlike the other men who present themselves as the 'rescuers', Geoff was different in that he and Margaret present themselves as also needing 'rescue' through formal support services.

In marked contrast to other participants with kinship care responsibilities across the four studies, Geoff's narrative also reflects an ambivalence towards the idea that formal care, namely outside of the family, is a bad option for his granddaughters. As described in Chap. 5, rescue and repair grandparenting was often initiated to prevent 'the social taking the children away'. Implicit was the two-fold belief that families were the best places for children and foster, or other state provided care, was not. In comparison, Geoff continues to question whether indeed the granddaughters need necessarily to live with their grandparents. This was so surprising to us, the authors, that in our QSA we paid additional attention to why this narrative worked against our own assumptions and confronted our normative expectations of how grandparents should behave towards grandchildren. Through this, we were also compelled to consider the longer family histories and related experiences described across Geoff's interviews to make sense of what were clearly enduring and distinctive views.

As part of our analytic consideration, we noted that the *character* of Geoff's ambivalence towards becoming a kinship carer differed from other cases across the studies, and also that observed in research about grandparents elsewhere. Mason et al. (2007), for example, discuss the axes of ambivalence in grandparents to centre on concerns about interference and non-interference in parenting of their grandchildren. In the 'Midlife Grandparents' study, grandparents expressed concern about the continued wellbeing of their grandchildren, their own financial wellbeing, and the longer-term independence and capabilities of their adult children in becoming satisfactory parents. Geoff's ambivalence includes two additional elements. The first is his long-term and ongoing frustration around his lack of meaningful choice in becoming a kinship carer. Here, Geoff expresses anger at what he describes as his entrapment by the social services who brought the two granddaughters in the middle of the night. The second is anger at his adult daughter, Abigail, the girls' mother, who failed to care for her own children, forcing him to take on the parental responsibility that he continues to question.

Although Geoff's more extended narrative expresses anger and frustration, he is keen to emphasise his efforts to do a good job on behalf of his granddaughters, efforts that have also been recognised by others, including support professionals. For example, Geoff attends a men's group on a regular basis to discuss his personal challenges with alcohol dependency and violence. He does this to manage his frustration at having to look after his granddaughters, the subsequent loss of his job, as well as his anger towards the eldest granddaughter who is, in his words, rebellious and a 'handful':

> I mean I'm quick tempered don't get me wrong I'm very quick tempered because me dad were same, but like say if [eldest granddaughter] started and all that I have to walk away. Cos I know I've told her many times I have to walk away and it's hard, it's an' hard thing to do walking away you know what I mean? A little kid's having a go at you and it's, it's an hard, your own grandkid's having a go at you…It's an hard thing to walk away, it is (laughs) you know what I mean it's, it's very hard, I find it difficult you know…
> *Geoff, Round One, Midlife Grandparents Study*

Here, walking away is important to Geoff, as it goes against what he describes as his inherited 'quick temper', and also what we come to learn is the more common physical violence he himself experienced as a young child when older people in parental relationships towards Geoff found him a 'handful'. The challenges of grandparent kinship care for Geoff and Margaret are additionally shaped by the economic fortunes of the locality in which they live. In Geoff's earlier extract, like Bob in Chap. 5, he directly links their family fortunes with those of the global economic recession of 2008, and explains that he had to give up his job to help parent his grandchildren and support Margaret. Like Bob, Geoff expresses frustration at how changing family responsibilities, and crises involving his adult children and consequently his grandchildren, affects his ability to fulfil expectations of breadwinning. Working identity was central to Geoff's self-esteem and pride, a finding noted in other research about men and work identity (Morgan, 1992). Across the interviews, we become aware that Geoff struggled to read and write as a child, and indeed met Margaret at a 'special school' organised for children with difficulties in these skills. Geoff describes a history of meaningful employment in which he is successful despite these challenges. Again, like Bob, having to leave his job led to depression and the need to take 'anxiety medication'. His interviews express an ongoing emotional struggle around this loss, and how not being in paid employment inhibits his efforts to provide financially. He explains:

> I just feel so annoyed with my daughter, you know what I mean? This is and obv…obviously, er, giving me job up, I mean it were only part time, but it were a job. Er, and that's the part I can't get me head 'round. I still can't today unfortunately I find it hard. You know I do find it hard…. I know for a fact I won't work again, I won't work again now….I've worked all me life and like I say, I had to give up a good job financially. I couldn't take it. There was so much pressure on me. The, the pressure I mean, I admire any woman who will look after their grandkids or anything but er, it's bloody hard work. Financially wise and everything else it's, it's tiring sometimes. I mean especially obviously at our age it's not easy because financial and you just think you know you get like Katie [*eldest granddaughter*] I mean she's 12 don't get me wrong she's a nice kid but, er, "Can you get me this gran, can you get me that?" and you can't tell her, you can't just tell her, "Oh we're sorry we can't afford it darling". *Geoff, Midlife Grandparents, Life Story interview*

Geoff has no hope nor anticipation that he will be able to work again, despite only being in his mid-fifties. Despite his difficulties, he volunteers in the third sector organisation that continues to support both him and Margaret, to 'pay back' and help others new to similar circumstances. He was highly motivated to participate in the research and any conversations with the researchers beyond the recorded interviews. He was additionally very positive about the help he had received and despite feeling challenged by his kinship care responsibilities, his engagements with professionals are key to his narrative of sustained effort and engagement in becoming a 'good' grandfather kinship carer.

Geoff's account of his experiences of grandparent kinship care supports insights into how intergenerational familial networks are shaped and sustained through broader relational terrains. These include formal and informal health and social care services and relationships, legal systems, and the broader economies of the locality and nation. Synthesising across the cases of other men in our studies, analytic attention to these multiple relational terrains and networks offers additional insights into the complex processes shaping how men in low-income families and localities 'do' work and family over time. In relation to his experiences of becoming a kinship carer and sustaining this role, Geoff describes a potentially punitive and regulatory health and social care system that shapes his kinship care responsibilities wherein individual service providers (e.g. social workers), and pivotal decision-makers (e.g. judges) are critical in gatekeeping the resources he needs. This dependency is not something that he and Margaret learn about, navigate and—as in the case of Sam—resist and challenge. Instead, they actively seek out support in the 'civic' ordering of their family arrangements, responsibilities, and resourcing through the rewriting of their grandparent identities as kinship carers.

Financial entitlements are determined by, and differ according to, the formalised kinship care relationship between grandparents and grandchildren. A lack of understanding about the different kinds of legal orders available for grandparents in kinship care arrangements, and the kinds of financial resources attached to each, can be especially problematic for families in hardship. Here Margaret and Geoff reflect on what kind of arrangement they might be expected to agree to in formalising the terms of their relationship to their granddaughters, and describe their reliance on the judge to help them to make this decision in a way which will not financially disadvantage them:

Margaret:	Well it depends on how the judge, on how the judge'll see it. If he thinks it's best to just have the Special Guardianship then he'll do it.
Geoff:	We might be doing that.
Margaret:	But he thinks it's best to have the full custody…
Interviewer:	Like adoption?
Margaret:	…like adoption then you know it's up to him at end of t' day.
Geoff:	You see the problem is you can't foster 'em because you know you don't get paid. The Social Services don't pay you for, for fostering kids out. And to me that's annoying, believe me that is really annoying.
Margaret:	That why now we've got to come… Yeah but we've got to come off Income Support now…
Geoff:	Yeah but you'll get …

Margaret: ...to sort this because with him getting the pension from January even though I'm seven years younger than him I also get the pension because I can't work ...erm, it means that we've got to go for like the Child Tax Credits...

Geoff: Which'll be better. *Geoff   and   Margaret,   Midlife Grandparents Study, Round Two*

Uncertainty about the legal status of their granddaughters is crucially tied up with an uncertainty about welfare benefit entitlements, and the necessary micromanagement of different benefits where any diminution in income is catastrophic. This extract also describes the uncertain status of kinship care in a broader context of policy and legislative systems and the challenges engendered for grandparents through how kinship care arrangements position them both in relation to their grandchildren and to the benefits and payments required for their care. These very issues were articulately expressed by Sam and his case when he asks 'Am I a worker, a job seeker, or a government employee?'.

In the longer interview, where Geoff questions whether formal care is necessarily a bad thing, like Sam above he 'brings his childhood forward' to contextualise his feelings, albeit describing markedly different experiences of family. Here, Geoff's wider narrative charts a life history that articulates the challenges of navigating an abused childhood that was financially and emotionally constrained, during which he experienced state care and attended 'special schools'. From a very young age, Geoff's narrative describes a boy and then a man who experienced life from the vantage of being 'in the system'.

Explanations for these elements were to be found in data generated in the family-oriented life history narratives in interviews with Geoff and Margaret. Geoff's account described an unhappy childhood in which family was not a safe space for him. In contrast, his own experiences of formal care as a child had been relatively positive in comparison to the constant danger and precarity of the different family situations in which he had been. Abuse at the hands of his biological father, and while living with a set of foster parents, meant that for Geoff, family relationships were not necessarily those best placed to provide the care of children. Geoff, however, is alone in this view of who should care for his granddaughters. Margaret, for example, had tried to commit suicide some period before they received their granddaughters and, for her, their arrival was overwhelmingly positive. This difference between them is articulated through their joint interviews, where their shared narrative throughout is one of subtle dispute around this vexed question: whether they need to continue looking after the girls, and if going into formal care is really such a bad thing after all.

Driven by Geoff's own experiences as a child, a key feature of their joint 'rescue' discussion centres on the safety of their granddaughters, where this can be best achieved and who is best placed to decide on this (here, it is 'the Judge'):

Geoff:	Well yeah, because the way life is now, recession on and, er, and it does, it affects family, it affects kids. Erm, whether it's because I were in care, and I were very... I mean at first I were with my parents, and then things happened, and then I got put in care with my other brothers. And, er, whether it's, that is because it's, I'm overprotective... I just don't know what it is. It's, it, it's hard to explain sometimes. Cos when you've been in care you feel safe. And I don't want them to wander off. Not of, er, not at the time now.
Interviewer:	So is, er, do you find it, the thought of them leaving quite difficult?
Geoff:	Yeah. I think so. It's probably... I don't know if it... It's like, well put it this way, if their mam come back on the scene now, and it went to court, I'd like 'em to go to their mam, er, and I wouldn't, in a way. Because we'd miss 'em.
Margaret:	I know. We get used to it.
Geoff:	I, I'll have, miss 'em. Believe it or not I would miss 'em, cos we've had 'em all this time. But I, like I say, er, I wouldn't like 'em to go to their mam because I'd, they wouldn't be really safe with her.
Margaret:	...if it had to go court, the Judge wouldn't allow it.
Interviewer:	Yeah. So you feel that despite the difficulties in the area that you're living in, they're still better off...?
Geoff:	Oh yeah, yes, with us.
Margaret:	Oh yeah.
Geoff:	No doubt about that. You know what I mean?
Margaret:	Oh no doubt about that.
Geoff:	I have...
Margaret:	Everybody's said it. Er...

Interviewer:	Because you can protect them at home.
Margaret:	Yeah. Everybody's said how different they've been since we've had them. Erm, I mean everyone's commented on it, even the family. They've all commented. Because they've said, "If they'd been with their mum, they wouldn't have got anywhere."
Geoff:	But like I say, it's, er…
Margaret:	…they like being with us.
Geoff:	…you can't predict, nobody can predict how they're gonna turn out, can you?
Interviewer:	But you're trying to, sort of…
Geoff:	That's right.
Interviewer:	…protect their personal safety (inaudible)…
Margaret:	Yeah.
Geoff:	That's what I'm saying. *Geoff and Margaret, Midlife Grandparents, Round Three*

As we have argued across the chapters so far, we caution against an overfocus on people's individual capacity 'to provide' through paid work, as this obscures how personal histories are entangled with and shaped through broader socio-economic processes that lead to the underresourcing of low-income families. This includes in circumstances where generational responsibilities for children are redistributed from parents to other family members. Such emphasis on paid work as the sole source of provision additionally obscures the diversity of relationships through which people may gain access to resources crucial to the everyday concern of making ends meet (Edin & Lein, 1997; Strange, 2012; Emmel et al., 2007; Emmel & Hughes, 2010, see also Chap. 5). For example, Geoff and Margaret's narratives focus intensively on the kinds of relationships they need to develop to address their struggle to afford the basic necessities of everyday life. Indeed, they adopt the language of 'kinship care' through their engagements with professionals to gain access to necessary resources that improve their financial situation, their ability to support their grandchildren, and to accept or at least rationalise the circumstances in which they find themselves.

Unlike Sam, Geoff and Margaret initially lacked the skills to deploy this policy-relevant language about their family circumstances, as well as lacking knowledge of the possible resources available to them. Consequently, Geoff and Margaret describe a significant degree of dependence on the local professional support they receive through the various organisations and health and social care services with which they are involved. Positive experiences with these professionals have tremendous transformative potential for the microfinancing of their unanticipated, extended family. For example, through the third sector support service in which Geoff and Margaret are involved, they gain access to a financial advisor able to advise them on the welfare benefits to which they were entitled. A modest increase of £17 per week radically changes their financial circumstances, enabling them to 'put a bit by' for a day trip in the summer as their annual family holiday. The importance of such financial support and guidance exemplifies how, where people lack an understanding of effective policy language of relevant services and benefits, and perhaps of additional support available through third sector services, they may continue to struggle not only to communicate their needs to those best placed to support them, but also fail to access the benefits they so sorely need for financial survival. In effect, in some circumstances, people need to be 'trained to work' with formal services, an approach that is being evaluated and tested in the *Following Young Fathers Further* study directed by Anna (Tarrant et al., 2020–2024).

These observations demonstrate a contrast between Sam, and Geoff and Margarent. Geoff and Margaret's connections across their locality involve two distinct networks, those of their adult children and grandchildren, and networks of formal and informal professionals and legal systems. When asked about their area they talk about their locality briefly, but focus immediately on their housing. We have not yet touched on this aspect of people's lives but Chaps. 1 and 3 show how these localities were primarily comprised of social housing. There were several incidences in relation to their housing that they discussed, primarily in terms of its repair and adaptation:

Geoff: …it, it, it's, it's a nice area. Er, like I say, we've had a few dealings…with, with council, with repairs and, er, things like that in general. Because they don't seem that bothered, council, sometimes. You have to, you know, if you want owt doing you've gotta …go through channels, get every, you know, get it all sorted out. I mean we had a problem a few year ago wi, wi, er, condensation, it were damp. And we had to get a Solicitor, and get it all sorted out. And some people do have trouble. But luckily enough for us now it's all come together.

But, erm, as I say, council to me, don't, I don't know, they don't seem to bother sometimes, do they?

Margaret: Well we asked 'em, we got 'em out to do some tap repair in the bathroom, because we couldn't turn the taps in the bath, we couldn't turn 'em off. So because he had some different ones in his van, he went, er, and got 'em, put 'em on for the bath... He altered 'em and put some new washers on ...without having, sort of like. To go through, back through the, the, the channels, it'll take you a bloody, a week...   *Geoff and Margaret, Midlife Grandparents, Round Three*

As we saw above, Geoff and Margaret are entirely dependent on formal and informal health and social care services in securing the smallest service or resource. Here, they casually reveal how their relationship with the council requires mediation through a solicitor, in order to get small plumbing jobs completed. Their surprise and relief that the plumber was able to fix dripping taps without having to go back to the council illustrates the efforts involved for low-income families in 'going through the channels', which in more resourced households only involves a microdecision rather than a significant undertaking.

It is when bringing insights concerning this couple's dependence on health and social services, that Geoff's struggles as a grandfather become more comprehensible. In elaborating their difficulties with their house, Margaret describes how she has recently had an over-the-bath shower with a shower rail installed in her house. This is revolutionary, not only for her but also for Geoff. Her disabilities have previously meant she needed assistance to get out of her bath:

Margaret: Because, erm, I were having, it were awkward for me to do their [her granddaughter's] hair with just a jug. And, erm, they asked me then if I wanted a walk-in shower, and I said, "No," for the simple reason, er, having the girls, they like a bath. I like a bath as well, cos I like to soak in my bath and relax. And then when he came out [*man from Occupational Therapy Services*] he says, "Wouldn't you like a walk...?" I says, "No," I said, "because," I says, "of the girls." And I says, "I like to soak. It's relaxing." I says. He says, "I must admit," he says, "I like a soak in the bath." So that's when he said, "Oh, I'll put you this rail up." Cos there is one for the shower. And he says, "Is that one all right for you there?" I said, "Yeah, because, er, (inaudible) I can get in, I can lean over and get into the shower." Erm, so he says, "Well I'll put you one above this a bit, and, and better for you to get out, and that.".... Because if I get stuck sometimes I have to shout for him. Or if the girls are upstairs in the bedroom, cos they, they are really good, cos they know that grandma's difficulties (inaudible). I shout, "(inaudible), go and get your granddad," if I get stuck. .... When I go for a bath, sometimes I'll say to him, "Oh, Geoff, just come, just come and do, shower my hair." Er, but, erm, he does, he does help me with, with stuff like that now. He does help me. *Geoff and Margaret, Midlife Grandparents, Round Three*

In this example, it becomes understandable why Geoff and Margaret focus on their social housing when asked about their locality. Margaret describes the physical labour of grandparenting, such as washing her granddaughter's hair, keeping the girls clean, and how she and they like to relax. Her reported conversation with the man from Occupational Therapy services, demonstrates how ostensibly mundane practices such as baths and washing, and private areas such as bathrooms and showers, emerge as publicly regulated, shaped, and equipped spaces. In this respect, they link to the relevant council departments for housing and symbolise 'locality' for this couple. These are also spaces for family negotiation, such as who can use the bathroom alongside whom, when, and how. For men, this can be particularly problematic. When these negotiations occur in kinship caring circumstances, the microdynamics of family life become exposed as matters of formal service involvement. As Tarrant (2021) demonstrates for example, state-imposed rules around the care of looked after children in the homes of grandparent kinship carers have gendered implications that have potential to impact on relations between husbands and wives and grandparents and their grandchildren. Empirical data analysed in the Men, Poverty and Care study identifies concerns raised by male and female kinship carers, where explicit requests that men do not accompany female children to the bathroom to reduce the risk of potential allegations of sexual misconduct, impact on the relationships of the carers.

We additionally gain insight into the everyday care that Geoff—and sometimes the granddaughters—provide for Margaret and how she depends on these because of her disabilities. This example serves to reiterate the limitations of focusing on single generational identities. Geoff and Margaret were interviewed specifically as *grandparents*. Our analyses of Geoff's narrative so far have been primarily concerned with his account of these experiences. It is when we encounter these details of his everyday life, however, that he emerges as a possible counterpart for Bob, in the previous chapter. Like Bob, Geoff is forced to step back from his job because of his caring responsibilities that run in multiple directions: to his granddaughters, his wife and, we also find, towards his adult daughters, his other grandchildren, and his new great-grandson. Our conceptual focus in this chapter, for example, *grandparent* kinship caring has shaped our analyses of men's participation in low-income families across the life-course. Had we focused solely on expressions and practices of care and caring for family members in what have been traditional 'nuclear' formations, Geoff's grandparenting may have been seen as unusual, inadequate, and emotionally problematic. Instead, Geoff's case demonstrates the necessity of a longitudinal lifecourse approach for understanding people's situated explanations of how and why their lives have unfolded in the ways they have, without retreating to analyses premised solely on evaluating individual choices and actions that may support blame for people's disadvantage. Furthermore, understanding these relational terrains enables us to consider the nuances of not only the relational configurations comprising a 'system' (e.g. social care system, benefits system, legal system), but also includes how this is navigated and experienced. Crucially, Geoff is dependent on third sector and formal social services support to remain present and engaged in the lives of his granddaughters, and indeed continues to be 'coached' as to the desired character of this involvement.[3] Such relationships ensure security and safety for Geoff, his granddaughters and Margaret.

Furthermore, as Geoff's interviews develop and he is asked about the locality in more detail, his responses provide some additional context for his frustration and anger about his eldest daughter's 'attitude'. In an extended section of their interview, for both Geoff and Margaret, their concern relates to how being disobedient, going out without permission,

---

[3] See also Emmel (2017), on the 'pivotal character of social care, legal services and welfare provision for explanations of vulnerability and flourishing', p. 645.

and rebelling against their authority moves her into parts of her locality where young people her age 'drink beer in the streets'. Specifically, however, their concern is that by hanging out in the streets, it makes their eldest granddaughter more vulnerable to violence in the locality:

Margaret: She already has [*been personally attacked*]. Erm, some lads, erm, set about her. They went to, went to (inaudible). And, erm, she phoned one day in tears. And I says, "What's the matter?" "Them lads." I says, "Well they go to your school?" I said, she said, "Yeah." Then she says, "I know who they are?" I says, "Well what were they doing?". She says, "They were hitting me," and then they said, "Oh you, you, you're different because you live with your grandma and granddad." And, "Why do you live with your grandma and granddad?" And she, then they kept saying, "Your mum's a bitch," and stuff like this. And it were, really upset her.

Geoff and Margaret, Midlife Grandparents, Round Three

Although this comes from Margaret, she is prompted to say this by Geoff, and he concurs throughout. For both of them, their only excursions are to the charity for grandparent kinship carers, to their two adult daughters' houses and, on occasion, to their grandchildren's school. The intergenerational dynamics of hardship at play here include the stigma of being raised by grandparents, intergenerational experiences of both familial and place-based violence, and the transmission of care across and also down generations, such as how Margaret's daughters and granddaughters are involved in her care. Through Geoff's case, with Margaret alongside him, we observe people whose life experiences have entailed high rates of involvement in health and social care, and legal systems throughout their lives, and thereby come to understand how these forms of involvement comprise the everyday localities of their lives. In particular, Geoff's profound dependence on these relationships is articulated through his struggles in managing them, exposing the implications of these both for the survival of his family and also his family participation.

Men as (Grandparent) Kinship Carers

Before concluding, we reiterate our commitment to sustained critical engagement of the cases we examine. Becoming kinship carers and sustaining these unexpected and often emotionally and financially difficult responsibilities over time is not necessarily an unalloyed 'good'. While kinship care is a more stable option for children and young people it can be a complex and demanding role for carers themselves, who are more likely to have disabilities and experience significant levels of deprivation (Wellard et al., 2017; Hunt, 2018). According to Mervyn-Smith (2018) outcomes for kinship carers mean many fare worse than peers of the same generational cohort, living in inadequate accommodation, financing sometimes two or more children unexpectedly with limited support via the welfare system, and losing connection to the labour market either voluntarily or through necessity. Both Sam and Geoff are illustrative of how problematic and challenging becoming a kinship carer may be, albeit in different ways.

Although the men live in similar localities and share experiences as grandfather kinship carers, they have different orientations to their roles and identities in this regard. For both men, their family histories are consequential in shaping their ideas around their unanticipated familial responsibilities and obligations. The circumstances in which they both become kinship carers are also distinctive; Sam explicitly 'rescues' his grandson while Geoff expresses continued ambivalence towards his granddaughters and questions whether kinship care is necessary. Geoff also requires much more support and intervention in taking on responsibilities for his grandchildren in ways that are out of step with his own expectations about how his life should unfold.

However, these cases are comparable in illustrating how the meanings associated with grandfather kinship care are shaped, both by hardship in the locality and in their lives, and by the professional and legal services they are required to interact with to secure resources on behalf of their younger relatives and themselves. Both are required to develop a policy-based language of family—kinship carer—to sustain particular familial relationships. This extends the changes in language concerning family identities introduced by Victor, who describes himself as a 'step-father' in Chap. 5. The term 'step-father' derives from a legalistic reconfiguration of family relationships and responsibilities consequent on couples with children who repartner. Nevertheless, the term 'step-father' still invokes the language of family. Kinship carer, by contrast, is derived solely through histories of policy formation and engagement in changing family arrangements and relationship, and is oriented primarily towards guardianship roles across the broadest range of family ties (grandfather, uncle, older brother, cousin, and so on). While using this policy-based language of family is essential for leveraging access to necessary resources, whether material or support, this language *writes in* specific modes of caring and responsibility for these grandfathers. Too, the language of kinship care rewrites their relationships to work and provisioning, and the need to establish care arrangements that remain subject to ongoing surveillance and monitoring. In these ways, not only do men enter 'the system' to become grandparent kinship carers, but so too do their family relationships, to the extent that these can be described as *'families* in the system', where such families are characteristic of these localities and simultaneously expressive of them. Consequently, our analyses of grandfather kinship carers help identify how families in low-income contexts come to have high rates of health and social care intervention (Hughes & Emmel, 2012), and how these interventions shape possibilities for the doing of families through poverty.

CONCLUSION

We have used these cases to explore and render visible men's family participation and generational responsibilities and investments later in the lifecourse, and to interrogate how the longitudinal dynamics of poverty shape the distinctive familial and intergenerational processes that are navigated by men in these contexts. Such investments include 'rescue and repair' grandparenting, including as kinship carers and here, as with other areas of research and policy on family life, men are often either hidden or unnoticed.

In this chapter, we have redressed this gap in existing evidence and established how men and women across the four linked studies drawn upon for this book take on unexpected care responsibilities for grandchildren in contexts of high dependency and hardship. In Chap. 4, using women's accounts of men, we establish how men sustain families from multiple generational positions. The cases of Bob and Victor in Chap. 5 enable us to develop a more nuanced account of how, in low-income circumstances, and against the backdrop of persistent economic decline, men continue to provision families. In considering grandfather kinship care, this chapter demonstrates how men (and women) facilitate the intergenerational *doing* of families through formal and informal health and social care involvements, how these processes may be gendered, and how these involvements are sometimes pivotal in shaping the possibilities for doing and even having family. Combined, these chapters work towards 'recovering' a more comprehensive account of men's intergenerational family participation through changing family configurations. In the next and final empirical chapter, we consider how the longitudinal dynamics of poverty shape and/or constrain the possibilities of families for men over their lifecourse.

REFERENCES

Bennett, F., & Daly, M. (2014). *Poverty Through a Gender Lens: Evidence and Policy Review on Gender and Poverty*. Joseph Rowntree Foundation Report.

Blaxland, M., Skattlebol, J., Hamilton, M., van Toorn, G., Thomson, C., & Valentine, K. (2021). From Being 'at Risk' to Being 'a Risk': Journeys into Parenthood Among Young Women Experiencing Adversity. *Families, Relationships and Societies, 0*(0), 1–20.

Buchanen, A., & Rotkirch, A. (2016). Twenty-first Century Grandparents: Global Perspectives on Changing Roles and Consequences. *Contemporary Social Science, 13*(2), 131–144.

Brandon, M., Philip, G., & Clifton, J. (2017). *'Counting Fathers In': Understanding Men's Experiences of the Child Protection System*. University of East Anglia Report.

Bywaters, P. et al., (2020). *The Child Welfare Inequalities Project: Final Report Paul Bywaters and the Child Welfare Inequalities Project Team*. https://pure.hud.ac.uk/ws/files/21398145/CWIP_Final_Report.pdf

Cunningham-Burley, S. (1984). 'We Don't Talk About it…': Issues of Gender and Method in the Portrayal of Grandfatherhood. *Sociology, 18*(3), 325–338.

Edin, K., & Lein, L. (1997). Work, Welfare, and Single Mothers' Economic Survival Strategies. *American Sociological Review, 62*(2), 253–266.

Emmel, N. (2017). Empowerment in the Relational Longitudinal Space of Vulnerability. *Social Policy and Society, 16*(3), 457–467.

Emmel N D & Hughes K. (2010). 'Recession, it's all the same to us son': the longitudinal experience (1999–2010) of deprivation, in Rosalind Edwards and Sarah Irwin, Lived experience through economic downturn in Britain—perspectives across time and across the life-course, Twenty-First Century Society, 5: 2, 119–124. https://doi.org/10.1080/17450141003783413

Emmel, N., & Hughes, K. (2014). Vulnerability, Intergenerational Exchange and the Conscience of Generations. In R. Edwards & J. Holland (Eds.), *Understanding Families Over Time: Research and Policy*. Palgrave Macmillan.

Emmel, N., Hughes, K., Greenhalgh, J., & Sales, A. (2007). Accessing Socially Excluded People—Trust and the Gatekeeper in the Researcher-Participant Relationship. *Sociological Research Online, 12*(2), 43–55.

Farmer, E., & Moyers, S. (2008). *Kinship Care: Fostering Effective Family and Friends Placements.* Jessica Kingsley.

Gupta, A., & Featherstone, B. (2016). What About My Dad? Black Fathers and the Child Protection System. *Critical and Radical Social Work, 4*(1), 77–91.

Halpern, A., Perez-Vaisvidovsky, N., & Mizrahi, R. (2021). Involving Fathers in Family Social Services in Israel: In the Shadow of a Conflicted Policy. *Families, Relationships and Societies.* https://bristoluniversitypressdigital.com/view/journals/frs/aop/article-10.1332-204674321X16297306778771/article-10.1332-204674321X16297306778771.xml

Hughes, K., & Emmel, N. (2012). *Analysing Time: Times and Timing in the Lives of Low-Income Grandparents,* Timescapes Methods Guides Series 2012 Guide No. 9. file:///Users/anna/Downloads/analysingtimeandtimingshughesandemmel.pdf

Hunt, J. (2018). Grandparents as Substitute Parents in the UK. *Contemporary Social Science, 13*(2), 175–186.

Hunt, J., Waterhouse, S., & Lutman, E. (2008). *Keeping Them in the Family: Outcomes for Abused and Neglected Children Placed with Family or Friends Carers Through Care Proceedings.* BAAF.

Jamieson, L., Ribe, E., & Warner, P. (2018). Outdated Assumptions About Maternal Grandmothers? Gender and Lineage in Grandparent–Grandchild Relationships. *Contemporary Social Science, 13*(2), 261–274.

Kinship. (2017). State of the Nation 2017 Survey Report, https://kinship.org.uk/report/state-of-the-nation-2017-survey-report/

MacDonald, M., Hayes, D., & Houston, S. (2018). 'Understanding Informal Kinship Care: A Critical Narrative Review of Theory and Research'. *Families, Relationships and Societies, 7*(1), 71–87.

Mann, R., Tarrant, A., & Leeson, G. (2016). Grandfatherhood: Shifting Masculinities in Later Life. *Sociology, 50*(3), 594–610.

Mason, J., May, V., & Clarke, L. (2007). Ambivalence and the Paradoxes of Grandparenting. *The Sociological Review, 55*(4), 687–706.

McCartan, C., Bunting, L., Bywaters, P., Davidson, G., Elliott, M., & Hooper, J. (2018). A Four-Nation Comparison of Kinship Care in the UK: The Relationship Between Formal Kinship Care and Deprivation. *Social Policy and Society, 17*(4), 619–635.

Mervyn-Smith, O. (2018). *Kinship Care: State of the Nation,* Grandparents Plus. https://www.basw.co.uk/system/files/resources/kinship_care_2018.pdf

Morgan, D. H. J. (1992). *Discovering Men: Sociology and Masculinities.* Routledge.

Nandy, S., & Selwyn, J. (2013). Kinship Care and Poverty: Using Census Data to Examine the Extent and Nature of Kinship Care in the UK. *The British Journal of Social Work, 43*(8), 1649–1666.

Nandy, S., Selwyn, J., Farmer, E., & Vaisey, P. (2013). *Spotlight on Kinship Care: Using Census Microdata to Examine the Extent and Nature of Kinship Care in the UK at the Turn of the Twentieth Century*. University of Bristol Report.

Neale, B., & Davies, L. (2015). *Hard to Reach? Re-thinking Support for Young Fathers*, Briefing Paper no. 6. https://followingfathers.leeds.ac.uk/wp-content/uploads/sites/79/2015/10/Brieifing-Paper-6-V7.pdf

Neale, B., & Lau Clayton, C. (2014). Young Parenthood and Cross Generational Relationships: The Perspectives of Young Fathers. In J. Holland & R. Edwards (Eds.), *Understanding Families Over Time*. Palgrave Macmillan.

Neale, B., & Patrick, R. (2016) Engaged Young Fathers? Gender Parenthood and the Dynamics of Relationships, *FYF Working Paper Series no. 1*. https://followingfathers.leeds.ac.uk/wp-content/uploads/sites/79/2015/10/FYF-Working-Paper-Engaged-young-fathers.pdf

Newsome, M., & Kelly, S. (2004). Grandparents Raising Grandchildren: A Solution-Focused Brief Therapy Approach in School Settings. *Social Work with Groups, 27*(4), 65–84.

Skoglund, J., & Thørnblad, R. (2019). Kinship Care or Upbringing by Relatives? The Need for 'New' Understandings in Research. *European Journal of Social Work, 22*(3), 435–445. https://doi.org/10.1080/13691457.2017.1364702

Smethers, S. (2015). What Are the Issues Affecting Grandparents in Britain Today? *Quality in Ageing and Older Adults, 16*(1), 37–43.

Sobo-Allen, L. (2019). The last resort? Initial findings of a PhD study exploring the circumstances, and motivations, of non- resident fathers taking on the full time care of their children though the involvement of social services. Link to Leeds Beckett Repository record: https://eprints.leedsbeckett.ac.uk/id/eprint/8141/

Sobo-Allen, L., & Howarth, S. (2020). Social Work with Single and Non-resident Fathers: How Inclusive Is Our Practice and Where Do We Go from Here? In B. Nikku (Ed.), *Global Social Work Cutting Edge Issues and Critical Reflections* (pp. 163–182). IntechOpen.

Strange, J.-M. (2012). Fatherhood, Providing, and attachment in Late Victorian and Edwardian Working-class Families. *The Historical Journal, 55*(4), 1007–1027.

Tarrant, A. (2013). Grandfathering as Spatio-temporal Practice: Conceptualizing Performances of Ageing Masculinities in Contemporary Familial Carescapes. *Social and Cultural Geography, 14*(2), 192–210.

Tarrant, A. (2014). Negotiating Multiple Positionalities in the Interview Setting; Researching Across Gender and Generational Boundaries. *The Professional Geographer, 66*(3), 493–500.

Tarrant, A. (2017). Getting Out of the Swamp? Methodological Reflections on Using Qualitative Secondary Analysis to Develop Research Design. *International Journal of Social Research Methodology, 20*(6), 599–611.

Tarrant, A. (2018). Care in an Age of Austerity: Men's Care Responsibilities in Low-income. *Families, Ethics and Social Welfare, 12*(1), 34–48.

Tarrant, Anna, & Hughes, Kahryn. (2019). Qualitative Secondary Analysis: Building Longitudinal Samples to Understand Men's Generational Identities in Low Income Contexts. *Sociology, 53*(3), 538–553.

Tarrant, A. (2021). *Fathering and Poverty: Uncovering Men's Participation in Low-Income Family Life*. Policy Press.

Tarrant, A., Featherstone, B., O'Dell, L., & Fraser, C. (2017). "You Try to Keep a Brave Face on But Inside You Are in Bits": Grandparent Experiences of Engaging with Professionals in Children's Services. *Qualitative Social Work, 16*(3), 351–366.

Valentine, G., & Hughes, K. (2010). Ripples in a Pond: The Disclosure to, and Management of, Problem Internet Gambling with/in the Family. *Community, Work & Family, 13*(3), 273–290.

Wellard, S., Meakings, S., Farmer, E., & Hunt, J. (2017). *Growing Up in Kinship Care: Experiences as Adolescents and Outcomes in Young Adulthood*. Grandparents Plus report.

Wenham, A. (2016). "I Know I'm a Good Mum - No-one Can Tell me Different": Young Mothers Negotiating a Stigmatized Identity Through Time. *Families, Relationships and Societies, 5*(1), 127–144.

Wijedasa, D. (2017). *Children Growing Up in the Care of Relatives in the UK*, Policy Bristol. https://www.bristol.ac.uk/media-library/sites/sps/documents/kinship/policy-bristol-report.pdf

Zanoni, L., Warburton, W., Bussey, K., & McMaugh, A. (2013). Fathers as 'core business' in child welfare practice and research. *Children & Youth Services, 35*, 1055–1070.

CHAPTER 7

The Limits of Family for Men in Poverty

Introduction

So far our analyses have demonstrated how men are actively involved in, and central to, families, yet place-based poverty and hardship shape the character of such participation. Informed by men's accounts, we have troubled the binary language of work and family life, and instead treated what men do as simultaneously comprising forms of provisioning *and* family participation (see also Strange, 2012; King, 2015; Doucet, 2020). We have also elaborated how longitudinal circumstances of poverty shape inequalities in health and other life chances relative to others better off in the same city over the same period (Emmel & Hughes, 2010). Thus, we have engaged both with how men are, inevitably, integral to families, as well as how poverty shapes the character of their participation over their lives, from and through multiple generational identities.

In 'recovering' accounts of men's family participation, we have sought to avoid an over-conflation of families with households, and of men as 'present' solely because they are resident in their family homes, or 'absent', solely because they are non-resident. However, it is here that this chapter takes its departure from considering how men participate in families, and instead consider how they may actively be excluded from families, such as from family households and thereby from certain forms of family

K. Hughes, A. Tarrant, *Men, Families, and Poverty*, Palgrave Macmillan Studies in Family and Intimate Life, https://doi.org/10.1007/978-3-031-24922-8_7

participation. This necessarily requires interrogation of what the limits of family might look like for men in poverty.[1]

In this chapter we present cases of men that describe patterns of being expelled from family households, sidelined and marginalised in certain family relationships (see also Neale & Lau Clayton, 2014), and other forms of familial exclusion over time and across place. We discuss how these link with experiences of substance abuse, neglect, social isolation, and imprisonment. In doing so, we develop our discussion of men's 'poverty of family' and consider how our theoretical family lifecourse framework facilitates insight into how men's longitudinal involvement in families may be actively constrained at certain junctures. This may occur through changing family configurations, such as when the children become adults, or when parents repartner.

This chapter uses two cases, one of which is Ben, through Sheila's interviews in the 'Midlife Grandparents' study, and the second is Joe in his own words from the 'Men, Poverty and Care' study. Additionally, throughout the chapter we use a range of participants from different studies as 'empirical counterparts'. An empirical counterpart, as we formulate the language here, refers to the use of cases of different, unrelated, participants, perhaps from different datasets, whose cases nevertheless share salient features. We use these empirical counterparts theoretically to situate one participant in relation to another intra- and intergenerationally. For example, as mothers of a young father, or—as with Bob and Ben—as intragenerational peers, and then with Ben and Joe intergenerationally, with Joe situated generationally as Ben's 'son'. A 'counterpart' operates as an analytic device to mobilise certain questions. We have discussed elsewhere (Tarrant & Hughes, 2019), when we sought to use 'generation' as a theoretical category to build longitudinal samples across different but linked datasets, we were unable to do so. The sample lacked generational continuity. However, for the analyses for this book, we have been able to bring certain cases from across the four datasets together to interrogate intra- and intergenerational dynamics of low-income life. In our discussions, we have sought to elaborate the complex of intergenerational relationships in which people are embedded and participate through

---

[1] McKenzie (2015) writes about how men occupy different spaces than the women in their families, such as in barbers' shops or boxing studios. We situate our work alongside hers by considering where they may go or which spaces they inhabit when their family homes are no longer an option.

circumstances of poverty, from multigenerational perspectives. For example, in Chap. 4, we used Josie's son to consider how he participated in, and sustained, his family simultaneously as a brother, son, young father, and uncle. Below, although focusing on two key cases, we continue to introduce empirical counterparts to develop and refine our analyses.

A Brief Overview of the Cases

Ben, *through Sheila's interviews.* Ben lives in a city in the North of England. He meets Sheila when he is around 18 years of age, and she moves in with him and his parents when he is 19. Sheila is already pregnant, and he becomes a young father to twin boys at around the age of 19, at which time he and Sheila move into their own social housing. By the age of 20 he has three children, and Sheila continues to give birth to a total of eight children until Ben is *circa* 32 years of age. Ben starts drinking in his early 20s, and experiences insecure working conditions. However, he continues to work and provide for Sheila, at one point working away for a long period of time, but returns with money on a regular basis. He provides support for his parents but loses his father by the time he is 46; precise age is unknown. It is likely Ben's father died prematurely. Ben has a brother, with whom he has a troubled relationship and in which Sheila says Ben is 'let down'. Ben is violent towards Sheila and occasionally physically rough with his children, although there is no suggestion that he beat or abused them. Ben is expelled from the family home when he is roughly 40 years old by Sheila, who is supported in this by their eldest twin sons, and several of his children refuse subsequently to visit or speak to him. We do not know where he lives immediately afterwards, but there is a suggestion that he spends time with his brother. Ben spends his final three years living with his widowed mother, and is repeatedly hospitalised for alcohol-related illnesses, during which time he is visited by Sheila and some of his children. Ben dies at around the age of 48, but he may have been slightly younger. He spends his final three days on his mother's sofa. Nobody speaks to him, or attends to him during that time.

Joe is a young father, age 22, who has two children by two different partners. He was born in a city in the North of England and has three brothers and two sisters. He is the eldest of his siblings. Both his parents were working when he was growing up. He completed high school and went to college. He left college in the second year of a three-year course when he became involved in criminal activity. His dad left home when he was 15 and his mum 'kicked him out' when he was 16 years old. His father died prematurely three years prior to the interview. During a period of sofa surfing and homelessness he struggles to secure, well-paid work and is sentenced to prison for five weeks for failing to attend probation and community service linked to drinking at a young age. He has a step-dad who his mum has been with for seven years. He had his eldest son at 19 years old and has a second son aged one. He used to see his eldest son but is no longer in contact with him. At 21 he met Carla, the mother of his second son. He had his own place at this time. The baby was unplanned, and they were no longer in a relationship when she told him she was pregnant. Following a period in prison for Joe, they got back together but Joe decided to secure a home via a housing charity to ensure that his son and mother of his son were not affected financially by them being a family together. They had broken up again at the time of interview, but Joe continued to see his son. Joe has longer-term aspirations to get a decent job, his own house, and a little family but in the short term he is trying to navigate through the challenges of getting secure housing and bettering himself for the sake of himself and his children. Joe has a family worker supporting him to keep in touch with his ex-partner so that he can continue to see his youngest son.

MEN'S EXCLUSION FROM FAMILIES: HUSBANDS/PARTNERS AND FATHERS

In Chap. 4, we discussed how women described their partner/marriage relationships in terms of a 'saviour to abuser' narrative, whereby the same man might indeed embody both roles over the course of their relationships. These 'saviour to abuser' relationships ended in various ways. In Chap. 4, we saw how Josie became able to divorce her abusive ex-husband when she was in prison, and her eldest son became a de facto coparent and protector until she repartnered with a man, who took on the protector role against her ex-partner who continued to harass her. Carolyn left her abusive ex-partner by repartnering with Victor, who became her protector. Susan divorced her ex-husband and gained social housing of her own with the help of her father. These cases contained multiple accounts of ex-partners/husbands being 'kicked out' of their houses by law, by force, and by family members, and the dynamics of their marginalisation and exclusion from, and reinvolvement in, certain family contexts. In considering the changing opportunities and limits of families for men as they are produced and shaped over time and through changing family configurations, this chapter addresses the often 'voluntaristic' character of men's family participation or otherwise, as they may be treated in literature and research, and policy orientation. We also become alerted to what happens to men beyond their family contexts, specifically family households, in terms of what's available to them. In other words, we are able to ask if men *are* absent from families, where they are, and how and why did they get there?

SHEILA AND BEN: EXCLUDING MEN FROM FAMILIES

To begin our analyses, we return to Sheila, first introduced in Chap. 4, and interrogate further the longitudinal dynamics of her 'saviour to abuser' experiences with her ex-partner Ben, who died from alcohol-related liver disease at circa 48 years old. There are multiple narratives about Ben developed across five rounds of interviews with Sheila. In Chap. 4, for example, she concisely details how, as she has more children, Ben's employment becomes increasingly precarious because the clothing industries, that have provided work and incomes to the residents of the purpose-built estate, disappear. He gradually withdraws from his family, begins to drink, becomes increasingly violent, and is described by Sheila as effectively 'absent', predominantly as a father.[2]

Across her interviews, Sheila describes a 'mouse' to 'lion' process in her relationship with Ben, where she moves from being too frightened and intimidated to say anything, to being able to 'stand up to' him. Here, in conversation with one of her sons, she describes her response to a violent incident where she witnesses Ben hurting her youngest daughter:

Sheila: He's basically been an alcoholic for nearly 25 years has Ben, and we've only, so for 23 years I was living with an alcoholic, and he was a verbally abusive, most of the time, he was physically abusive 'til I belted him, and that was when he was a baby [talking about her 4th son]. One day he's just, I'd come out of hospital

---

[2] All of Sheila's interviews commonly include some or all her children, and Ben's family history is therefore 'told' not only by Sheila, but also collectively over a period of six or so years by all her immediate family until Ben dies. After this point, Sheila's eldest daughter says that she does not want her father discussed in interviews any longer, and Sheila no longer focuses on him in her interviews.

hadn't I? I'd come down, I'd come out of hospital with him I'd gone to school to surprise these [meaning her adult children who were also in the interview], left him and Anya [youngest daughter] with a mate up the street and Ben's gone up there pissed, and I said I'm just going to surprise kids let 'em know I'm home, I've walked in me front door through a living room door just in time to see Ben pick Anya three foot of the floor with her hair, put her on the sofa and bung him [4th son] on her knee and say here feed the baby. She was three years old, so that is the first time.

Sheila's 4th Son: You don't pick a three-year-old up by their hair.

Sheila: That is the first time I laid him out and I didn't half lay him out.

Sheila and several of her children, Accessing Socially Excluded Study

This excerpt from Sheila's narrative resembles that of women researched by others, where threats or violence to children are productive of defensive action against the husband/partner (Gillies, 2006; Daly & Kelly, 2015; Erhard, 2020). However, the process of Sheila's increasing resistance to Ben tracks alongside other important changes in their broader family configuration. Her two eldest sons grow taller and stronger between the Accessing Socially Excluded study and the Midlife Grandparents study. During her first interview for the Midlife Grandparents Study, Sheila indicates that they became able to stand up to Ben on her behalf. Also, while Sheila's younger children were still small, her eldest daughter had her own child, moved out and got a council house in the neighbourhood, providing Sheila with somewhere to 'sit' during the day away from Ben. This, for Sheila, was life changing, because her eldest daughter is able to exclude her father from her house.

Sheila: Erm., but, er, for a, for me, it, it, it was, it was new when I had grandchildren. I mean, I could do what I wanted then because I took no notice of Ben whatsoever and, erm, I mean if I wanted to go sit in Tanya's house all day, I'd go and sit in Tanya's house all day. You know, and he'd come, and he'd go, "What the f- you

doing round here?" "Er, nothing to do with you. I'm sat here."
And Tanya wouldn't put up with it because she'd lock the door
and shut him out. You know, whereas I couldn't do that at home.
Sheila, Accessing Socially Excluded Study

As Josie's example in Chap. 4 illustrated, for Sheila the conditions
through which she is able to remove herself from Ben or embark on a
process of isolating him from her household, involves her children as they
become adults and are either physically strong enough or gain access to
their own resources to provide her with the help she needs.

These insights contribute to, and in some way extend, existing scholarship in this area which focuses on women's emotional states, or how they
navigate shifting conditions of threat and autonomy in relation to their
husbands/partners in low-income circumstances (e.g. Lister, 2005; Daly
& Kelly, 2015; Erhard, 2020). Rather than observing situations in which
Sheila exercises 'agency' or 'autonomy' through individual acts of resistance or rebellion, instead we see how she strategically mobilises resources
through her family relationships across the locality, as well as those available through welfare provision. Because they were not married, for example, Sheila retained all rights to her social housing and to the various
welfare benefits as the main parent to her eight children. These changes—
the maturation of her older children, the security of economic/welfare
independence from Ben, and Ben's physical decline from alcoholism—
combined to create a situation in which Sheila is able finally to expel Ben
from the home:

Sheila: Yeah. Because I can't, I didn't actually ask him to leave. He went
           to help his mum and dad move, erm, to this bungalow where
           they're staying now, and he basically came home once a week on
           a payday to give me some money and then go again. And he did
           this for 6 weeks and during that 6 weeks I got a taste of what it
           was like without him and I went, "I like it." So, when he came
           home, I locked the door and told him he wasn't coming in... I
           told him to go back to his mum. So that was it. It was great. It
           was just me and the kids. There wasn't half as many arguments.
           There was no, "You fat slag," or this, that and other going
           through the house you know ...
           Sheila, Accessing Socially Excluded Study

Sheila's account exemplifies how moments of resistance and rebellion against abusive partners are more than 'turning points' in women's emotional states. Rather they are part of longer-term processes involving the accumulation of a diverse range of resources or, more properly here, relationships which support women in realising such change. A focus on the emotionality of Sheila's account may obscure the extended strategising women need to engage in, in moving out and moving away, or—as in Sheila's case forcing Ben to do so. Such focus, on an individual's capacity to effect change in their lives may inadvertently responsibilise women in such decision-making. Instead, Sheila's account demonstrates how persistent hardship constrains possibilities for decision-making as momentary and, in that moment, effective of change. By focusing on the importance of cumulative and shared resourcing for Sheila in excluding Ben from her household, we are reorientated away from such responsibilisation.

Ben's expulsion from the residential home was continued as a form of exclusion from his family with Sheila, broadly sustained by their children. Several children refused either to visit him or let him come to visit them in their own houses as they grew up and gradually moved away from home, while at the same time continuing to sustain close and connected relationships with each other.

In the final rounds of interviews for the 'Midlife Grandparents' study, Sheila tells of how her older sons take their nieces and nephews to primary school everyday, there being so many of them of a similar age, that they fill the classrooms of the local primary school. Her eldest daughter Tanya comes round and cleans Sheila's house, because Sheila has developed mobility problems, and Sheila's grandchildren visit regularly. We make this point because existing research has identified the erosive character of poverty for family relationships and a reliance on fleeting, informal ties beyond the family by women as a strategy for getting by (e.g. Desmond, 2012). In contrast, for Sheila's family, the strength of these family relationships is essential to their shared security. This strength is reflected in how this family 'does kinship' in and on behalf of each other, even where this means excluding one family member (Ben) who is not serving the family through his destructive behaviours.

Nevertheless, Ben's expulsion from the family may have longer-term consequences in rupturing intergenerational connections for his children and grandchildren. For example, in Sheila's own account, she describes how, as a child, she and her brothers lost contact with her maternal grandparents, and all their relations on her mother's side, because of the death of her mother at a young age, which results in her and her brothers being placed in foster care. Sheila says the loss of these relationships results in a wider lack of familial support that characterises her childhood more generally. Sheila blames these older relatives for her having to experience foster care, because they did not step in and support Sheila's father with the care of his three children while he was in full-time work. Such absence of support meant, for Sheila, that when she returned to her father's home, an event tangentially linked to her father's remarriage, she was required to take care of her younger brothers (one of whom has learning disabilities), both in the home and then at school. Such longer-term consequences of ruptured intergenerational relationships may be imputed in Ben's case as, after he died, some of Sheila's children embargoed any further discussion of Ben in the research interviews. From this, we can observe how men who have been physically excluded from families may nevertheless come to have a new form of 'presence', such as through a protected identity as a deceased parent, while simultaneously remaining absent from the lives of their children and grandchildren.

Through Sheila's interviews, and the comments by her children, we gain a partial, yet detailed, view of Ben's longer trajectories. For example, Sheila and her sons provide a vivid visual commentary on Ben's physical deterioration linked to his alcoholism as he ages and his gradual decline. Below they describe him in one of his final hospitalisations, which occurred just prior to the first study:

Sheila:	But I mean Ben's only 46 years old but he looks…
2nd Daughter:	96.
4th Son:	He looks older than my granddad.
Sheila:	He looks really, really old.
4th Son:	Older than my granddad used to look.
Sheila:	Well, the people at the hospital thought he was my Dad. I said "no love. I'm his ex-partner, he's only three years older than me".
4th Son:	But he is getting bad, he can hardly walk, he's skinny as owt, I'd say he weighs about seven, seven and a half stone.

Sheila and two of her adult children, Accessing Socially Excluded study

We also learn that after he is expelled from the family home, Ben is 'let down' by his brother, and is uncared for by his mother with whom he lives until he dies, a form of family exclusion by neglect. It would be easy to adopt the language of the women in Chap. 4 to describe Ben as a 'crap partner and a crap dad', but Ben's biography supports the need for a life-course perspective to understand the relationship between poverty and family participation as these have consequences for how men's lives may unfold and how their presence/absence may shape the fortunes of younger relatives, especially younger men. For example, the quality and character of intergenerational relations among men are often invoked to explain poorer social outcomes (Roy, 2014), and our analyses of Ben in this regard address a gap in existing knowledge about how such intergenerational relationships are shaped through, or characterise, longer-term experiences of poverty for men (see also Anderson, 1999).

Chapters 5 and 6 recover men's accounts of a complex array of caregiving and intergenerational exchanges in the low-income families of which they are a part, and in which they participate. Ben's case exemplifies the consequences for men when these relationships and connections are either absent or withdrawn. It is here that we found the use of empirical counterparts to be particularly useful in interrogating Ben's life history, and we identified Bob as a significant empirical counterpart to Ben see Chap. 5, not least because they grew up in the same area, at the same time, and knew each other. More than this, like Ben, Bob is made redundant and develops drinking problems, but his case differs considerably, as his narrative demonstrates how he continues to be highly involved in sustaining his family, walking the estate for his sister and his father-in-law, taking a parental role towards his grandson and looking after Dianne as she becomes increasingly disabled. Bob's situation is materially different from Ben. Unlike Ben, and because of the character of his family participation, Bob has a place to 'go' to when he can no longer secure paid work. This 'place' is both material and affective: he has both his home, and also in (for and with), his family relationships. He is valued, integral to his family, and is critical to the ongoing care of family members as they age. Although as we argue in Chap. 5 that it can be problematic to conflate families with households when recovering accounts of men's intergenerational participation in families, for men like Ben who are rejected from their family households, lose their partner/spouse relationship, and do not repartner, this loss is important. Ben's case in particular demonstrates that where men become increasingly vulnerable as they age, if they lack engaged family members to look after them, they become increasingly isolated. This can be productive of further mental and physical ill health, and even potentially fatal consequences, as reflected in higher-than-average suicide rates for men in these circumstances (Rojas & Stenberg, 2010; Kerr et al., 2017). What we find when we compare Ben and Bob's cases is that, when younger, Ben's own family circumstances were ambivalent, with tensions and conflicts across his extended family carried forward into his adult life. These tensions, such as with his adult sister, also affected Sheila. At one point, while they struggled with housing, Sheila stayed for a period with Ben's sister. However, his sister would insist that Sheila stayed outside the home from early morning to early evening, meaning she often sat for hours on the front doorstep with her young children. Sheila's narrative describes a persistent lack of extended family support, especially from Ben's side of the family. In contrast, Bob and Dianne describe wider family interconnections, micro-exchanges of help and care, which sustain them over the longer course of their lives. We are reluctant to over-claim here, but suggest that in these localities where micro exchanges of food, money and other resources were critical to making ends meet on a day-to-day basis through persistent hardship, such extended family relations may have a prophylactic effect in mitigating some of the isolations and extremes of poverty.

Sheila's account of Ben's alcoholism and premature ageing is also a qualitative illustration of the impacts of place-based poverty, articulating with statistical evidence on health inequalities in the area, highlighting the relationship between poverty and increased ill health,[3] and unemployment and mental illness, experienced also by so many participants across the four studies (Martikainen et al., 2003; Murali & Oyebode, 2004; Kahneman & Deaton, 2010). His story furthermore illustrates a commonality of experience for men across these localities of lower life expectancy and higher rates of drug and alcohol dependency (see also, Staley, 1992; Wacquant, 1995; Crutchfield & Wadsworth, 2003; Manhica et al., 2021).

It is worth briefly including an extract from an interview with Bob to illustrate precisely the ages at which people commonly die in these localities. Here he discusses the ages at which he lost his parents and other family members, many of which are way below the average life expectancy:

---

[3] In the 'Midlife Grandparents' study, almost all the participants over the age of 45 all experienced significant health problems and disabilities. In discussions about their adult children and grandchildren there were frequent stories of miscarriage and stillbirth.

Me mam were 59, me dad were only 63. Lost them in the space of 6 months…I were 18 then. Say there's only me an' April [older sister] now cos other two have passed away, there's only me an' our April, she's 71, 72 in't she? Our Ada [aunt] died at 63, Fred [uncle] died at 51, Irving died at birth [father's twin brother].[4] *Bob and Dianne, Midlife Grandparents, Round One Interview*

While these relatives are from the previous generation in Bob's family, the ages at which they die are reflected in more recent life expectancy data. For example, in 2018 to 2020, the life expectancy of healthy men at birth was 54.2 in the most deprived areas, compared with 67.6 years in the least deprived areas (ONS, 2018). Developing a comparative analysis of cases across the four studies, and situated in broader debate, men's trajectories track alongside the economic fortunes of the locality which is characterised by the decline of manufacturing work and widespread deindustrialisation that have implications for men's breadwinning identities (Nayak, 2006; MacDonald et al., 2020). This decline has affected many Northern English cities, so graphically described by Dianne in Chap. 3 when she describes the changes in her estate, and resulted in a shift to longer-term patterns of unemployment, poor health, and a reliance on service providers (Emmel & Hughes, 2010) for men and women more generally, reflected in the cases used in the empirical chapters for this book.

An absence of recognition of this broader complex in the interior logics that families might produce in evaluating the 'worthiness' of individuals in families and what they do and how they behave, might lead to a simplistic reading of people as 'good' and 'bad', or as deserving and undeserving poor (e.g. Dorey, 2010; McKenzie, 2015; Shildrick & MacDonald, 2013). While we in no way seek to redeem Ben as either a father or partner, we do endeavour to interpret moral accounts of family members in context. Narrow analytic attention to moral accounts may in their formulation obscure the broader dynamics of localities and longitudinal poverty, that are embodied, observable, and violent in their effects. The longitudinal capture of the four linked studies demonstrates how these socio-economic pressures have shaped the lives of these families for five decades. Recognition of the longer histories of places and the families that comprise

---

[4] By the conclusion of the 'Midlife Grandparents' study, both Dianne's father and Bob's older sister, the oldest people tracked across the study, had died. The other deaths included deaths of young men in the Accessing Socially Excluded study from drug overdoses, and a possible drug suicide of one of the adult children in the 'Midlife Grandparents' study; and in the 'Men, Poverty and Care' study, there was the death of Joe's father, and at the community centre accessed during the study, multiple suicides amongst single men were also discussed.

them requires us to reject a narrow focus on, and explanations of, within-family poverty, but also to identify the need for a more critical examination of the interconnections between families and longitudinal and life-course experiences of poverty for different family members.

In our focus on Ben's case, we have been able to examine the longer-term trajectories of older men living in low-income localities. Further, across our studies we have been able to track deprivation as experienced by men across the lifecourse and intergenerationally. What is so compelling about our data and analyses of them, are the similarities of their trajectories across cases and how these link to the socio-economic fortunes of places. We also observed how these longitudinal processes shaped the lives of the younger men across the studies, albeit in different ways and in more detail, because we have interviewed men in these circumstances when they are young. While our secondary analyses of accounts of Ben through Sheila's narratives are rich and revealing of men's trajectories through poverty, we were not able to explore in any detail whether and how he intersects with different services and institutions across his life, nor were we able to understand his lifecourse experiences, including the earlier stages of his life, from his own perspective. This is much more visible in interviews with young men from the studies aimed at eliciting such accounts from men. In the next section, we consider the case of Joe, interviewed for the Men, Poverty and Care study.

Joe's Case: Men's Exclusion from Families: Sons and Welfare

Although we have interview data from several of Ben's sons, we are choosing instead to use part of Joe's case as an empirical counterpart for Ben. Joe is a young father who lost his own father at a young age to alcoholism, but also has alcohol dependency problems of his own. Using empirical counterparts as an analytical strategy enables us to observe commonalities of experiences within generations, but also how certain experiences can be observed *inter*generationally and in place. Bringing Joe and Ben's cases together, albeit in a partial way, reinforces the value of longitudinal analyses for understanding the consequences of certain experiences on how men participate in families, as well as where the limits of families are for these men. We can track Ben through different family arrangements across Sheila's interviews, (and also in Bob's) observing him in and out of work, and in and out of different households. We are able to make a case for Ben that he is not absent from his families' lives. However, Joe's case operates as a point of departure in this respect, and allows us to ask, if men are indeed absent, and not in their families, where do they go?

Albeit with distinctive features, Joe's trajectory is very similar to that of a number of young men in both the Following Young Fathers and Accessing Socially Excluded studies. Joe lost his father young and while we have no data about the age of his father when he died, it is likely that this was prematurely, like Ben, and given that Joe is only 22. Joe's father had also been expelled from the family home, and there had been numerous violent encounters subsequently between Joe's parents, in which he was also involved (see below). At 22, Joe is the eldest of six children, and the loss of his father at a young age resembles that of Sheila's oldest sons, who were approximately 26 when Ben died. The life and death of Joe's father shape his trajectory and relationships with his family:

Joe: My mum had kicked me out when I was sixteen. I thought there was bigger and better out in the world. I just thought I'd go and get a job that would be easy. Then obviously like I ended up getting in with the wrong crowd. Since all that's happened I just know that now I'm getting the help. I always took things on the chin and blamed myself. So that's it really.

Interviewer: Why did your mum kick you out at sixteen?

Joe: My dad left when I were fifteen. They broke up and I was just being like a little rogue. She couldn't cope with me.

Joe, Men, Poverty and Care Study

Joe's case is an exemplar of situations described elsewhere across the datasets, particularly in the *Accessing Socially Excluded* study, when a father dies young, at a similar age to Ben, or leaves. For young men who turn 16[5]

---

[5] Sixteen was an important 'coming of age' across the datasets as this age coincided with changes in how and by whom young people were treated in formal and health and social care settings. At 16, young people became able to decide who they lived with, for example, and Josh (Chap. 5) decided to leave his mother and return to his grandparents Bob and Dianne, with whom he had lived since he was a baby. Young parents, particularly young fathers, lose certain contact rights to their children at this age because they lose their 'child' status, (see Tarrant & Hughes, 2019) and the datasets include numerous accounts of young men moving out of home and sofa surfing at around 16 years of age (see Joe's case, this chapter) (see also Bonner-Thompson & McDowell, 2020).

this may represent a pivotal moment, where they either remain in the family home as a source of support for their mothers or are required to leave:

> The life I went through with my dad and that. I used to have disputes. At the end of the day, he was coming to mum's house. My mum never stopped him from seeing us. He used to come and be drunk and that. He'd see us. And then my mum would see that we'd had enough. My eldest brother was eleven. My eldest sister, about nine. My youngest sister, about one or two. I basically didn't want that. I didn't have the contact with him. I didn't see him. I was at that age, fifteen or sixteen. I knew what was going on. But obviously they were like 'Oh Dad's here'. If I had to go, I'd go and stand with the kids. I wouldn't speak to my dad. I knew he was just babbling on. I was like 'Come in now mum and say bye to dad'. That's when he'd kick off. I had to do what I had to do. I never did it in front of him, but I always basically just took him away and just told him don't be coming to the house like this. At the end of day, I had to look after my brothers and sisters and my mum… My dad was like six foot something, but my mum was only little. About five six. She's not going to obviously stand there and not hit him with something. She never did it in front of the kids. At the end of the day, I know everyone has been through stuff. Everyone has problems. I just know it's my time to change. I don't need friends. I do need family to an extent. Cos I'm old enough now, I've got to like stand on my own two toes. *Joe, Men, Poverty and Care Study*

Here, Joe expresses in narrative form what elsewhere has been described as a process of adultification, experienced by young men in response to 'institutional power, violence and trauma, and complex relationships with adults' (Roy et al., 2014, p. 56). In this, young men are required to navigate risks in both their families *and* their communities (ibid.). Adultification involves acting as peer, spouse, or even parent for one's own parents (Burton, 2007), and an acceptance of advanced responsibilities of provision and care for family members as part of an acceleration of young peoples' transitions to adulthood in socio-economically disadvantaged families (Roy et al., 2014). While Joe attributes his behaviour and his mum's exclusion of him from his family home to his dad leaving, he goes on to explain more about his experiences of the locality, which he links narratively with 'going off the rails', drinking alcohol, and taking drugs. Joe's account of his mother's relationship breakdown with his father is similar in many respects to those recounted in this book (e.g. Sheila's, Carolyn's, Josie's) where sons need to become protectors of their mothers and their younger siblings (see below). Joe links this period of his life with becoming 'a rogue' and too difficult for his mother to manage. We note here that Joe does have a step-father with whom he says he has a good relationship. However, in examining Joe's narrative for the sorts of engagements and exchanges with his step-father, this person figures more as a shadowy figure whose support of Joe is not fully described or developed and therefore remains difficult to comment on.

Across the datasets we observed these processes of 'adultification', which are distinctive for these localities relative to their wealthier neighbourhoods. Elsewhere, we demonstrate how, in these localities, the age of 16 becomes entrenched as the moment of 'coming of age', underscored through the shifting emphases of formal health and social care services and interventions that render those over the age of 16 as adults. At this point, young people are both tasked with new forms of responsibility and independence by health and social care professionals whilst simultaneously losing a raft of protections that may otherwise secure their relationship to other family members (e.g. their own children) (Tarrant & Hughes, 2019).

Joe's account of leaving home resembles that of many young men across the four studies, whereby moving out is narratively linked with a process of destablisation for young men in their families. This process may be continued through circumstances of homelessness for young men who begin to lead nomadic lives where neither state nor family provides for them (Neale & Ladlow, 2015). This ongoing destabilisation increases the importance of friendship networks in young men's neighbourhood (Harding, 2009) and reliance on formal and informal health and social care services. Young men turn to friends in the locality to survive, sofa surfing from one friend to the next, using friends to graft with. Problematically during these nomadic phases, when people are most in need of support and resources, they become least visible to services (Hughes, 2007). When asked to observe whether his experience was typical of other young men in the neighbourhood, Joe says:

Interviewer: All your experiences. Is that typical to other lads from [Estate]?

Joe: Yes and no. My best mate, who I know, he went through a hard time. He got kicked out. His mum didn't do owt. He had to do everything. He ended up going to jail. Six times in one year. That was from being young. He had a bad bringing up.

Joe, Men, Poverty and Care Study

Had interviews been conducted with the families of either Joe or his 'best mate', both would have been described as absent. In comparing himself to other young men in the locality, a key similarity for Joe is time in prison. In the case of both himself and his best mate, Joe links going to prison to his upbringing and the limits of support provided by his family, and the dangers and risks of the very friendships and relationships on which he depended as part of his nomadic existence. Such dangers include trajectories into drugs and then prison (see also Maguire, 2020):

> When I were younger I were good fun. From the age of being little. 'Til I was sixteen. I've lived round [locality] all my life. When I come to sixteen and me getting kicked out. Now I've realised the friends that I've had, they weren't there for my help. They were there to use me or like we'd go out and do something silly. At the end of the day, you've all got to look after yourself but I never did that. I always put all them in front. Instead of thinking why am I doing this, they are not looking after me. Some of them were but you don't realise it till you come to it. *Joe, Men, Poverty and Care Study*

Like so many of the participants in our studies, this excerpt illustrates how Joe internalises responsibility for how his life has unfolded. Sam, Chap. 6, for example, talks about 'luck', and Bob, Chap. 5, talks about life as a hand of cards and being responsible for playing that hand as well as possible (Emmel & Hughes, 2010). As in Sheila's interview extracts above, and those throughout this book, we observe how people in the various studies seek to make sense of, and indeed theorise, the world around them. Their narratives are so often shaped through individualising discourses (Shildrick & MacDonald, 2013) which echo the 'doxa' of poverty as the fault of those who experience it (Dorey, 2010). These narratives are part of an ongoing production of 'interior logics' of poverty, where 'interior' does not refer to the individual or their psyche, but to *collective* narratives of poverty based on shared and longitudinal experiences across families and neighbourhoods, elsewhere described as 'lifeworlds' (Erhard, 2020). We reemphasise that, in interrogating such interior logics, or narratives of poverty, people seek to 'tell about society' (Becker, 2007) through their own experiences in order to address a fundamental lack of recognition of the realities of living through hardship (McKenzie, 2015).

In his interview, Joe explicitly links family troubles and bad friends with his alcoholism and drug taking, and eventual prison sentence, where his narrative about his time in prison expresses certain forms of ambivalence. Prisons are violent and risky places for young men (e.g. Jones & Pratt, 2008; Trammell, 2012; Gooch, 2019) and Joe himself says prison is 'not a nice place to be'. However, he also described his time in prison as form of respite, and says:

> I won't lie it was the best five weeks of my life. A lot of people probably tell people the same. Basically, you can get a shower whenever you want. You get three meals a day. TV. Your own bed even though you've got someone else in your pad. I don't want to go back but it was like I didn't have nothing to worry about. I didn't have to be out in reality. When you are in there. You don't have to think about nothing. You just do what you have to do.
> *Joe, Men, Poverty and Care Study*

Like other young men in the 'Accessing Socially Excluded' study, prisons were sometimes places where young men got themselves 'sorted out'. This was particularly relevant for young men with a drug dependency, where people described 'going bareback' in prison when detoxing (see Hughes, 2007).[6] Research with young fathers in prison also indicates the importance of tailored and structured support offered by some prisons around the benefits of fatherhood (Meek, 2007; Bulman & Neale, 2017) and educational programmes around sex and relationship education (Robinson et al., 2022; Lohan et al., 2022). In this excerpt, Joe describes how prison provides stable accommodation and food for a reliable period of time, and a break from the disordered chaos that characterises his life prior to incarceration. Later in his interview he also describes the counselling he receives which provides him with a language around self-care and self-help, which he says he needs to fulfil his intentions to be a good father to his children. In effect, prison becomes a form of 'social care' intervention and certainly an interlude for Joe in an otherwise chaotic and difficult life in which he lacks consistent family support.

There are four points we would make based on these observations. The first is how Joe's experiences reveal the extent of vulnerability and insecurity longitudinal hardship produces for people, at different stages of their

---

[6] However, we also know that people are more exposed to drugs in prison, and prisons are places where people develop substance dependencies (Baltieri, 2014; Wakeling & Lynch, 2020).

lives. It also indicates the potential mitigating protections that families might provide for people, even if those families too are sometimes risky and violent. Our datasets contain numerous examples of young men whose families were steadfast in their support during their trajectories through drugs and prison.[7] The second point is that avoiding an 'angels and demons' narrative about institutions enables us to consider how prisons constitute a form of state-based social care intervention. In turn, this also indicates the critical importance of effective state interventions in people's lives when stability (if not security) is so highly valued as belonging to a period in prison, and why people continue to need formal, stable, structured support in lives characterised by longitudinal hardship (Lupton & Tunstall, 2008; Kearns et al., 2013). Third, and relatedly, that prisons might be places where 'displaced' social need becomes visible (Livingstone & Macmillan, 2015). Social need does not disappear simply through the production of government rhetoric, such as that promulgated through the 'austerity' narrative and, ultimately, the continued programme of welfare retrenchment seen in the UK (Beatty et al., 2021; Webb et al., 2022). Since the introduction of 'austerity measures', death rates have soared (Public Health England, 2018), achieving post-Second World War levels within the first three years. As welfare was retracted and state funding to charitable, third sector organisations withdrawn (Macmillan & Ellis Paine, 2020), there was a surge in visibility of people in need of the basics such as food, clothes, and care who presented themselves in schools, hospitals, police stations, and food banks in search of these (e.g. Beatty et al., 2021; Garthwaite et al., 2015; Garthwaite, 2016).

Joe's and Josie's accounts indicate that prisons, too, are where people are now appearing that otherwise might have been supported through different welfare arrangements, although prisons have long been recognised as places for the delivery of social care (Tucker et al., 2018, 2021). The decimation of services and funding for health and social care services additionally means that people in these circumstances will become almost impossible to access through the usual channels, namely informal and formal service organisations (see also Emmel et al., 2007), and therefore increasingly invisible for in-person research. Finally, in extension of this last point, these analyses lend themselves to a similar reading by that of

---

[7]We would raise caution here, as families may also be comprised of relationships wherein different forms of emotional dependency, such as of parent on their adult child, serves to further embed the adult child in substance dependency.

Waquant (2009), albeit using a somewhat different language, that prisons effectively serve to manage civil disorder in the neoliberal reordering of marginal populations, rendering them invisible *as* marginalised. In effect, it may be that men are indeed absent*ed*, as a result of being poor, and consequently in prison.

In contrast to Joe's story, there is evidence across the datasets, and supported by the broader literature, that suggests that for young men who do not participate in gangs, family plays a role in the 'moral rejection' of crime and violence (Baird, 2012). Roy (2006) argues that local ecological processes are also implicated in men's transitory participation in family life as providers and caregivers. We would add to this by including families in such local ecologies. Our data indicate that young men's trajectories are shaped by within-family dynamics, which change as fathers/partners are lost, and young men become positioned either as protectors of mums and/or younger siblings. This involves a realisation by those young men of the risks for family members when families 'destabilise' through death or separation, and even problematic repartnering by their mother with violent men. For example, Joe explains how he sought to protect his siblings from his father when he was being abusive as a younger boy, and his father was alive (see second quote in this section by Joe, for example). However, when women repartner, those dynamics necessarily shift again, and the role of protector, or 'saviour' may pass onto the new adult male.

We have established how vulnerability, uncertainty, and risk are core to experiences of poverty, but these may also be described as integral dimensions of place by our participants. As Joe's account illustrates, vulnerability, uncertainty, and risk have a two-fold character. The first is risks *from* the locality, risk of violence, and exposure to drugs and alcohol. But also, risks associated with *becoming* part of the locality, namely the uncertainties and vulnerabilities promulgated *through* the use of drugs and alcohol, and the potential for violence and abuse embedded in relationships with other people in the locality.

We draw on accounts from across the studies to interrogate the implications of shifting family configurations for young men in more detail and found the case of Carolyn and Victor, discussed in Chaps. 4 and 5, to be especially useful. Across their four interviews, Victor and Carolyn acknowledge the risks *of* and *in* place, and we consider how far Victor may be used as a 'data proxy' (Tarrant & Hughes, 2019) for Joe's step-father. As a couple, they develop 'predictive narratives' on behalf of Carolyn's four children and her grandson, namely that, as they grow older and live more in their friendship groups rather than within their family setting, they become exposed to these. In an extended reflection on the violence in their local area in their third interview, Carolyn and Victor describe the challenges for parenting where not only are risks to violence enhanced but also forms of civic protection, such as through the police, are difficult to secure or pose a risk through neighbourhood surveillance (such as from neighbours) when contacted:

Victor: You can't teach your children that if they go out there don't worry there are adults out there, if you have a problem go and talk to an adult or go to the shop keeper or go and see the Policeman, you're not gonna see a Policeman anyway and you're not gonna see a Traffic Warden and you know, so they go out there…

Carolyn: There's no protection.

Victor: Yeah, we've been out in situations where we've had to step in to help somebody and we've watched other adults do nothing.

Carolyn: I've seen grown men watch a young lad with his school coat and his school bag on, getting beaten up by a man, they just sat there and watched. I went and intervened and got rid of this fella, but the fellas, the men in, the taxi drivers just parked up at the side of the road just sat watching.

Victor: And that seems to be, I mean on these estates if you call the Police you can run into difficulty cos when we've called the Police many a times but then we're prepared to get on the doorstep, you know, poke somebody back in the chest and…

Carolyn: I did call the Police and I don't care.

Victor: So do something about it but if you're a weaker, more vulnerable person and you call the Police the chances are your windows are you gonna go through or whatever it is, it's gang, it's gang culture. If you…

Carolyn: If you can't hit, it's like the kids, they can't have a fight with somebody in their own year or their own age without the rest of the family getting involved….if they beat them then the cousins will get involved. And it ends up being a big family affair and it's ridiculous really that a kid can't stand up for themselves without…

Victor: So you've gotta work a pattern of living that try…negotiates
           all these little problems that are coming along and with
           younger kids like… *Carolyn and Victor, Midlife Grandparents*

In this richly expressive excerpt, Carolyn and Victor detail the need for
purposeful demeanour and interventions, specifically for younger relatives—their children, grandchildren—in their locality. Traditional forms of
formal protection are not available so Carolyn and Victor describe an
ongoing process involving the careful negotiation of their identities and
involvements. They neither consider themselves to belong to their locality
through becoming part of broader activities, nor being apart from it,
which renders them different and consequently vulnerable to the violence
that might arise from that. This emerges specifically in response to the
questions guiding the Midlife Grandparents study, namely what it is that
the participants did for younger relatives in order to change their life
chances. Here, Victor may be treated as a 'data proxy' for Joe's step-father,
albeit with some differences. Where Joe's step-father remains a shadowy
figure that emerges occasionally in his narrative, Victor is able to describe
himself as an engaged step-father, and his concerted intervention in the
life of Carolyn's eldest son, Liam, who he supported to join the army:

Victor: Luke left because it was his only chance to do anything with his
           life. But that's because of my family history though, cos my fam-
           ily have always been military, when Carolyn and I got together
           it was, it became an option that we discussed, wasn't it?
           Round Three

Victor's narrative is one in which he bases his identity as a 'good' step-
father/step-grandfather in recognising and seeking to ameliorate the risks
and vulnerabilities of place, especially for Carolyn's son. Such protection
also extends to forms of discipline and ordering by older siblings of their
younger relatives. In the Accessing Socially Excluded study, Sheila's eldest
sons describe 'looking out' for their youngest brother to make sure he did
not 'make the same mistakes as they had'. They both considered it was
'too late' for them, at the age of 24, to change their life trajectories. Both
had extensive criminal records for petty crime, and there was informal
evidence of drug dependency. This 'looking out' sometimes involved
physical domination in their efforts to ensure that their youngest brother
would not get into drugs or trouble with the police:

| Interviewer: | ...you stopped [younger brother] doing what you and [Jamie's twin brother] had done (getting in trouble around the estate). |
| Jamie (son of Sheila): | Well that's obvious, he's my younger brother, you know what I mean? I wouldn't let him do the things what I did when I was younger. I might not have been caught for anything like it, you know what I mean, but it still, I didn't do it, but I still want, I wouldn't want my younger brother to do it. |

Jamie, Sheila's son, Accessing Socially Excluded

Below, Adam's narrative from the Following Young Fathers study demonstrates how the fates of older relatives operate as cautionary tales, existing as examples of trajectories that should be avoided:

Adam:	Me first brother he's, he's in, he's, he's in [name] Prison...like all Uncles and all them have all been in prison and all that, you see. So...in a way I...seen it all. Like prison and...and it's horrible, you see. It's just...horrid really.
Interviewer:	Yeah. Have you learnt anything from them then in a way, with them being in prison?
Adam:	Yeah, keep outta trouble [laughs].

Adam, Following Young Fathers

Returning to our main case in this section, Joe's own narrative serves to emblematise these processes of reflection, involving 'looking out for', or 'trying to avoid' the fates of other men that may play out across a variety of age differences. Here, Joe observes the fates of other men on the estate, and reflects on how his best friend whom he earlier said did not look out for him has become a 'role model':

| Joe: | He's working now. Had four or five jobs in't past two years. And he's been to jail. Done his crime. When I look up to him, I feel like I've got a role model now. A decent one. If he didn't want to speak to me, he could have. I'd say he's one of the best things that happened to me when I got older anyway. |

Joe, Men, Poverty and Care Study

In this short section, we have combined excerpts from three different studies with different foci, at different times, but in similar localities and about young men in similar circumstances. These provide cumulative and compelling evidence of how stubborn longitudinal poverty shapes distinctive trajectories for men who may otherwise be treated as 'absent' from their families. While there are distinct nuances in these described trajectories that move beyond a simplistic reading of men as disinclined to be part of, or disinterested in, their families, they provide a broader account of familial dynamics through which Joe grows up and develops self and other relationships. In particular, they demonstrate how the 'in/out' character of Joe's father figures shaped his relationship to his younger siblings, and additionally how his own fatherhood with two young children is shaped in turn by this intergenerational hardship expressed as relational volatility. In this respect, then, Joe's case provides detailed insight into how longitudinal and intergenerational hardship limits the possibilities of family for him.

Since turning 16 and leaving home, Joe loses access to his birth family, and during the subsequent six years fathers two children, one at 19 and one at 22, each with different partners. Prison, insecure, low-income work, and lack of money disrupt his relationship with his first child. The mother moves away to a different city, and he ultimately loses contact with her. In contrast, he has regular contact with his second child, which he makes efforts to preserve, not least because his son had severe medical needs when he was born. However, his relationship with the mother is fraught, and his life continues to be unstable. Joe was accessed for the research via a housing support charity, who supported him to identify his potential. He has also been in contact with a drug and alcohol support charity.

When we analysed his interview to see who else he could turn to, his account reveals repeated absence of support in relationships in his life. In contrast to others in the dataset who, on leaving prison, had homes and families to go, or effective bail hostels that supported their journeys out of prison and into independent housing (see also Binswanger et al., 2012), Joe had nobody to turn to:

> My stepdad has done quite a lot for me. He still does more than my mum does. My ex-partner had all my clothes at the time I came out. I was still staying there. We had a bit of an argument. Last Saturday or week before. She kicked me out. I moved all me stuff to one of her mates. And basically, he's robbed me and took all my stuff. But it doesn't bother me. It's only

clothes. It's all replaceable. Couple of days later she asked me to come down. Wanted to speak to me. I feel like people are sometimes playing mind games with me. I will fall into that trap because I love her to bits. *Joe, Men, Poverty and Care, Round One*

The processes of reflection described above, of 'looking out for', or 'trying to avoid the fates' of others are critically important, embedded as they are in expectations of, or failure to experience, reciprocity from people that are considered 'mates'. Such expectations relate to peoples' access to the essential elements for everyday survival, such as 'a place to lay my head' where such resources are not available through their family relationships.

Specifically, Joe's case, and the others we discuss across the empirical chapters, permit us to 'see' men when they are not in family contexts, physically occupying different places. These include working in men's clubs, in young women's flats dealing in drugs, in hostels, prisons and halfway houses, in mates' houses, living on their own in blocks of social housing flats living on their own, on the streets, either in gangs, or with mates, in gambling shops and pharmacies, in community centres if there are any in the locality, and in drugs outreach centres. In the context of young fatherhood, Neale (2016) describes these trajectories as nomadic, whereby expulsion from the family home contributes to significant volatility linked with the violence of place. Informal 'mate' relationships may thus operate as prophylactic networks that sustain young men and protect them from the endemic risks of being seen as 'out of place' by other young men in these or neighbouring localities, and in this way protect them from the violence of others.

All of these spaces can offer forms of community to men through peer engagement. For some, this may create opportunities for more positive trajectories, such as supported by community-based interventions and support (Tarrant, 2021). For others, particularly through informal and even criminal networks, which may involve unequal and risky exchanges of certain forms of security and resources (e.g. money, drugs, companionship, and housing), the possible benefits of these relationships may fail to materialise. In the excerpt above, Joe describes the profound precarity and uncertainty in what emerge as risky friendships and relationships and his vulnerability to the predation of others. More generally, Joe's overall family history indicates how old and new families as they change and reform can be problematic for young men. Joe's efforts to secure a new family have been unsuccessful, as have his efforts for stable work. In his case, the only relationships or situations that have provided stability have been those associated with formal services. His case additionally demonstrates how poverty processes limit the possibilities of family for men in certain ways that render them absent, not just as fathers but as sons, brothers, and uncles. We have compared Joe's case with that of Ben to demonstrate the continuities of these lifecourse trajectories for these two men, across two different studies separated by over a decade, but which are linked through shared experiences of place and poverty. Their lives are similarly shaped in relation to drug and alcohol dependency, involvement and exclusion from families, and persistent employment and housing insecurity. By bringing these cases together we can see how families might have mitigating effects against social isolation, as observed in other research (Eckhard, 2018), but may also be exclusionary and produce additional vulnerabilities for men across their lives.

Discussion

It is in this chapter that the distinctive analytical affordances of QSA are most prominently displayed. We are not only able to cluster together people from within a study or series of studies, but able to cluster people and localities, across differently constituted datasets from research by different research teams. Here, our 'cases' therefore become theoretical, and through casing people in these ways (Emmel & Hughes, 2009), we can interrogate not only the dynamic relational nexuses of which they form a part, but also how these relate to their broader localities, and how these change according to the different analytical foci we bring to the narratives, including generational identity, locality, time period, age, family circumstances, employment, housing, education, and parental responsibilities.

Sheila and Ben's case addresses a gap in the literature and adds to existing evidence on what happens to men in poverty as they age. The predominant empirical focus on boys and young men in family poverty research, as well as men's studies, has led researchers to describe the field as (young) men's studies (Calasanti & King, 2005). While there have been modest attempts to establish a sociology of adulthood (e.g. Pilcher et al., 2003), middle-aged and older men are rarely considered, a theme we have addressed throughout the empirical chapters of this book. Notwithstanding the generational emphasis on young men and their economic circumstances and trajectories, economic restructuring also disproportionately affects older generations of working-class men (McDowell, 2000; Stewart et al., 2021) and their family dynamics. Thus, as Haywood and Johansson (2017) argue, marginalisation is simultaneously relational but also manifests at a generational level. Older men tend to attract less media, government, and even academic attention, not least because they are less likely to create disruptive social 'noise' or demand widespread attention, such as in rioting, than their youthful counterparts, rendering them less visible. Their 'troubles' also tend to be downgraded in the context of portrayals of young men as a social 'problem' (Ruxton, 2002). As Ruxton highlights however, the increasing pace of globalisation has meant that while some men have been able to increase their power, for working-class men, downsizing, retrenchment, and unemployment are very real challenges to their identities and experienced masculinities (ibid.). In 2000, one-third of all British men currently not in employment were aged between 50 and 65, meaning that some 2.5 million were economically inactive and reliant on state or private benefits in some form (McDowell, 2000). This period neatly fits with the cases of men in the 'Midlife Grandparents' Study, specifically Ben, but also with Bob (in Chap. 5) and Geoff (in Chap. 6). Our analytical approach therefore directly engages with questions of generational experience (e.g. Tarrant & Hughes, 2019a), and in this chapter we begin to build a comparative analysis of accounts from older and younger men. In doing so, we become aware of how the longitudinal impacts of poverty profoundly shape the character, and possibilities, of men's family participation across their lifecourse, and the processes through which they may be systematically excluded from families through the investments women make through circumstances of separation, repartnering, and having more children.

This chapter also echoes the themes of contempt and disdain first encountered in Chap. 4, and how violent men are excluded from their families by their partners, adult children, and then their grandchildren. In considering the consequences of men's expulsion and then exclusion from their families, we observe how men become increasingly exposed to different forms of violence that extend beyond interpersonal, physical violence, to institutional forms of discipline and management. Our findings demonstrate that when people consciously strive not to integrate into networks of relationships characterised by violence, drugs, and crime, which in turn stigmatise the locality, they render themselves vulnerable to being identified as 'outsiders', an identity which again attracts distinctive risks. In Victor and Carolyn's case, we observe how predictive trajectories of hardship in place are developed and mobilised, to manage and regulate the behaviours of their children and grandchildren in relation to what they describe as a culture of place. These interventions are nevertheless fraught with their own risks that produce vulnerabilities in place, and highlight the vulnerabilities *of* place. Equally apparent across the interviews, therefore, is how people's trajectories through family relationships are shaped through place, and may intensify certain visibilities such as of young men in either drug-using, or criminal justice, networks, and systems. In turn, these processes serve to shape localities over time.

In their discussion of how research may both engage with and explain 'the texture of hardship', Newman and Peeples Massengill (2006, p. 436) discuss what they describe as 'the forces of disorder', in relation to young men in low-income localities in America. Their review of existing scholarship, predominantly of immersive ethnography of young men's gang lives (Harding, 2009), street lives (Anderson, 1999), and drug lives (Venkatesh, 2000), demonstrates the efforts required by young men to navigate unsafe and risky places. These efforts occur through friendship networks that—through their elaboration and participation—are productive of subversive forms of public disorder (Newman & Peeples Massengill, 2006).

Central to Joe's account is his vulnerability and exposure to violence, where such violence might be seen as part of informal process of 'civilising' (Ray, 2018), or informal social ordering. For example, one of Sheila's sons describes getting stabbed by someone from a rival gang from a neighbouring estate because he and his friends had crossed a symbolic boundary between the two estates, namely through a children's park. Violence, as a form of social ordering by people within localities, enforces boundaries, establishes affiliations, and supports we/I discourses of belonging[8] to the extent that it becomes *characteristic* of place. The 'texture of hardship', we suggest, is therefore not simply related to lack of resource, and the difficulty of 'making ends meet', but includes embodied hardships through exposure to multiple forms of violence—whether physical or symbolic—interpersonal, such as in families on the estates, or state-sanctioned, through disciplinary and surveillancing processes (Ray, 2018; Waquant, 2009). Our analyses add to these debates by demonstrating how family relationships are profoundly implicated in, and shaped by, such 'ordering' processes of hardship more commonly approached from individualised or

---

[8] We would like to thank Dr Esben Houborg, University of Aarhus, for alerting us to the role violence plays in social ordering, specifically in drug-using networks.

locality-based perspectives. We therefore seek to elucidate the complex of family networks and relationships over time in these places without stigmatising the people who comprise them but understanding the processes through which they and/as their localities come to be stigmatised. Critically important here are how the narratives of men and women across the studies express processes of internalisation of civic ordering within and across families and neighbourhoods. Simultaneously, they describe the profound lack of civic investment and support needed to sustain stability and security for those who live there. Ultimately, in considering the violent ordering of everyday lives, through families, friendships, and place, these cases demonstrate not only violence *in* poverty, but the violence *of* poverty.

Finally, in terms of the central questions of this book, Ben and Joe's cases demonstrate how the longitudinal character of their participation, including Ben's early fierce protectiveness of Sheila, and Joe's fierce protectiveness of his younger siblings, their involvement, and then absence from the lives of their children is not simply reducible to these men at these times. In effect, the continuities and similarities of their lifecourse trajectories express more than these men's adequacy or otherwise as men in families, but describe and illustrate how longitudinal experiences of poverty serve to limit the possibilities of family for men.

References

Anderson, E. (1999). *Code of the Street: Decency, Violence, and the Moral Life of the Inner City*. Norton.

Baird, A. (2012). The Violent Gang and the Construction of Masculinity Amongst Socially Excluded Young Men. *Safer Communities, 11*, 179–190.

Baltieri, D. (2014). Order of Onset of Drug Use and Criminal Activities in a Sample of Drug-Abusing Women Convicted of Violent Crimes. *Drug and Alcohol Review, 33*(2), 202–210.

Beatty, C., Bennett, C., & Hawkins, A. (2021). Managing Precarity: Food Bank Use by Low-Income Women Workers in a Changing Welfare Regime. *Social Policy Administration, 55*, 981–1000.

Becker, H. (2007). *Telling About Society*. University of Chicago Press.

Binswanger, I. A., Nowels, C., Corsi, K. F., Glanz, J., Long, J., Booth, R. E., & Steiner, J. (2012). Return to Drug Use and Overdose After Release from Prison: A Qualitative Study of Risk and Protective Factors. *Addiction Science Clinical Practice, 7*(1), 3.

Bonner-Thompson, C., & McDowell, L. (2020). Precarious Lives, Precarious Care: Young Men's Caring Practices in Three Coastal Towns in England. *Emotion, Space and Society, 35,* 100684.

Bulman, K., & Neale, B. (2017). Developing Sustained Support for Vulnerable Young Fathers: Journeys with Young Offenders. In A. Tarrant & B. Neale (Eds.), *Learning to Support Young Dads,* Responding to Young Fathers in a Different Way: Project Report, https://followingfathers.leeds.ac.uk/wpcontent/uploads/sites/79/2017/04/SYD-final-report.pdf

Burton, L. (2007). Childhood Adultification in Economically Disadvantaged Families: A Conceptual Model. *Family Relations: An Interdisciplinary Journal of Applied Family Science, 56*(4), 329–345.

Calasanti, T., & King, N. (2005). Firming the Floppy Penis: Age, Class, and Gender Relations in the Lives of Old Men. *Men and Masculinities, 8*(1), 3–23.

Crutchfield, R. D., & Wadsworth, T. (2003). Poverty and Violence. In W. Heitmeyer & J. Hagan (Eds.), *International Handbook of Violence Research.* Springer.

Daly, M., & Kelly, G. (2015). *Families and Poverty: Everyday Life on a Low-Income.* Policy Press.

Desmond, M. (2012). Disposable Ties and the Urban Poor. *American Journal of Sociology, 117*(5), 1295–1335.

Dorey, P. (2010). A Poverty of Imagination: Blaming the Poor for Inequality. *The Political Quarterly, 81*(3), 333–343.

Doucet, A. (2020). Father Involvement, Care and Breadwinning: Genealogies of Concepts and Revisioned Conceptual Narratives. *Genealogy, 4*(1), 14.

Eckhard. (2018). Does Poverty Increase the Risk of Social Isolation? *Insights Based on Panel Data from Germany, The Sociological Quarterly, 59*(2), 338–359.

Emmel, N., & Hughes, K. (2010). 'Recession, It's All the Same to Us Son': The Longitudinal Experience (1999-2010) of Deprivation. *Twenty-First Century Society, 5*(2), 171–181.

Emmel, N., Hughes, K., Greenhalgh, J., & Sales, A. (2007). Accessing Socially Excluded People—Trust and the Gatekeeper in the Researcher-Participant Relationship. *Sociological Research Online, 12*(2), 43–55.

Emmel, N., & Hughes, K. (2009). Small-N Access Cases to Refine Theories of Social Exclusion and Access to Socially Excluded Individuals and Groups. In D. Byrne & C. Ragin (Eds.), *The SAGE Handbook of Case-Centered Methods.* SAGE.

Erhard, F. (2020). The Struggle to Provide: How Poverty Is Experienced in the Context of Family Care. *Journal of Poverty and Social Justice, 28*(1), 119–134.

Garthwaite, K. (2016). *Hunger Pains: Life Inside Foodbank Britain.* Policy Press.

Garthwaite, K., Collins, P., & Bambra, C. (2015). Food for Thought: An Ethnographic Study of Negotiating Ill Health and Food Insecurity in a UK Foodbank'. *Social Science and Medicine, 132,* 38–44.

Gillies, V. (2006). Working Class Mothers and School Life: Exploring the Role of Emotional Capital. *Gender and Education, 18*(3), 281–293.

Gooch, K. (2019). Kidulthood': Ethnography, Juvenile Prison Violence and the Transition from 'Boys' to 'Men. *Criminology and Criminal Justice, 19*(1), 80–97.

Harding, D. J. (2009). Violence, Older Peers, and the Socialization of Adolescent Boys in Disadvantaged Neighborhoods. *American Sociological Review, 1, 74, 3*, 445–464.   https://doi.org/10.1177/000312240907400306.   PMID: 20161350; PMCID: PMC2776742.

Haywood, C., & Johansson, T. (2017). *Marginalized Masculinities: Contexts, Continuities and Change.* Routledge.

Hughes, K. (2007). Migrating Identities: The Relational Constitution of Drug Use and Addiction. *Sociology of Health & Illness, 29*, 673–691. https://doi.org/10.1111/j.1467-9566.2007.01018.x

Jones, T., & Pratt, T. (2008). The Prevalence of Sexual Violence in Prison: The State of the Knowledge Base and Implications for Evidence-Based Correctional Policy Making. *International Journal of Therapy and Comparative Criminology, 52*(3), 280–295.

Kahneman, D., & Deaton, A. (2010). High Income Improves Evaluation of Life but Not Emotional Wellbeing. *Proceedings of the National Academy of Sciences, 107*(38), 16489–16493.

Kearns, A., Keanrs, O., & Lawson, L. (2013). Notorious Places: Image, Reputation, Stigma. The Role of Newspapers in Area Reputations for Social Housing Estates. *Housing Studies, 28*(4), 579–598.

Kerr, W. C., Kaplan, M. S., Huguet, N., Caetano, R., Giesbrecht, N., & McFarland, B. H. (2017). Economic Recession, Alcohol, and Suicide Rates: Comparative Effects of Poverty, Foreclosure, and Job Loss. *American Journal of Preventative Medicine., 52*(4), 469–475. https://doi.org/10.1016/j.amepre.2016.09.021

King, L. (2015). *Family Men: Fatherhood and Masculinity in Britain, C. 1914-1960.* Oxford University Press.

Lister, R. (2005). *Poverty.* Polity Press.

Livingstone, I., & Macmillan, R. (2015). More Than a Provider: The Voluntary Sector, Commissioning and Stewardship for a Diverse Market in Criminal Justice. *Voluntary Sector Review, 6*(2), 221–230.

Lohan, M., Brennan-Wilson, A., Hunter, R., Gabrio, A., McDaid, L., Young, H., French, R., Aventin, A., Clarke, M., McDowell, C., Logan, D., Toase, S., O'Hare, L., Bonell, C., Gillespie, K., Gough, A., Lagdon, S., Warren, E., Buckley, K., et al. (2022). Effects of Gender-Transformative Relationships and Sexuality Education to Reduce Adolescent Pregnancy (the JACK Trial): A Cluster-Randomised Trial. *The Lancet Public Health, 7*(7), 626–637.

Lupton, R., & Tunstall, R. (2008). Neighbourhood Regeneration Through Mixed Communities: A 'Social Justice Dilemma'? *Journal of Education Policy, 23*(2), 105–117.

MacDonald, R., Shildrick, T., & Furlong, A. (2020). 'Cycles of Disadvantage' Revisited: Young People, Families and Poverty Across Generations. *Journal of Youth Studies, 23*(1), 12–27.

Macmillan, R., & Ellis Paine, A. (2020). The Third Sector in a Strategically Selective Landscape - The Case of Commissioning Public Services. *Journal of Social Policy, 50*(3), 606–626.

Maguire, D. (2020). *Male, Failed, Jailed: Masculinities and "Revolving-Door" Imprisonment in the UK*. Palgrave Macmillan.

Manhica, H., Straatmann, V. S., Lundin, A., Agardh, E., & Danielsson, A. (2021). Association Between Poverty Exposure During Childhood and Adolescence, and Drug Use Disorders and Drug-Related Crimes Later in Life. *Addiction, 116*(7), 1747–1756.

Martikainen, P., Adda, J., Ferrie, J., Smith, G. D., & Marmot, M. (2003). Effects of Income and Wealth on GHQ Depression and Poor Self Rated Health in White Collar Women and Men in the Whitehall II Study. *Journal of Epidemiology & Community Health, 57*(9), 718–723.

McDowell, L. (2000). The Trouble with Men? Young People, Gender Transformations and the Crisis of Masculinity. *International Journal of Urban and Regional Research, 24*(1), 201–209.

McKenzie, L. (2015). *Getting By: Estates, Class and Culture in Austerity Britain*. Policy Press.

Meek, K. (2007). Parenting Education for Young Fathers in Prison. *Child & Family Social Work, 12*(3), 239–247.

Murali, V., & Oyebode, F. (2004). Poverty, Social Inequality and Mental Health. *Advances in Psychiatric Treatment, 10*(3), 216–224.

Nayak, A. (2006). Displaced Masculinities: Chavs, Youth and Class in the Post-industrial City. *Sociology, 40*(5), 813–831.

Neale, B. (2016). Introduction: Young Fatherhood: Lived Experiences and Policy Challenges. *Social Policy and Society, 15*(1), 75–83.

Neale, B., & Ladlow, L. (2015). Finding a Place to Parent? Housing Young Fathers, Briefing Paper no. 7. https://followingfathers.leeds.ac.uk/wp-content/uploads/sites/79/2015/10/Brieifing-Paper-7-V3.pdf

Neale, B., & Lau Clayton, C. (2014). Young Parenthood and Cross Generational Relationships: The Perspectives of Young Fathers. In J. Holland & R. Edwards (Eds.), *Understanding Families Over Time*. Palgrave Macmillan.

Newman, K. S., & Peeples Massengill, R. (2006). The Texture of Hardship: Qualitative Sociology of Poverty. *Annual Review of Sociology, 32*(1), 423–446.

Office for National Statistics. (2018). *Health Inequalities Current Patterns and Trends in Ill Health and Death by Measures of Socio-Economic Status*, https://www.ons.gov.uk/peoplepopulationandcommunity/healthandsocialcare/healthinequalities#:~:text=Male%20healthy%20life%20expectancy%20(HLE,53.3%20and%2070.2%20years%2C%20respectively

Pilcher, J., Williams, J., & Pole, C. (2003). Rethinking Adulthood: Families, Transitions, and Social Change. *Sociological Research Online, 8*(4), 181–185.

Public Health England. (2018). A Review of Recent Trends in Mortality in England, PHE Publications Gateway Number: GW-686. https://assets.publishing.service.gov.uk/government/uploads/system/uploads/attachment_data/file/827518/Recent_trends_in_mortality_in_England.pdf

Ray, L. (2018). *Violence and Society* (2nd ed.). SAGE.

Robinson, M., Templeton, M., Kelly, C., Grant, D., Buston, K., Hunt, K., & Lohan, M. (2022). Addressing Sexual and Reproductive Health and Rights with Men in Prisons: Co-production and Feasibility Testing of a Relationship, Sexuality and Future Fatherhood Education Programme. *International Journal of Prisoner Health*, https://doi.org/10.1108/IJPH-02-2022-0008.

Rojas, Y., & Stenberg, S.-A. (2010). Evictions and Suicide: A Follow-up Study of Almost 22,000 Swedish Households in the Wake of the Global Financial Crisis. *Journal of Epidemiological Community Health, 70*(4), 409–413.

Roy, K. (2006). Father Stories: A Life Course Examination of Paternal Identity Among Low-income African American Men. *Journal of Family Issues, 27*(1), 31–54.

Roy, K. (2014). Fathering from the Long View: Framing Personal and Social Change Through Life Course Theory. *Journal of Family Theory and Review, 6*, 319–335.

Roy, K., Messina, L., Smith, J., & Waters, D. (2014). Growing Up as "Man of the House": Adultification and Transition into Adulthood for Young Men in Economically Disadvantaged Families. In K. Roy & N. Jones (Eds.), *Pathways to Adulthood for Disconnected Young Men in Low-Income Communities. New Directions in Child and Adolescent Development*, (pp. 55–72), Jossey-Bass.

Ruxton, S. (2002). *Men, Masculinities and Poverty in the UK*. Oxfam.

Shildrick, T., & MacDonald, R. (2013). Poverty Talk: How People Experiencing Poverty Deny Their Poverty and Why They Blame 'The Poor.' *The Sociological Review, 61*(2), 285–303.

Staley, S. (1992). *Drug Policy and the Decline of American Cities*. Transaction Publishers.

Stewart, K., Reeves, A., & Patrick, R. (2021). *A Time of Need: Exploring the Changing Poverty Risk Facing Larger Families in the UK*. https://sticerd.lse.ac.uk/CASE/_NEW/PUBLICATIONS/abstract/?index=8275

Strange, J.-M. (2012). Fatherhood, Providing, and attachment in Late Victorian and Edwardian Working-class Families. *The Historical Journal, 55*(4), 1007–1027.

Tarrant, A. (2021). *Fathering and Poverty: Uncovering Men's Participation in Low-Income Family Life*. Policy Press.

Tarrant, A., & Hughes, K. (2019). Qualitative Secondary Analysis: Building Longitudinal Samples to Understand Men's Generational Identities in Low Income Contexts. *Sociology, 53*(3), 538–553.

Trammell, R. (2012). *Enforcing the Convict Code: Violence and Prison Culture.* Lynne Rienner Publishers.

Tucker, S., Hargreaves, C., Roberts, A., Anderson, I., Shaw, J., & Challis, D., (2018). Social Care in Prison: Emerging Practice Arrangements Consequent Upon the Introduction of the Care Act 2014. *The British Journal of Social Work, 48*(6), 1627–1644.

Tucker, S., Hargreaves, C., Cattermull, M., Roberts, A., Walker, T., Shaw, J., & Challis, D. (2021). The Nature and Extent of Prisoners' Social Care Needs: Do Older Prisoners Require a Different Service Response? *Journal of Social Work, 21*(3), 310–328. https://doi.org/10.1177/1468017319890077

Venkatesh, S. A. (2000). *American Project: The Rise and Fall of a Modern Ghetto.* Harvard University Press.

Wacquant, L. (1995). Pugs at Work: Bodily Capital and Bodily Labour among Professional Boxers. *Body & Society, 1*(1), 65–93.

Wakeling, K., & Lynch, K. (2020). Exploring Substance Use in Prisons: A Case Study Approach in Five Closed Male English Prisons. *Ministry of Justice Analytical Series.* https://www.drugsandalcohol.ie/33284/1/HMPPS_Exploring-substance-use-prisons.pdf

Walsh, D., Wyper, G. M. A., & McCartney, G. (2022). Trends in Healthy Life Expectancy in the Age of Austerity. *Journal of Epidemiology and Community Health, 76*(8), 743–745.

Walsh, D., Dundas, R., McCartney, G., Gibson, M., & Seaman, R. (2022). Bearing the Burden of Austerity: How Do Changing Mortality Rates in the UK Compare Between Men and Women? *Journal of Epidemiology and Community Health, 76*(12), 1027–1033.

Waquant, L. (2009). *Urban Outcasts: A Sociology of Advanced Marginality.* Polity Press.

Webb, C., Bennett, D., & Bywaters, P. (2022). Austerity, Poverty, and Children's Services Quality in England: Consequences for Child Welfare and Public Services. *Social Policy and Society*, 1–22. https://doi.org/10.1017/S147474642200001X

CHAPTER 8

Conclusion: Trajectories of Families Through Poverty

INTRODUCTION

Our empirical focus when starting to develop the work elaborated in this book was men living in low-income families. We began with the observation that the empirical absence of men in literatures considering family and poverty precludes a fuller understanding of the longitudinal dynamics of hardship, as well as of the broader intergenerational trajectories and relationships for men in these localities. As our analyses of men's accounts have evolved, we have developed more cogent and nuanced insights of *family* trajectories through poverty with varying implications for men and women across generations.

We began with the observation that static representations of 'absent men' obscure the dynamics of men's longitudinal family participation through various phases of their lifecourse, sustain deficit representations of men in low-income localities, and constrain analytic attention to how and when men are vulnerable in families. In contrast, attention to the intricacies of men's family relationships intergenerationally and from multiple generational identities, across place, with employment, to other men and women, and over time helped us to identify and explain what emerged as longitudinal 'in/out' processes of family participation.

The novel use of a 'data ethnography' facilitated this detailed and longitudinal engagement via the reuse of qualitative data from four linked

K. Hughes, A. Tarrant, *Men, Families, and Poverty*, Palgrave Macmillan Studies in Family and Intimate Life, https://doi.org/10.1007/978-3-031-24922-8_8

longitudinal studies. Indeed, as far as we are aware and certainly in our fields of expertise, this is the first full length book entirely based on Qualitative Secondary Analysis (QSA) amalgamating multiple qualitative datasets to generate findings addressing contemporary debates. The men from the four studies detailed in Chaps. 1 and 3 were interviewed for different research purposes and at different times. We link their accounts along the theoretical dimensions shared by the four studies, including their connections to the *Timescapes: Changing Lives and Times* programme of research (Neale et al., 2012); questions oriented towards temporality; comparable socio-economic and geographical localities; shared participants; and linked researchers and methodological concerns. The people and families we write about experience stubborn, intergenerational, and place-based poverty. These studies capture first- and second-hand accounts of men's participation in families across their lives and in relation to an array of generational identities, including as fathers, sons, grandfathers, brothers, and uncles. The wealth of qualitative longitudinal data on which we are able to draw provides compelling evidence of how men's family participation is integral to the doing and sustaining of low-income families.

Such participation is not always straightforward, however, and to address the longitudinal dynamics of men's family participation, we established and refined a theoretical multigenerational analytic framework. Using this, we built longitudinal cases from both men and women from across the four studies to examine the diversity and range of men's intergenerational participation in families, from multiple generational positions in and through low-income circumstances over time. This case-based approach enabled interrogation of *the experience of family life* that is, the complex and dynamic positioning of individuals within families, their transitions in and through different family configurations and generational positions and their interdependencies over time, and *the lives of families*, that is, the shifting, complex of longitudinal trajectories of family networks shaped through, and shaping, involvements, transitions, and trajectories. Below we summarise the advances we make on the basis of these methodological and theoretical innovations.

Advancing Existing Debate: Beyond 'Absent' Men

Combined, our analyses demonstrate that men are not straightforwardly disinvested from family life in the ways described and implied by the policy language of absence. Chapters 4, 5, 6, 7 evidence men's own perceptions, insights, theories, and understandings of their family lives and relationships over time. We consider how these interweave with experiences and meanings of their working lives, over their lifecourse, against a backdrop of intergenerational poverty, and through complex governmental, third sector, and legal relationships. Via these processes, it is evident that men are not always able to sustain family relationships through the disruptive effects of poverty, which shapes men's lives and interdependencies over time, and women and children's lives by implication. Our understanding and explanation of men's longitudinal trajectories through poverty and family build across two interconnected analytic domains.

Men as Partners/Husbands and Fathers: the 'In/Out' Character of Low-income Men's Family Participation

A major theme is the discursive and evidentiary 'absenting' or *'process of absenting'* of men in low-income families in two areas. First, in family-orientated policy, which frames these men as absent from their families. Second, the inadvertent exacerbation of this 'absenting' by the theoretical framing of questions and research approaches on families in poverty, where the focus on men is commonly through their 'breadwinner' or fatherhood identities (see also Tarrant, 2021). Such absenting is underscored by assumptions that, when men leave households, or when relationships end, there is no continued interdependency among family members across households (see also Hamer, 2001). Our analyses strongly counter these assumptions. Non-resident fathers have been noted as an important example of how men's familial roles and responsibilities become obscured, or even ignored, when they are no longer resident with their children (e.g. Dermott, 2016; Sobo-Allen and Howarth, 2022).

Women's accounts both confirmed and disrupted these arguments. Although providing compelling and detailed evidence about how and when men were absent from their lives and families, they simultaneously supported new insights into how men participated in, and sustained, their families over time. We began with the observation that women's narratives about men frequently chime with policy representations of men as absent, and by implication, position them as the cause of, and solution to, their family problems and hardships. Mirroring the static policy accounts of men we describe above, women often focused on certain men, at certain times. First, they concentrated on men in particular generational positions, namely as partners/husbands and as the fathers of their children. Second, their interviews tended towards discussing the tenor of these particular men's behaviours and practices in their family contexts at specific moments in the lifecourse of their family. Women's accounts described violence, abuse, and neglect in these relationships, and included narratives of ex-partners/husbands as 'crap dads' and 'absent', the very discourses prevalent in literature and policy and those we seek to nuance here. Consequently, we concluded that where research relies solely on one-off or snapshot accounts from women of family life through poverty, such framings may both produce and confirm narratives of male absence, especially when the focus is on men who have left the 'family home' and their biological children.

Yet women's accounts were also replete with evidence of distinctive changing family configurations wherein men and boys of all ages are an essential part of everyday family life. The life history cases of the women describe myriad instances of men's participation in the context of often ruptured and discontinuous intergenerational family networks in which parent and grandparent generations are lost. In the interviews, experiences of intergenerational ruptures, parents repartnering with people who do not take on parental roles towards existing children, moving in and out of care settings when young, all combine to produce difficult family situations from which the women consider they have been 'rescued' by their partner. However, subsequently, many women's marital/partnership trajectories include instances of violence, abuse, separation, and divorce. Essentially, we observe longitudinal patterns in which women need rescuing from the very men they have been rescued by. These men continue to have a symbolic 'presence', even if they are not directly engaged in sustaining family life, and even after they die, which their ex-partners and children continue to navigate.

In these and other often difficult family situations, the women recount the involvement of other men at particular moments and from multiple generational positions, playing an essential role in supporting women, and their children, to leave violent partners. These men provide opportunities, resources, and services (cash, cars and vans, help with removals, help with children) during these times. They also engage in interpersonal forms of family 'ordering', such as physically excluding violent men from households, protecting their families, and taking on caring responsibilities for younger relatives when women are unable to or are absent such as through a prison sentence. Here, sons and brothers, sometimes uncles, may 'step in' and provide essential support in the longer-term survival and protection of families in myriad ways.

In troubling the character of men's 'absence' from families, we identified the need for research to continue to track where men go when relationships end and they leave the family home, as well as *why* to those places, and *what* it is they do there. Working from a view of men as partners/husbands and 'fathers', we observe how men may be absent in some households at certain points in time, or phases in changing family life-courses, yet continue to draw on and reinforce particular generational identities, such as 'father', 'step-father', and 'grandparent kinship carer'. This 'in/out' character of their family participation, and how men assert or prioritise particular generational identities, links strongly to their strategic resourcing of one set of family relationships over others. Hardship plays a significant role in such selective resourcing where men simply lack the money to financially support previous as well as current families, especially those that include dependents. Victor's case, for example, allowed us to interrogate how processes of moving in, moving out, and moving on in partnering relationships produce changing family configurations, resulting in the 'absence' of men from one family, yet their 'presence' in another. Victor was notably 'visible' in his second family with Carolyn to some policy services and organisations—in his case as a foster parent—yet 'invisible' for other services from his first family, such as from the perspective of the Child Support Agency, Victor's ex-wife, and his biological son. Our analytical focus therefore disrupts simplistic narratives of men's 'absence', and works to clarify and explain how men's 'in/visibility' is shaped by certain perspectives, such as those from ex-partners, and policy organisations.

Patterns of 'presence' and 'absence' from families apply for *women*, as well as men, including the effects of these for their children and grandchildren. Josie spends a three-year period in prison during which, in her absence, her two youngest children are subject to abuse and violence from their father, her ex-husband. Josie also observes the repeated mistakes her daughter makes in continually repartnering with men who are violent and abusive. Susan's eldest daughter dies from an inadvertent drug overdose, leaving Susan with four young grandchildren to look after. This involved her managing an uneasy relationship with the father of those children, wherein he had access to the two youngest children but not to the older two. Susan is tasked with managing the emotional impacts on her grandchildren through their loss of their mother, her own grief at the loss of her daughter, and the problematic character of her grandchildren's father's participation in the lives of his children, which is additionally proscribed through social work management and involvement. As we demonstrate, developing a longitudinal and intergenerational approach to family participation is a conceptual innovation that can facilitate important insight into the dynamic interplay of both men and women's absence and presence in changing family configurations.

Men as Kinship Carers: Longitudinal and Intergenerational Hardship and Higher Levels of Kinship Care

Working from a consideration of the consequences of longitudinal poverty on changing family forms and configurations, we see how and why families in hardship are more likely to experience kinship care arrangements. When analysing men's accounts of becoming kinship carers, their narratives describe a more constrained degree of 'choice' around their decision-making in comparison to their narratives about becoming fathers and husbands, narratives already expressive of considerable constraint. Such constraint typifies the informal yet critical 'rescue and repair' work in which men and women engage. While we recognise women are more likely to become kinship carers, the four datasets demonstrate high rates of kinship care for older men, especially as grandfathers. 'Rescue and repair' grandparenting includes a range of family living arrangements on a spectrum of involvement from occasional to permanent residential care of grandchildren, and consequently a continuum of informal to formal kinship care. An example of informal kinship care is Bob, whose grandson lived with him and his wife Dianne from babyhood until he was a teenager. Bob's case is especially valuable in interrogating the challenges for older men in sustaining working lives as the impacts of poverty affect their, and their partners' health, and as they gradually assume full-time caring responsibility for others, often unexpectedly (see also Yeandle & Buckner, 2017; Fisher & Buckner, 2018). An empirical counterpart for Bob is Geoff, who is forced to become a formal kinship carer for his two granddaughters, a role which creates considerable stress and anger for him, and continues to be a point of contention across the four years of his research involvement. Geoff, too, is a carer for his wife Margaret, and combined these responsibilities impinge on his work identity and his forced retirement from a job through which he gained considerable self-esteem. These two cases illustrate the diversity of emotional experience in relation to kinship care, whilst also illustrating shared experiences of increasing levels of mental ill health associated with job loss and challenges to masculinity because of ageing (Tarrant, 2014), additionally linked with complex family caring responsibilities and arrangements. These shared experiences are further shaped through shared experiences of deindustrialisation and employment decline in the locality.

'Rescue and repair' grandparenting by male kinship carers is both characteristic of, and critical to, the sustaining of low-income families over time and to how men 'do kinship'. However, their contributions and the associated financial pressures of sometimes unexpected additional family responsibilities are often invisible and undervalued. We develop a more complex understanding of processes of strategic decision-making through these family circumstances, including how men make constrained choices about their management of financial and emotional resources, often with limited knowledge about their rights and in a context of dwindling financial and legal support. As in Victor's case above, in *becoming* male kinship carers, men consciously strive to take on, or describe themselves from, certain familial identities in order to access the resources they need to sustain their changing families. These are often hard won, and are frequently dependent on additional professional help, such as through social workers or legal advisors. These relationships are frequently challenging, and men's histories of struggles with health and social care providers, that themselves sometimes require legal intervention, demonstrate the importance of men's 'professionalisation' in the language and associated rights and benefits of kinship care. Men's accounts additionally alert us to the ostensible absence or problematic presence of women, including mothers and grandmothers, where women's family participation, including their involvement with children, is not necessarily a social good. We refer here to Sam's case, where the maternal grandmother was identified as responsible for neglect and abuse not only towards her grandson, Leo, but also historically towards her children. We only have a partial picture of her case and circumstances, and are reluctant to draw any further conclusions or points on the basis of the limited data available to us. Our argument here is that gender does not straightforwardly link to caring for younger relatives. We raise this point as part of a more general argument, that in conflating gender with caring arrangements where women are seen as the default caregiver, men in different generational positions can be overlooked in caring arrangements for vulnerable children, who may lose their connection to their broader families in the longer term (Sobo-Allen and Howarth, 2022;

Tarrant, 2021). Furthermore, such gendering of care may entrench women even further family arrangements that depend on, and reinforce, an intensification of women's responsibilities for the care and sustenance of their dependents.

The Volatility of Hardship in the Lifecourse Trajectories of Men and Women

Considering the intergenerational dynamics of poverty supports attention to the volatility produced by hardship in the lifecourse trajectories of men and women. Across the cases, similarities and continuities in the patterning and trajectories of men's lives through poverty and family are observable. We interrogated the dynamics of their lifecourse trajectories to both illustrate and explain how experiences of longitudinal and intergenerational poverty may serve to limit the possibilities of family for men. In this way, we consider how, when, and why men may be actively *absented* from their families, either by their relatives or through formal service intervention.

To explore such absenting of men from families by their relatives, we used 'empirical counterparts' and questions of generational experience. In interrogating the longitudinal dynamics of this active absenting, we were alerted to the volatility of men's trajectories through their families. For example, Chap. 7, comparing the cases of Ben, an older man, and Joe, a young man, highlights patterns of men being expelled from family households, sidelined and marginalised in certain family relationships (see also Neale & Lau Clayton, 2014), and other forms of familial exclusion over time and across place, to the extent they experience a 'poverty of family'. These forms of expulsion and marginalisation are narratively connected, by both themselves, the women in their families and other family members, with a range of events. Men's exclusion from families often coincides when they turn 16 years of age and consequently both gain and lose particular welfare rights (Ladlow, 2021; McKenzie, 2015; Tarrant & Hughes, 2019; Tarrant & Neale, forthcoming), which may make them expensive for families in hardship. They may also be incarcerated and therefore forcibly removed from family contexts by formal agencies (e.g. Roy, 2006, 2014). Across the datasets men and boys were expelled from families when they were violent and abusive, when they developed problematic substance dependency, but also when their parents repartnered and the young men's position in the family became precarious. Importantly, men's expulsion and then exclusion from their families exposes them to different forms of violence, extending beyond interpersonal, physical violence, to include institutional forms of discipline and management specific to the localities in which they reside. We discuss this further below.

We analytically connect these longer trajectories of presence and absence of men in families with broader social trends, more usually discussed in research which foregrounds different dimensions of poverty, such as un/employment, inequality, crime, and violence. Our research, in its focus on longitudinal hardship in families for men, as well as in place-based relationships with other men proved fruitful for interrogating the extended nexuses of relationships in which the men in our studies were situated and how these were typified variously by asymmetrical interdependencies: with relatives, work colleagues, neighbours, friends, health and social care professionals, and professionals in welfare and legal systems. In capturing and accounting for these we were able to establish a connective analytical thread between the concerns of family and poverty sociology, developing the conceptual foundations and conceptual tools for a new sociology of family poverty.

Towards a 'New' Sociology of Family Poverty

Our work adds to existing literature on how men's relationships with their families intersect with and are imbricated in their relationships with other men in the localities in which they live, where both modes of relating entail uncertainty and risk. Academic knowledge and understanding of families are largely premised on middle-class rather than low-income families. Instead, low-income families have been considered, albeit in an interdisciplinary way, predominantly by social policy scholars or those whose work raises questions about welfare and the intersections of welfare change with families. Notable areas of analysis include the lived experiences of welfare (e.g. Patrick, 2018; Millar, 2019), the troubled families programme (e.g. Crossley, 2017; Lambert, 2017), foodbank use (Garthwaite et al., 2015; Garthwaite, 2016), policy and low-income family life (Daly, 2018; Cordon & Millar, 2010), families and austerity (Hall, 2019; Beatty et al., 2021; Jensen & Tyler, 2012), and so on.

In recovering and interpreting longitudinal experiences of 'absent men' in low-income families and localities, we have developed a detailed understanding of the interrelations between poverty and family life with a specific focus on how poverty shapes families, namely key dimensions of the ripple effect of poverty on intergenerational family configurations. We see our work in this respect as establishing a distinctive sociology of family poverty. This endeavour has been supported by the development of a theoretical family lifecourse framework comprising the conceptual tools developed in past research about the longitudinal dynamics of poverty and families. These have permitted an investigation of how family configurations emerge, endure, and change through poverty, as well as engaging with the longitudinal trajectories of family members from multiple intergenerational family identities through such changing circumstances. Engaging across micro to macrodynamics, we account for how people *do* family and kinship through poverty, considering the continuities and difference of poverty for men and women. In shifting to macro-level engagement with the broader circumstances through which families are shaped, and the localities they comprise, we advance the need to consider the impacts of a place-based understanding of socio-economic decline and the consequences of these in developing understandings and explanations of the violence of family poverty.

Doing Families

Well-established literature in the sociology of the family has supported consideration of how families are formed and performed in broader networks, such as those comprising health and social care, and investigation of the changing lives of families through the changing forms of 'kinship' (Comas d'Argemir & Soronellas, 2019) comprising them. Kinship has emerged as a set of normative expectations held by our participants that accrue to multiply held generational identities that both undergird and frame peoples' explanations of how and why they do what they do in and for their families. Kinship identities transcend considerations of gender and are irreducible to gendered identities. Above we consider the personal impacts of kinship care. Here, we turn to the rewriting of intergenerational identities and responsibilities effected through formal kinship care of both men and women in relation to younger relatives. Prime examples here are Sam, in Chap. 6, who simultaneously holds a father and grandfather relationship to his grandson, Leo, and works to sustain his son's (Mike's) relationship and Ruth, in Chap. 4, who is treated by professionals in her role as a grandmother, which confounds her support for her daughter (see also Emmel & Hughes, 2014). Engaging analytically with narratives and practices of kinship has been useful for enhancing our use of existing literature on the complexities of 'doing families' (Morgan, 2011, 2020), especially where specific generational identities have been rewritten through legal jurisdiction, such as in *kinship* care arrangements. This tells us more about the importance of formal and legal interventions which may serve to 'reorder' families and the kin relationships comprising them.

This was particularly apparent in Chaps. 6 and 7. In Chap. 6, in considering the *formal* 'rescue and repair' grandparenting undertaken by the men across the studies, our investigations travel in two directions. First, we are required to engage in national-level evidence on the relationship between poverty and high rates of kinship caring, and second, we are required to 'recover' accounts of the implications for family members of becoming kinship carers in their endeavours to preserve and sustain younger relatives. Such endeavours work towards producing particular family arrangements which themselves are shaped through the professional relationships and 'systems' they are required to navigate. In these undertakings, men are required to develop a *policy-based* language of kinship, that is kinship carer, deriving also from a legalistic reconfiguration of family relationships and responsibilities which, in turn, are exposed to and contingent on particular forms of social monitoring and surveillance. Becoming a kinship carer thus *writes in* specific modes of caring and responsibility for these grandfathers, as well as rewriting—indeed either disrupting or ending—their relationships to work and provisioning. Families involving kinship care arrangements can be described as 'families in the system'.

This analytic theme, of how families are configured through changing policy contexts, highlights the importance of how they are resourced, who in the family is resourced, how peoples' movement in and through families is managed by others, the significance of who does the resourcing in this regard, and how men, of all ages, may get 'left out' of family life. Building on these insights, we were able to see when men experience a 'poverty of family'. This may be caused through active exclusions from their families because of their behaviours, such as experienced by Ben, and the capacity of family members (Ben's twin sons) to exclude them. It may also be consequent on changing relationships within families such as through repartnering, how they are resourced, or men's absence through families because of imprisonment. Understanding when, why, and how men indeed might be absent from families required us to take an analytical 'step back' from a focus solely on families, to consider men in their localities. This engendered a dual-fold analytical move. First, it resisted an individualisation of experiences of, or responsibility for, people's poverty. Second, it necessitated a move away from focusing solely on individuals within families in the formulation of our findings on intergenerational experiences of poverty.

Our analyses demonstrate that poverty produces distinctive forms of intergenerational disruption and rupture with ripple effects across generations, to the extent that it is not possible to understand family lives and family poverty without accounting for this effect. Our analytic engagement with questions concerning the longitudinal, multi- and intergenerational dynamics of family life through poverty, was supported by our theoretical family lifecourse framework. The framework enabled the capture of the changing composition and character of family connections over time as they related to the impacts of poverty. These are most graphically articulated by the high rates of midlife morbidity, mental illness, and shorter life expectancy of our participants, and for those in their localities, compared with others living in more affluent and proximate neighbourhoods. The interrogation of the innumerable instances of 'absence' of both men and women from their families across the datasets using intergenerational timeframes brought these into sharp focus. For example, in the 'Midlife Grandparents' study, when tracking 'up' the generations, there are multiple accounts of 'absent' mothers, fathers, grandparents, and so on, and tales of childhood vulnerability for the participants in the studies and their older relatives. Analytically tracking 'down' the generations, there are numerous accounts of people taking on unexpected parental responsibility for younger relatives. Bob, in Chap. 5, provides an especially graphic recounting of the premature deaths of his parents' generation, and by the end of the study he is unusual as the only member of his own generation in his family who is still alive.

Poverty for Men

The longitudinal and multigenerational character of the research data, and time gaps between the four studies, enabled us to build empirical cases both of young and older men, to provide detailed qualitative narratives that articulate personal accounts of macroprocesses of national economic decline. Our attention to older men has allowed us to address gaps in existing research, albeit situated within a scholarship that has examined the trajectories of boys and men in evolving labour market and policy contexts. The predominant empirical focus on boys and young men in family and poverty research, as well as men's studies, has led researchers to describe the field as (young) men's studies (Calasanti & King, 2005). The older men in these studies describe histories of early employment and later life long-term unemployment involving working in manufacturing on leaving school, the loss of these employment opportunities in the early 1980s, followed by infrequent employment thereafter. They experience disabilities and mental illness requiring medication, with many on long-term incapacity benefit. The younger men experience the insecurity of a 'low pay, no pay' churn (Shildrick et al., 2012), with long periods of unemployment, insecurity in relation to their education and housing, high rates of drug and alcohol misuse, prison sentences and periods of time spent in bail hostels. Those who are in employment work in non-manual skilled (shop assistants, hospital porters); manual skilled (van drivers, joiners); partly skilled (security guards, refuse collectors); and unskilled work (building labourers and hospital cleaners). These findings accord with a broader literature that identifies how the deindustrialisation of towns and cities has impacted and disadvantaged men in these places and in low-income localities (McDowell & Bonner-Thompson, 2021; Nayak, 2006; Ward et al., 2017).

Notwithstanding the generational emphasis on young men and their economic circumstances and trajectories in wider scholarship, we concur with McDowell's (2000) argument that economic restructuring disproportionately affects older generations of working-class men. Our selection of older men's cases was in response to our familiarity with data, where we had a strong sense of the longitudinal impacts of economic restructuring on them and their parent generation. We sought to interrogate themes raised by Haywood and Johansson (2017) who argue that marginalisation is simultaneously relational but also manifests at a generational level. Older men tend to attract less media, government, and even academic attention, not least because they are less likely to create disruptive social 'noise' or demand widespread attention, such as in rioting, than their youthful counterparts, rendering them less visible. Their 'troubles' also tend to be downgraded in the context of portrayals of young men as a 'problem' (Ruxton, 2002).

Chapter 7 detailed the shared 'problems' for men in different generations such as alcohol and drug dependency, as well as precarious and diminishing employment prospects. These tracked across all generations, and again accounted for periods of 'absence' for men from some family configurations and accounting for them in other places, such as with friends, or in single-occupancy housing. However, there were also some generational differences, particularly in relation to changing welfare rights and support, as well as expectations by young fathers (Neale, 2016). As Ruxton (2002) highlights, the increasing pace of globalisation has meant that while some men have been able to increase their power, for working-class men downsizing, retrenchment, and unemployment are very real challenges to their identities and masculinities. We observed for the older men a persistent decline and challenge for their 'breadwinner' identities and narratives. In 2000, one-third of all British men not in employment were aged between 50 and 65, meaning that some 2.5 million were economically inactive and reliant on state or private benefits in some form (McDowell, 2000). This period neatly fits with the cases of men in the 'Midlife Grandparents' study, specifically Bob, Geoff, and Ben (Chap. 7), and this evidence has been used to support our reading of these transcripts.

Poverty for Women

The narratives of the women we have written about, including Sheila, Carolyn, Josie, and Susan (discussed in Chap. 4) and Margaret, Dianne (Chaps. 5 and 6), share distinctive similarities with those of the men we discuss in terms of the impacts of longitudinal poverty, especially across the dimensions of health, education, and employment (Cummins et al., 2007; Beatty et al., 2021). Josie, Sheila, Margaret, and Dianne are all in their 40s or late 40s, and all four women have some form of significant poverty-related disability. In these respects, disadvantages for women are consequent on economic instability, uncertain employment, and welfare retrenchment on the women's working and family lives. Women too experienced high rates of mental and physical ill health, disability, midlife morbidity, and shorter life expectancy. These engender rapidly changing and intensifying caring responsibilities for people during their 40s. Caring focus shifts from children towards partners/spouses *and* grandchildren, often at a time during which people are either caring for, or losing, their parent generation (see also Ben-Galim & Silim, 2013). In Bob and Geoff's cases, as we detail above, these caring responsibilities may migrate to older daughters, but more commonly to women's partners/husbands, and require additional resourcing through home adaptations provided through occupational therapy or other healthcare service provision. Such provision is not necessarily benign, and may position men as risky especially in relation to intimate spaces, such as bathrooms, especially where kinship care arrangements are in place (Tarrant, 2021). While in Chap. 6 we fore-ground the implications of sometimes problematic framings of men in families, it is worthwhile here considering how risky service interactions might be for women who are dependent on their partners for every-day cares.

Reflecting on the implications of our findings for understanding the impacts of policy which either absents men, or frames them as risky, further exposes the limitations of framing men's participation in families solely in terms of their breadwinning, and highlights an unintended obscuring of the gendered impacts of poverty. First, an over focus on men as breadwinners in low-income contexts obscures the impacts of low pay no pay work on *both* men and women, and their experiences of the often-challenging interlayer-ing of family and working responsibilities through hardship. Second, it obscures the consequences of poverty-related ill health on the broader fam-ily in terms of who takes on associated caring responsibilities, when and in relation to whom. An overfocus on men's breadwinning roles also obscures how labour intensive the work of poverty is for all family members (Lister, 2005; Ridge, 2009; Daly & Kelly, 2015) including for women. Caregiving and interdependencies often change over the lifecourse, where men are more likely to be carers and disabled (Yeandle & Buckner, 2017) or, as is the case for many women in low-income families, are required to be kinship carers (Hunt, 2018; Tarrant, 2021).

Socio-economic Decline and Change

It is not possible to make sense of the microdynamics of family poverty without bringing them into analytical dialogue with broader locality-based evidence on the longitudinal impacts of poverty for peoples' housing, employment, health, and longevity. Longitudinal engagements with fami-lies living in poverty and experiencing economic hardships confirm that the evolving, multidirectional, and myriad interlayerings of the 'fortunes' of the locality, as well as the changing possibilities and types of work, or experiences of unemployment, occur against a backdrop of 'a semi-permanent *constellation of external socio-economic pressures*' (MacDonald et al., 2020, p. 12). These have borne down on successive generations of families in low-income localities for decades, and have continuously sus-tained the intergenerational ripple effect of persistent disadvantage and hardship. Developing comparative empirical insights across numerous British towns and cities, MacDonald et al., (2020, p. 27) describe 'a shared context of declining job opportunities but extended to a contracting and disciplinary Welfare State, punitive criminal justice systems, poor-quality education, and the physical decline of working-class neighbourhoods' (see also Tarrant, 2021).

These multiple forms of deprivation have been exacerbated by decades of social disinvestment (Wacquant, 2004) and instances of policy driven civic intervention by local and regional councils, that have persistently reduced or removed locality-based resources to produce architectures of deprivation (Elias, 1997; Foucault, 1976). Consequently, the dual-fold retreat of industry and the intensification of locality-based, deprivation have produced 'estate enclosures' (Ray, 2018), where mobility in and out of these areas is further constrained through lack of transport infrastructure. The wider city, of which these localities in our studies are a part, has experienced a long-term decline in rates of violence as part of longer social processes involving the more general reduction of levels of violence in the UK. However, these low-income areas nevertheless continue to experience high levels of crime, interpersonal violence, and distrust and surveillance by the police, demonstrating an unevenness in the decline of violence across deindustrialised localities (Soja, 2000).

Rather than the breakdown or weakening of 'social solidarity', described by Wirth (1938) and others (Desmond, 2012, see also Chap. 1), hardship may intensify people's familial interdependencies, through the sharing of microresources, such as time, support, and care across these localities. Even where family estrangement has occurred, this has been gendered, and experienced as a significant loss with potentially catastrophic effects, such as suicide in men and mental illness in women, although not exclusively so and, indeed, our cases demonstrates mental illness for several men (including Geoff andBob), and attempted suicide by women (including Margaret and Susan's now-deceased daughter). Furthermore, hardship has intensified people's longer-term dependencies on local services, producing experiences of family, and family arrangements that, as we have illustrated above and throughout the book, express these relational entanglements.

The 'Ordering' of Families Through Poverty

The theme of how low-income families are configured through formal services described above, has supported an analysis of the 'civic' and interpersonal ordering of family relationships, arrangements, and their changing configurations over time. The 'ordering' of family relationships and arrangements may be undertaken by individual family members, such as through re/partnering and divorce, but may also occur through broader institutional involvements. 'Civic' ordering refers primarily to how health and social care interventions, legal adjudications, and other formalised (such as employment) and institutional involvements are both characteristic of and characterise families in low-income circumstances. We again use the example of kinship care. In both seeking, and securing, the resources required to sustain grandparent kinship care relationships and responsibilities, a new language of 'family' must be learned and deployed by the grandparent kinship carers, new institutional relationships must be forged and navigated, and new ways of 'doing' family must be learned and effectively 'displayed' (Finch, 2007). Again in relation to Sam and Geoff in Chap. 6, we discussed how becoming a grandparent kinship carer involves a 'rewriting' of people's normative expectations of grandparenting, alongside a *reordering* of family relationships and responsibilities.

In exploring how relationships with health and social care professionals may be understood to shape families intergenerationally, the language of 'civic ordering' conveys how hardship *necessitates* involvements in professional relational processes, such as through the legal system, or health and social care services in the sustaining and doing of family. In turn, such relationships involve asymmetrical power dynamics between different family members, and between family members and service providers and professionals. These manifest as risk, uncertainty, and multiple opportunities for intervention, some of which include the essential provisioning of everyday life, yet may also be punitive, including the removal of financial or other resources, and decision-making about the placement of younger dependents to create alternative family arrangements. In these ways, such involvements simultaneously entail forms of civic ordering through the *dis*ordering of family arrangements and through rewriting intergenerational responsibilities, relationships, and family configurations. These experiences predominate in the accounts of men as well as women about their efforts to sustain and manage their families 'through the system'.

Interpersonal forms of ordering within family relationships refers, in contrast, to how people in their family relationships may organise or reorder them, including through violence. Violence is endemic to the interview narratives across all four studies, and violence manifests in interpersonal forms of ordering of and through family and other relationships. Here, violent 'ordering' refers to behaviours involving the subjugation and dominance of others, but also, in contrast, the protections by parents of themselves and their children, perhaps against other parents but also other relatives.

Violence and Family Poverty

The theme of violence was extremely challenging for us to write about and analytically to navigate from the outset, but impossible to ignore. This theme runs in multiple directions with innumerable consequences for our understanding of men and families living through poverty. Multiple forms and experiences of violence are prevalent in both men and women's accounts, and are integral to men's narratives about their trajectories through poverty and their locality-based relationships. Rather than 'telling sad stories' (Jensen, 2014), our intention has become to clarify how persistent, intergenerational poverty is productive of *distinctive* challenges for the 'doing' and sustaining of families for people over time, core to which are both interpersonal and collective (often civic) forms of violence (see also Ray, 2018) and correspondingly forms of informal and formal social ordering.

Experiences and narratives of interpersonal violence suffused the interviews with the women and men across generations, but especially the women analysed for Chap. 4, where they described violent partners. They spoke of how men in their families used violence against other men in the protection of their families, including their mothers, siblings, and partners. Violence was also used as a means of disciplining and managing younger relatives, and boundarying families, such as through excluding problematic or violent relatives, whether partners, parents, or children. Sheila, in Chap. 7 for example, describes how she and her twin sons physically excluded her ex-partner Ben from their family home. Carolyn and Victor developed 'predictive narratives' concerning the risks of violence in their localities which underscored how they guided their children's educational and career trajectories, as well as how they intervened in Carolyn's grandson's life, informing their joint decisions about removing him from his young mother when her life became exposed to other young men in the locality and, as the research progressed, to interpersonal violence in these relationships. In effect, violence emerges in these accounts as an ordering practice, through which relationships are regulated, managed, boundaried and ended.

Restricting analyses to interpersonal violence, however, either ignores or obscures the broader swathe of experiences of violence narrated in the studies. Considering multimodal and multidirectional forms of *collective* violence enabled us to reconceive the wider nexuses of relationships of which the participants are an integral part. While we do not elaborate on interpersonal violence to any great extent, we consider how it may be operationalised in the informal 'ordering' of interpersonal relationships, described above. It is precisely this form of interpersonal ordering through violence in locality-based relationships (see also Houborg et al., 2022) that is treated as *characterising* these localities by formal services including policing, such that the residents become treated as a form of threat to the wider localities. Here, violence reemerges *as threat* (Stanko, 2001) especially to the wider city, but so too do people's experiences of hardship as a form of symbolic disorder. In this way those that live there become infused with multiple forms of stigma that constrain their ability to seek work elsewhere, or are treated with suspicion and hostility in the wider city (Hughes, 2007). Violence intrinsic to modes of 'civic ordering' by the broadest gamut of formal services thus produces distinctive experiences of marginalisation and exclusion for people in these localities. In effect, by interrogating collective forms of violence we become better able to situate and understand interpersonal forms of violence as contextualised experiences of poverty. Combined, these themes of interpersonal and collective violence allow insight into the textures of hardship both in place and for families as they endure intergenerationally in these localities.

Critically, then, families, for men, emerge as ambiguous but important places. While families may be violent places they are far safer for men than the street. Nevertheless, men are often expelled from families—for money, for being violent, by other men—and their lives become incredibly precarious in consequence. There is a two-fold character to violence between men. Men's very survival is dependent on other men as families operate as difficult spaces of obligation and provision in localities experiencing high rates of unemployment. However, men's accounts describe the need for their persistent, longitudinal navigation of violence *from* other men. Lewis rescues his brothers and sisters, his mum and nephews from his violent father; Joe describes violence and predation in relationships with his 'mates'; Geoff describes how violent families are and the violence to which his granddaughter is exposed on the street outside their home; Sheila talks about 'beyond the garden gate' as a space of lawless vulnerability for her children and grandchildren; Bob fights to be a man and breadwinner in bullying work relationships; Victor fights for a moral father identity with children that are not his in challenging engagements with health, social care and welfare professionals.

Finally, in respect to this theme of violence, there were additional challenges in both the *reading* and *reporting of* the descriptive content of the interviews, including the emotional difficulties for us reading these accounts.[1] Our concern has been to address how the many narratives of violence, abandonment, coercion, and abuse, especially of spouses and of children have been amplified through our innovative synthesis of women's interview narratives with men's. We have sought to ensure, in our handling of these data and

[1] See especially Hubbard et al. (2001) for a discussion of the emotional management of research data by researchers.

the stories we have foregrounded, a balanced and even-handed (re)presentation of both men's and women's experiences of violence, including that which occurs between men and other men, men and women, women and other women, and adults and children. In presenting our analyses of women's accounts, we have prioritised the need to be responsible, nuanced, and sensitive in our representations, and the arguments we advance, especially of experiences of abuse. We are especially mindful of our own authority and responsibility in our positions as academics as we intervene in the production of knowledge about individuals living in poverty.

Our approach is governed by an ethics that attends to these considerations, to ensure that our analyses are empirically driven rather than unreflexively governed by 'prenotions' of men's (and women's) relationship to violence in low-income circumstances (see also Dobash & Dobash, 2004; Roberts & Elliott, 2020). Indeed, our efforts to provide a balanced account is predicated on foregrounding accounts from men, alongside women's accounts of them, as legitimate informers on their own experience. In this way we redress a problematic gap in existing literature where such accounts have been only rarely included in research, especially those which focus on men's family participation across their lifecourse. Our analyses in no way seek to either deny the experiences of the research participants, whether women or men, nor promote exculpatory explanations of violence against others that may tend towards 'sanitising' men's violence in women's accounts of family life, or sanitising violence perpetrated by women. Instead, we have sought to provide a carefully situated and nuanced account of longitudinal experiences of poverty, without retreating to a singular moral explanation, obscuring, condoning, or ignoring interpersonal violence, nor dismissing gendered power asymmetries and inequalities. In this way we provide empirical accounts of the erosive character of poverty, rather than the lack of character of those experiencing it (Jensen, 2014; McAra & McVie, 2016; Feltwell et al., 2017).

This has been supported by an approach which interlayers our own qualitative evidence with broader statistical data in a form of synthetic analysis, and we have sought to avoid furthering the persistent stigmatisation of people in circumstances of poverty through their association with violence and other social issues (Jensen, 2014; Feltwell et al., 2017). Yet to mute narratives of violence constitutes a form of 'double silencing' via a process of academic erasure, that inhibits an inclusive account of the character of persistent, intergenerational hardship and thereby a failure to grasp precisely the broader social histories and processes through which these lives are shaped (McAra & McVie, 2016). Indeed, to obscure these narratives is to fundamentally ignore what has been described as 'the texture of hardship'

(Newman & Peeples Massengill, 2006), and thereby prohibit the 'empirical telling' of challenges for the doing and sustaining of families for people who experience intergenerational poverty, and of how poverty produces and shapes the possibilities and limits of and for families.

CAUTIONS

We raise several cautions about the work presented here, especially those to do with representation, the specificity of the data on which we draw, and the language of family participation that we ourselves put forward. First, we have striven to sustain a feminist epistemological reflexivity throughout the book (Stanley, 1993; see also Mason, 2007). This alerted us to the multiplicity of occasions in which we write both from an 'outsider' perspective, wherein we have 'othered' the experiences of our participants (Merton, 1972). In turn, this has illuminated how we write from distinctive socially inscribed vantages (Stanley, 1993). Consequently, although throughout this book we have taken to task existing scholarship for problems of representation, it is important to acknowledge how we have also produced particular accounts and representations of the people in these studies. Furthermore, those interview accounts were also shaped in distinctive ways through specific relational dynamics with other researchers (Ezzy, 2010). We have sought to address these ongoing problems of representation by establishing comparisons and linkages across the four studies, and formulating new analytic directions harnessing our own relational distance both from the formative contexts of those studies but also the lives of the participants (see also Hughes et al., 2022).

Second, and relatedly, we wish to forestall concerns about the ostensibly fragmented and diverse character of the data on and from men on which we draw. Over a considerable period of time and in working across these four, data rich studies, we have done a great deal of theoretical work to test and refine our ideas and theories and to establish the theoretical, substantive, and methodological links between the datasets (see also Tarrant & Hughes, 2019). In this process we repurposed interviews and orientated them to new questions and lines of enquiry (see also Bishop, 2007; Irwin & Winterton, 2011a, 2011b; Tarrant, 2016; Tarrant & Hughes, 2019). However, there are limitations in terms of the modest 'histories' we have sought to develop. We have used detailed case studies of men of different ages, from different studies across different time points, to create a discursive space in existing scholarship about the broader gamut of men's family participation through poverty. Neither the datasets on their own, nor the cases we develop, can be treated as providing comprehensive historical accounts of men over these historical periods (see also Edwards & Gillies, 2012).

Relatedly, we have simultaneously treated women as narrators of men's stories, positioning certain participants as 'gatekeepers' to particular accounts and details.[2] We have acknowledged how, in the context of very specific research interests and questions, an interviewee edits and hives off certain details, foregrounds some narratives over others, and describes others from their own perspective at given moments in their own lives. Thus, our interviewees (and our very research approach) shape what and who and how we can see the people of whom they do or do not speak. Not only might they produce amplifications of particular themes, narratives and representations, but through their focus, will also produce 'silences'(Bornat, 2004; Irwin et al., 2012). For the purposes of this book, the significance of these silences, or emphases have been treated as empirical materials in our analyses, particularly in regard to how men may be 'absented' from accounts of family poverty, and in our discussion of how the impacts of poverty for families may be gendered. Our methodological innovation in using women's accounts was as a first step in developing an empirically driven case for our own programme of research on men in families in poverty, and we have sought carefully to account for our analytic orientation towards the datasets and the analytical strategies we used with the data.

Finally, although we make a case for shifting to a language of family participation, we caution against a reading of such participation as universally benign. As the examples described in the empirical chapters demonstrate, in some cases men's family participation may be destructive of family lives through violence and abuse, and a source of distress. However, we continue to assert this language as current binary conceptualisations of absence and presence, in their association with men as fathers, rather simplistically posit that men's family presence (as fathers) is positive and their absence is negative (Tarrant, 2021). Some of these men in these accounts were very present in these family contexts but with pernicious effects for the mothers and their children.

---

[2] We would like to thank Lauryn Healey, Social Research MA student, University of Leeds, for this idea of participants' narratives as 'gatekeeper' narratives into the lives of others.

Methodology and Slow Scholarship: The Value of QSA and Our Iterative Programme of Work

We conclude with some brief final reflections on our engagement in 'slow scholarship' (see also Hartman & Darab, 2012; Mountz et al., 2015; Bozalek, 2017). Our research and intellectual engagement have endured over a long period, showcasing the value of reusing historical data and accordingly demonstrating its continuing value for new research. Our work also illustrates how, using a limited number of emblematic cases (Tarrant & Hughes, 2019) based on an extensive and continuous familiarity with the broader datasets, we can formulate extended critiques of existing research, advance our own QSA methodology, develop a new intergenerational analytic framework, and thereby new substantive findings concerning men's family participation through circumstances of place-based hardship. There were two particular sorts of temporality involved in our work. We worked across *conceptually* extensive analytical timeframes that sought to address the 20-year period covered by the aggregated datasets. Yet, they were also *pragmatically* time consuming. The careful work of QSA, so valuable for tracking through the intricacies of multigenerational family participation, involved a constant return to the data. As our arguments developed, so too did our analyses and every stage of our writing involved a repeated return to the transcripts of our chosen cases. In turn, each rereading alerted us to new evidence in transcripts we had already used, and supported further theoretical development. This analytical process has additionally served to reinforce our social justice agenda for the importance of archiving these sorts of data from research with those with such highly constrained access to public participation. Archiving serves to preserve a diverse social history for future researchers, providing for endlessly creative and insightful interpretations of research data into the future (Hughes & Tarrant, 2020).

Also, drawing on the work of others we consider the value of slow scholarship as a means of not only resisting the hyper-speedy pacing of neoliberal rationality characterising university agendas (Hartman & Darab, 2012; Edwards, 2022), but also for demonstrating the endlessly creative ways to which qualitative research data may be put (Neale, 2020; Hughes & Tarrant, 2020). Our work here thus demonstrates the creative potential of reapprehending datasets in new and novel ways to support and develop new thinking and address knowledge gaps through the reuse of existing resources (see also Tarrant, 2016; Hughes et al., 2022).

Finally, a central ethical tenet of this 'slow scholarship' links to what we might describe as 'long engagement', whereby efforts in relation to the preservation and reuse of peoples' data should be towards preserving rather than silencing their accounts. Amalgamating the four datasets has enabled us to capture the cumulative effects of multiple deprivation for people in poverty over long timeframes (15 PLUS_SPI years). The QSA we present here is undertaken with data in the Timescapes Archive (https://timescapes-archive.leeds.ac.uk) and demonstrates the value of digital preservation and curation of research data. A temporally attuned ethics towards data reuse, as discussed in Chap. 3, supports our broader commitment to ensuring the social histories of those with least access to digital participation are nevertheless available long into the future (see also Dencik et al., 2019; Hughes & Tarrant, 2020; Tarrant & Hughes, 2020). In these key respects, our 'slow scholarship' is not solely a process of resisting some of the worse aspects of work intensification and acceleration (Wajcman, 2015), but showcases the dialogic *character* of scholarship, whereby those 'dialogues' are neither necessarily in-person, synchronous, nor co-present, but describe much longer timeframes of interdisciplinary development and engagement. Furthermore, our work 'writes against' assumptions that temporal distance from the original contexts of research can solely be treated as a form of deficit. In other words, our work demonstrates how, as they age, data *accrue* rather than lose value and, as we demonstrate, can be treated in ways which emphasise their value for 'contemporary' questions, as this 'contemporary' too, is a constantly changing 'present' (Hughes et al., 2022).

This 'slow scholarship', then, foregrounds our use of synthetic analysis, where such synthesis draws on and develops disciplinary expertise (Hughes et al., 2022). We have found the language of 'expert synthesis' useful here, which refers to synthesising across a broad terrain of differently constituted data, explicitly addressing questions of how we may treat these as different forms of evidence. These may include, but are not limited to, our own expertise and disciplinary knowledge, our own research histories and specialisms, the broader literature, different data, and so forth. The language of 'synthesis' additionally entails a shift from conflating 'empirical' with a preoccupation with 'fieldwork' as the sole crucible through which new findings or theorising can be forged. This often happens uncritically, whereby there is a tacit assertion that the only 'real' or 'valid' or 'authentic' evidence comes from participants, for example, interview data, or ethnographic observations, or creative methodological engagement. If we were to follow this assumption to its logical conclusion, we would effectively be writing against 'scholarship', the notion of disciplinary training, professional development, the development of expertise, and our own role within the knowledge production of a discipline. Finally, we are keen to unpick an uncritical tendency to treat participants' accounts in ways which do not acknowledge how these too are inflected with a diverse array of theoretical formulations, that in turn draw on long disciplinary development such as in psychology, history, biomedicine, and of course, sociology. Here again, our task is to critically engage with how we theorise, on what basis, how we cast 'stuff' as evidence, and how this evidence can be used to 'speak of the social world' (Becker, 2007). Our approach is exemplified both in how we formulate and utilise the theoretical bases for the selection of what we describe as the emblematic cases for each of the empirical chapters, and how in turn we interrogate the extent to which these cases can or cannot be repurposed to answer the new questions we bring to them.

A Legacy for Recovering Men in Low-income Contexts Through QSA

As well as recovering absent men empirically in low-income families and localities and establishing new theoretical frameworks through which to make sense of their family lives in poverty, and longitudinal family poverty more generally, we have also established the value of QSA as a methodology for new research. QSA may have connotations of retrospective research, a means of 'looking back' at empirically generated contexts, which may only be used to speak of the conditions of their becoming (Hughes et al., 2022). However, the arguments we present here serve as an exemplar of the enormous possibilities and affordances of QSA for research seeking to question afresh existing ideological orthodoxies, perhaps produced over long timeframes, through different and competing intellectual commitments. An example we have addressed is how men have been, inadvertently, 'absented' in research focused on explicating women's experiences of poverty. Such research has been essential in the broader feminist project of redressing the political and evidentiary muting of women that has been used to further delegitimise their accounts. However, rather than contradicting or discounting such research, the QSA we present here draws on data that track alongside the development of such literature. We suggest that our insights concerning men's participation in families in poverty support a more complex reading precisely of the broader social histories involved in people's longitudinal experiences of poverty, thereby enriching existing understandings of the 'feminisation' of poverty by including accounts from men. Indeed, as we articulate above, through such analytic retrieval, we have found ourselves able to build more comprehensively towards a sociology of family poverty.

REFERENCES

Beatty, C., Bennett, C., & Hawkins, A. (2021). Managing Precarity: Food Bank Use by Low-Income Women Workers in a Changing Welfare Regime. *Social Policy Administration, 55*, 981–1000.

Becker, H. (2007). *Telling About Society*. University of Chicago Press.

Ben-Galim, D., & Silim, A. (2013). The Sandwich Generation: Older Women Balancing Work and Care, IPPR Report.

Bishop, L. (2007). A Reflexive Account of Reusing Qualitative Data: Beyond Primary/Secondary Dualism. *Sociological Research Online, 12*(2). http://www.socresonline.org.uk/12/3/2.html

Bornat, J. (2004). Oral History. In C. Seale, G. Gobo, J. F. Gubrium, F. Jaber, & D. Silverman (Eds.), *Qualitative Research Practice*. London: Sage.

Bozalek, V. (2017). Slow Scholarship in Writing Retreats: A Diffractive Methodology for Response-Able Pedagogies. *South African Journal of Higher Education, 31*(2). https://hdl.handle.net/10520/EJC-6ee594b1c

Calasanti, T., & King, N. (2005). Firming the Floppy Penis: Age, Class, and Gender Relations in the Lives of Old Men. *Men and Masculinities, 8*(1), 3–23.

Comas-d'Argemir, D., & Soronellas, M. (2019). Men as Carers in Long-Term Caring: Doing Gender and Doing Kinship. *Journal of Family Issues, 40*(3), 315–339.

Cordon, A., & Millar, J. (2010). Time and Change: A Review of the Qualitative Longitudinal Research Literature for Social Policy. *Social Policy and Society, 6*(4), 583–592.

Crossley, S. (2017). *In Their Place: The Imagined Geographies of Poverty*. Pluto Press.

Cummins, S., Curtis, S. V., Diez-Roux, A., & Macintyre, S. (2007). Understanding and Representing 'Place' in Health Research: A Relational Approach. *Social Science & Medicine, 65*(9), 1825–1838.

Daly, M. (2018). Towards a Theorization of the Relationship Between Poverty and Family. *Social Policy & Administration, 52*(3), 565–577.

Daly, M., & Kelly, G. (2015). *Families and Poverty: Everyday Life on a Low-Income*. Policy Press.

Dencik, L., Hintz, A., Redden, J., & Trere, E. (2019). Exploring Data Justice: Conceptions, Applications and Directions. *Information, Communication & Society, 22*(7), 873–881.

Dermott, E. (2016). Non-resident Fathers in the UK: Living Standards and Social Support. *Journal of Poverty and Social Justice, 24*(2), 113–125.

Desmond, M. (2012). Disposable Ties and the Urban Poor. *American Journal of Sociology, 117*(5), 1295–1335.

Dobash, R. P., & Dobash, R. E. (2004). Women's Violence to Men in Intimate Relationships: Working on a Puzzle. *The British Journal of Criminology, 44*(3), 324–349. https://doi.org/10.1093/bjc/azh026

Edwards, R. (2022). Unfunded Research: Why Academics do it and its Unvalued Contribution to the Impact Agenda, https://blogs.lse.ac.uk/impactofsocialsciences/2020/08/13/unfunded-research-why-academics-do-it-and-its-unvalued-contribution-to-the-impact-agenda/

Edwards, R., & Gillies, V. (2012). Farewell to Family? Notes on an Argument for Retaining the Concept. *Families, Relationships and Societies, 1*(1), 63–69.

Elias, N. (1997). Informalization and the Civilizing Process. In J. Goudsblom & S. Mennell (Eds.), *The Norbert Elias Reader*. Blackwell.

Emmel, N., & Hughes, K. (2014). Vulnerability, Intergenerational Exchange and the Conscience of Generations. In R. Edwards & J. Holland (Eds.), *Understanding Families Over Time: Research and Policy*. Palgrave Macmillan.

Ezzy, D. (2010). Qualitative Interviewing as an Embodied Emotional Performance. *Qualitative Inquiry, 16*(3), 163–170.

Feltwell, T., Vines, J., Salt, K., et al. (2017). Counter-Discourse Activism on Social Media: The Case of Challenging "Poverty Porn" Television. *Computer Supported Coop Work, 26*, 345–385.

Finch, J. (2007). Displaying Families, *Sociology, 41*(1), 65–81.

Fisher, P., & Buckner, L. (2018). Time for "Resilience": Community Mediators Working with Marginalised Young People Offer a Novel Approach. *International Journal of Sociology and Social Policy, 38*(9/10), 794–808.

Foucault, M. (1976). *Discipline and Punish*. Allen Lane.

Garthwaite, K. (2016). *Hunger Pains: Life Inside Foodbank Britain*. Policy Press.

Garthwaite, K., Collins, P., & Bambra, C. (2015). Food for Thought: An Ethnographic Study of Negotiating Ill Health and Food Insecurity in a UK Foodbank'. *Social Science and Medicine, 132*, 38–44.

Hall, S. M. (2019). *Everyday Life in Austerity: Family, Friends and Intimate Relations*. Palgrave Macmillan.

Hamer, J. (2001). *What it Means to Be Daddy: Fatherhood for Black Men Living Away from Their Children*. Columbia University Press.

Hartman, Y., & Darab, S. (2012). A Call for Slow Scholarship: A Case Study on the Intensification of Academic Life and Its Implications for Pedagogy. *Review of Education, Pedagogy, and Cultural Studies, 34*(1–2), 49–60.

Haywood, C., & Johansson, T. (2017). *Marginalized Masculinities: Contexts, Continuities and Change*. Routledge.

Houborg, E., Kronbæk, M., Kappel, N., Relsted Fahnøe, K., Mørch Pedersen S., & Schepelern Johansen, K. (2022). Marginaliserede stofbrugeres hverdagsliv i København – stofmiljøer og velfærdstilbud. https://www.researchgate.net/publication/362932106_Marginaliserede_stofbrugeres_hverdagsliv_i_Kobenhavn_-stofmiljoer_og_velfaerdstilbud

Hubbard, G., Backett-Milburn, K., & Kemmer, D. (2001). Working with Emotion: Issues for the Researcher in Fieldwork and Teamwork. *International Journal of Social Research Methodology, 4*(2), 119–137.

Hughes, K. (2007). Migrating Identities: The Relational Constitution of Drug Use and Addiction. *Sociology of Health & Illness, 29,* 673–691. https://doi.org/10.1111/j.1467-9566.2007.01018.x

Hunt, J. (2018). Grandparents as Substitute Parents in the UK. *Contemporary Social Science, 13*(2), 175–186.

Hughes, K., & Tarrant, A. (2020). *Qualitative Secondary Anlalysis.* London: Sage.

Hughes, K., Hughes, J., & Tarrant, A. (2022). Working at a remove: continuous, collective, and configurative approaches to qualitative secondary analysis, *Quality & Quantity, 56,* 375–394.

Irwin, S., Bornat, J., & Winterton, M. (2012). Timescapes Secondary Analysis: Comparison, Context and Working Across Data Sets. *Qualitative Research, 12*(1), 66–80.

Irwin, S., & Winterton, M. (2011a). *Debates in Qualitative Secondary Analysis: Critical Reflections,* Timescapes Working Paper No. 4. http://www.timescapes.leeds.ac.uk/assets/files/WP4-March-2011.pdf

Irwin, S., & Winterton, M. (2011b). *Qualitative Secondary Analysis: A Guide to Practice,* Timescapes Working Paper, Guide 19. chrome-extension://efaidnbmnnnibpcajpcglclefindmkaj/https://timescapes-archive.leeds.ac.uk/wp-content/uploads/sites/47/2020/07/timescapes-irwin-secondary-analysis.pdf

Jensen, T. (2014). Welfare Commonsense, Poverty Porn and Doxosophy. *Sociological Research Online, 19*(3), 277–283.

Jensen, T., & Tyler, I. (2012). Austerity Parenting: New Economies of Parent-Citizenship. *Studies in the Maternal, 4*(2), 1.

Ladlow, L. (2021). *Housing Young Parents: A micro-dynamic study of the housing experiences and support needs of young mothers and fathers.* PhD thesis, University of Leeds.

Lambert, M. (2017). "Problem Families" and the Post-war Welfare State in the North West of England, 1943-74, PhD Thesis, Lancaster University.

Lister, R. (2005). *Poverty.* Polity Press.

MacDonald, M., Hayes, D., & Houston, S. (2018). 'Understanding Informal Kinship Care: A Critical Narrative Review of Theory and Research'. *Families, Relationships and Societies, 7*(1), 71–87.

MacDonald, R., Shildrick, T., & Furlong, A. (2020). 'Cycles of Disadvantage' Revisited: Young People, Families and Poverty Across Generations. *Journal of Youth Studies, 23*(1), 12–27.

Mason, J. (2007). 'Re-Using' Qualitative Data: On the Merits of an Investigative Epistemology. *Sociological Research Online, 12*(3). https://doi.org/10.5153/sro.1507

McAra, L., & McVie, S. (2016). Understanding Youth Violence: The Mediating Effects of Gender, Poverty and Vulnerability. *Journal of Criminal Justice, 45,* 71–77.

McDowell, L. (2000). The Trouble with Men? Young People, Gender Transformations and the Crisis of Masculinity. *International Journal of Urban and Regional Research, 24*(1), 201–209.

McDowell, L., & Bonner-Thompson, C. (2021). Digital geographies of austerity: young men's material, affective and everyday relationships with the digital. *Geoforum, 120*, 113–121.

McKenzie, L. (2015). *Getting By: Estates, Class and Culture in Austerity Britain.* Policy Press.

Merton, R. K. (1972). Insiders and Outsiders: A Chapter in the Sociology of Knowledge. *American Journal of Sociology, 78*(1), 9–47.

Millar, J. (2019). Self-Responsibility and Activation for Lone Mothers in the United Kingdom. *American Behavioural Science, 63*(1), 85–99.

Morgan, D. (2011). Locating Family Practices. *Sociological Research Online, 16*(4), 14.

Morgan, D. (2020). Family Practices in Time and Space. *Gender, Place and Culture, 27*(5), 733–743.

Mountz, A., Bonds, A., Mansfield, B., Lloyd, J., Hyndman, J., Walton-Roberts, M., Basu, R., Whitson, R., Hawkins, R., Hamilton, T., & Curran, W. (2015). For Slow Scholarship: A Feminist Politics of Resistance Through Collective Action in the Neoliberal University. *ACME: An International Journal for Critical Geographies, 14*(4), 1235–1259.

Nayak, A. (2006). Displaced Masculinities: Chavs, Youth and Class in the Post-industrial City. *Sociology, 40*(5), 813–831.

Neale, B. (2016). Introduction: Young Fatherhood: Lived Experiences and Policy Challenges. *Social Policy and Society, 15*(1), 75–83.

Neale, B. (2020). *The Craft of Qualitative Longitudinal Research.* Sage.

Neale, B., Henwood, K., & Holland, J. (2012). Researching Lives Through Time: An Introduction to the Timescapes Approach. *Qualitative Research, 12*(1), 4–15.

Neale, B., & Lau Clayton, C. (2014). Young Parenthood and Cross Generational Relationships: The Perspectives of Young Fathers. In J. Holland & R. Edwards (Eds.), *Understanding Families Over Time.* Palgrave Macmillan.

Newman, K. S., & Peeples Massengill, R. (2006). The Texture of Hardship: Qualitative Sociology of Poverty. *Annual Review of Sociology, 32*(1), 423–446.

Patrick, R. (2018). *For Whose Benefit? The Everyday Realities of Welfare Reform.* Policy Press.

Ray, L. (2018). *Violence and Society* (2nd ed.). SAGE.

Ridge, T. (2009). *Living with Poverty: A Review of the Literature on Children's and Families' Experiences of Poverty,* Department for Work and Pensions Research Report No 594. http://www.bris.ac.uk/poverty/downloads/keyofficialdocuments/Child%20Poverty%20lit%20review%20DWP.pdf

Roberts, S., & Elliott, K. (2020). Challenging Dominant Representations of Marginalised Boys and Men in Critical Studies on Men and Masculinities. *Boyhood Studies, 13*(2), 87–104.

Roy, K. (2006). Father Stories: A Life Course Examination of Paternal Identity Among Low-income African American Men. *Journal of Family Issues, 27*(1), 31–54.

Roy, K. (2014). Fathering from the Long View: Framing Personal and Social Change Through Life Course Theory. *Journal of Family Theory and Review*, 6, 319–335.

Ruxton, S. (2002). *Men, Masculinities and Poverty in the UK*. Oxfam.

Shildrick, T., MacDonald, R., Webster, C., & Garthwaite, K. (2012). *Poverty and Insecurity: Life in Low Pay, No Pay Britain*. Policy Press.

Sobo-Allen, L., & Howarth, S. (2022). Social Work with single and non-resident fathers: How inclusive is our practice and where do we go from here? In B. Niku (Ed.) *Global Social Work Cutting Edge Issues and Critical Reflections* (163–182). IntechOpen.

Soja, E. W. (2000). *Postmetropolis: Critical Studies of Cities and Regions*. Blackwell.

Stanko, E. A. (2001). The Day to Count: Reflections on a Methodology to Raise Awareness about the Impact of Domestic Violence in the UK. *Criminal Justice*, 1(2), 215–226. https://doi.org/10.1177/1466802501001002005

Stanley, L. (1993). On Auto/Biography in Sociology. *Sociology*, 27(1), 41–52.

Tarrant, A. (2014). Negotiating Multiple Positionalities in the Interview Setting; Researching Across Gender and Generational Boundaries. *The Professional Geographer*, 66(3), 493–500.

Tarrant, A. (2016). The Spatial and Gendered Politics of Displaying Family: Exploring Material Cultures in Grandfathers' Homes. *Gender, Place and Culture*, 23(7), 969–982.

Tarrant, A. (2021). *Fathering and Poverty: Uncovering Men's Participation in Low-Income Family Life*. Policy Press.

Tarrant, A., & Hughes, K. (2019). Qualitative Secondary Analysis: Building Longitudinal Samples to Understand Men's Generational Identities in Low Income Contexts. *Sociology*, 53(3), 538–553.

Tarrant, A., & Hughes, K. (2020). Collective Qualitative Secondary Analysis and Data-Sharing: Strategies, Insights and Challenges. In K. Hughes & A. Tarrant (Eds.), *Qualitative Secondary Analysis* (pp. 101–118). Sage, London.

Tarrant, A., & Neale, B. (forthcoming). *Following Young Fathers: Lived Experiences, Policy Challenges*. Policy Press.

Wacquant, L. (2004). Decivilizing and Demonizing: The Weakening of the Black American Ghetto. In S. Loyal & S. Quilley (Eds.), *The Sociology of Norbert Elias* (pp. 95–121). Cambridge University Press.

Wajcman, J. (2015). *Pressed for Time: The Acceleration of Life in Digital Capitalism*. Chicago University Press.

Ward, M., Tarrant A., Terry, G., Featherstone, B., Robb, M., and Ruxton, S. (2017). Doing gender locally: The importance of 'place' in understanding marginalised masculinities and young men's transitions to 'safe' and successful futures, *The Sociological Review*, 65(4), 797–815.

Wirth, L. (1938). Urbanism as a Way of Life, *The American Journal of Sociology*, 44(1), 1–24.

Yeandle, S., & Buckner, L. J. (2017). Older Workers and Care-giving in England: The Policy Context for Older Workers' Employment Patterns. *Journal of Cross-Cultural Gerontology*, 32, 303–321.

REFERENCES

Aassve, A., Davia, M., Iacovou, M., & Mazzuco, S. (2007). Does Leaving Home Make You Poor?: Evidence from 13 European Countries. *European Journal of Population, 23*, 315–338.

Abdill, A. (2018). *Fathering from the Margins: An Intimate Examination of Black Fatherhood*. Columbia University Press.

Alber, E., & Thelen, T. (2021). *Politics and Kinship: A Reader*. Taylor & Francis Ltd.

Allen, S. M., & Hawkins, A. J. (1999). Maternal Gatekeeping: Mothers' Beliefs and Behaviors That Inhibit Greater Father Involvement in Family Work. *Journal of Marriage and the Family, 61*(1), 199–212.

Anderson, E. (1999). *Code of the Street: Decency, Violence, and the Moral Life of the Inner City*. Norton.

Appadurai, A. (1996). *Modernity at Large: Cultural Dimensions of Globalization*. University of Minnesota Press.

Arendt, H. (1970). *On Violence*. Allen Lane.

Atkinson, P. (2017). *Thinking Ethnographically*. Sage.

Atkinson, R., & Kintrea, K. (2000). Owner Occupation, Social Mix and Neighbourhood Impacts. *Policy and Politics, 28*, 93–108.

Bailey, J. (2010). 'A Very Sensible Man': Imagining Fatherhood in England c. 1750–1830. *History, 95*(319), 267–292.

Baird, A. (2012). The Violent Gang and the Construction of Masculinity Amongst Socially Excluded Young Men. *Safer Communities, 11*, 179–190.

© The Author(s), under exclusive license to Springer Nature
Switzerland AG 2023
K. Hughes, A. Tarrant, *Men, Families, and Poverty*, Palgrave
Macmillan Studies in Family and Intimate Life,
https://doi.org/10.1007/978-3-031-24922-8

Baltieri, D. (2014). Order of Onset of Drug Use and Criminal Activities in a Sample of Drug-Abusing Women Convicted of Violent Crimes. *Drug and Alcohol Review, 33*(2), 202–210.

Bane, M., & Ellwood, D. (1986). Slipping Into and Out of Poverty: The Dynamics of Spells. *Journal of Human Resources, 21*(1), 1–23.

Barg, K., & Baker, W. (2021). Better Than Average? Parental Competence Beliefs and Socioeconomic Background, *Families, Relationships and Societies* (published online ahead of print 2021). Retrieved July 3, 2022, from https://bristoluniversitypressdigital.com/view/journals/frs/aop/article-10.1332-204674321X16316937949373/article-10.1332-204674321X16316937949373.xml

Bastos, A., Casaca, S. F., Nunes, F., & Pereirinha, J. (2009). Women and Poverty: A Gender-Sensitive Approach. *The Journal of Socio-Economics, 38*(5), 764–778.

Bauman, Z. (1992). *Mortality, Immortality, and Other Life Strategies.* Stanford.

Beatty, C., Bennett, C., & Hawkins, A. (2021). Managing Precarity: Food Bank Use by Low-Income Women Workers in a Changing Welfare Regime. *Social Policy Administration, 55*, 981–1000.

Beatty, C., & Fothergill, S (2016). *The Uneven Impact of Welfare Reform: The Financial Losses to Places and People.* Project Report. Sheffield, Sheffield Hallam University. http://shura.shu.ac.uk/15883/

Becker, H. (2007). *Telling About Society.* University of Chicago Press.

Beckert, J. (2016). *Imagined Futures: Fictional Expectations and Capitalist Dynamics.* Harvard University Press.

Ben-Galim, D., & Silim, A. (2013). The Sandwich Generation: Older Women Balancing Work and Care, IPPR Report.

Bengston, V., Copen, C. E., Putney, N. M., & Silverstein, M. (2008). Religion and Intergenerational Transmission Over Time. In K. W. Shale & R. P. Abeles (Eds.), *Social Structures and Aging Individuals: Continuing Challenges.* Springer Publishing.

Bennett, F., & Daly, M. (2014). *Poverty Through a Gender Lens: Evidence and Policy Review on Gender and Poverty.* Joseph Rowntree Foundation Report.

Berthoud, R., & Bryan, M. (2011). Income, Deprivation and Poverty: A Longitudinal Analysis. *Journal of Social Policy, 40*(1), 135–156.

Binswanger, I. A., Nowels, C., Corsi, K. F., Glanz, J., Long, J., Booth, R. E., & Steiner, J. (2012). Return to Drug Use and Overdose After Release from Prison: A Qualitative Study of Risk and Protective Factors. *Addiction Science Clinical Practice, 7*(1), 3.

Bishop, L. (2007). A Reflexive Account of Reusing Qualitative Data: Beyond Primary/Secondary Dualism. *Sociological Research Online, 12*(2). http://www.socresonline.org.uk/12/3/2.html

Bishop, L. (2009). Ethical Sharing and Reuse of Qualitative Data. *Australian Journal of Social Issues, 44*(3), 255–272.

Bishop, L., & Kuula-Luumi, A. (2017). Revisiting Qualitative Data Reuse: A Decade On. *Sage Open, 7*(1), 2158244016685136.

Bjørnholt, M. (2014). Changing Men, Changing Times – Fathers and Sons from an Experimental Gender Equality Study. *The Sociological Review, 62*(2), 295–315.

Blaxland, M., Skattlebol, J., Hamilton, M., van Toorn, G., Thomson, C., & Valentine, K. (2021). From Being 'at Risk' to Being 'a Risk': Journeys into Parenthood Among Young Women Experiencing Adversity. *Families, Relationships and Societies, 0*(0), 1–20.

Bonner-Thompson, C., & McDowell, L. (2020). Precarious Lives, Precarious Care: Young Men's Caring Practices in Three Coastal Towns in England. *Emotion, Space and Society, 35*, 100684.

Bornat, J. (2004). Oral History. In C. Seale, G. Gobo, J. F. Gubrium, F. Jaber, & D. Silverman (Eds.), *Qualitative Research Practice*. Sage.

Bornat, J., & Bytheway, B. (2012). Working with Different Temporalities: Archived Life History Interviews and Diaries. *International Journal of Social Research Methodology, 15*(4), 291–299.

Bosoni, M. L. (2014). "Breadwinners" or "Involved Fathers?" Men, Fathers and Work in Italy. *Journal of Comparative Family Studies, 45*(2), 293–315.

Bozalek, V. (2017). Slow Scholarship in Writing Retreats: A Diffractive Methodology for Response-Able Pedagogies. *South African Journal of Higher Education, 31*(2). https://hdl.handle.net/10520/EJC-6ee594b1c

Bradbury, B., Jenkins, S., & Micklewright, J. (2001). *The Dynamics of Child Poverty in Industrialised Countries*. Cambridge University Press.

Bradshaw, J., Stimson, C., Skinner, C., & Williams, J. (1999). *Absent Fathers?* Routledge.

Brandon, M., Philip, G. and Clifton, J. (2017). *'Counting Fathers In': Understanding Men's Experiences of the Child Protection System*. University of East Anglia Report.

Brannen, J. (2015). Fathers and Sons: Generations, Families and Migration. Palgrave Macmillan.

Britton, J. (2019). Muslim Men, Racialised Masculinities and Personal Life. *Sociology, 53*(1), 31–51.

Brooks, R., & Hodkinson, P. (2020). *Sharing Care: Equal and Primary Carer Fathers and Early Years Parenting*. Policy Press.

Buchanen, A., & Rotkirch, A. (2016). Twenty-first Century Grandparents: Global Perspectives on Changing Roles and Consequences. *Contemporary Social Science, 13*(2), 131–144.

Bucholc, M. (2013). Outside the Moral Circle: Polish Political Refugees in Norway: Between the Established and the Outsiders. *Everyday Practices and Long Term Processes: Overcoming Dichotomies with the Work of Norbert Elias, 2*(3).

Bullock, H. (2013). *Women and Poverty: Psychology, Public Policy, and Social Justice*. Wiley Blackwell.

Bulman, K., & Neale, B. (2017). Developing Sustained Support for Vulnerable Young Fathers: Journeys with Young Offenders. In A. Tarrant & B. Neale (Eds.), *Learning to Support Young Dads, Responding to Young Fathers in a Different Way: Project Report*, (pp. 5–14). https://followingfathers.leeds.ac.uk/wpcontent/uploads/sites/79/2017/04/SYD-final-report.pdf

Burgess, A. and Davies, J. (2017). *Cash or Carry? Fathers Combining Work and Care in the UK*, (Full Report). Contemporary Fathers in the UK series. Marlborough: Fatherhood Institute.

Burn-Murdock, J. (2022). *Britain and the US Are Poor Societies with Some Very Rich People*. The Financial Times. Retrieved October 18, 2022, from https://www.ft.com/content/ef265420-45e8-497b-b308-c951baa68945

Burton, L. (2007). Childhood Adultification in Economically Disadvantaged Families: A Conceptual Model. *Family Relations: An Interdisciplinary Journal of Applied Family Science, 56*(4), 329–345.

Busby, N., & Weldon-Johns, M. (2019). Fathers as Carers in UK Law and Policy: Dominant Ideologies and Lived Experience. *Journal of Social Welfare and Family Law, 41*(3), 280–301.

Butera, K. (2006). Manhunt: The Challenge of Enticing Men to Participate in a Study on Friendship. *Qualitative Inquiry, 12*(6), 1262–1282.

Bywaters, P. et al. (2020). *The Child Welfare Inequalities Project: Final Report Paul Bywaters and the Child Welfare Inequalities Project Team*. https://pure.hud.ac.uk/ws/files/21398145/CWIP_Final_Report.pdf

Calasanti, T., & King, N. (2005). Firming the Floppy Penis: Age, Class, and Gender Relations in the Lives of Old Men. *Men and Masculinities, 8*(1), 3–23.

Carsten, J. (2004). *After Kinship*. Cambridge University Press.

Chant, S. H. (2006). Re-thinking the "Feminization of Poverty" in Relation to Aggregate Gender Indices. *Journal of Human Development, 7*(2), 201–220.

Charles, N., Aull Davies, C., & Harris, C. (2008). *Families in Transition: Social Change, Family Formation, and Kin Relationships*. Policy Press.

Comas-d'Argemir, D., & Soronellas, M. (2019). Men as Carers in Long-Term Caring: Doing Gender and Doing Kinship. *Journal of Family Issues, 40*(3), 315–339.

Connell, R. (1995). *Masculinities*. California University Press.

Cooper, K. (2021). Are Poor Parents *Poor* Parents? The Relationship between Poverty and Parenting among Mothers in the UK. *Sociology, 55*(2), 349–383.

Cordon, A., & Millar, J. (2010). Time and Change: A Review of the Qualitative Longitudinal Research Literature for Social Policy. *Social Policy and Society, 6*(4), 583–592.

Corlyon, J., Gieve, M., Stock, L., & Sandamas, C. (2009). *Separated Families: How Mainstream Services Support Disadvantaged Children & Their Non-Resident Parents*. Tavistock Institute of Human Relations for Fatherhood Institute & Big Lottery Fund.

CPAG. (2021). *200,000 More Children Pushed into Poverty the Year Before the Pandemic - Dismal Data Warning.* https://cpag.org.uk/news-blogs/news-listings/200000-more-children-pushed-poverty-year-pandemic-dismal-data-warning

Crossley, S. (2017). *In Their Place: The Imagined Geographies of Poverty.* Pluto Press.

Crutchfield, R. D., & Wadsworth, T. (2003). Poverty and Violence. In W. Heitmeyer & J. Hagan (Eds.), *International Handbook of Violence Research.* Springer.

Culliney, M., Haux, T., & McKay, S. (2013). *Family Structure and Poverty in the UK: An Evidence and Policy Review.* Joseph Rowntree Foundation Report.

Cummins, S., Curtis, S. V., Diez-Roux, A., & Macintyre, S. (2007). Understanding and Representing 'Place' in Health Research: A Relational Approach. *Social Science & Medicine, 65*(9), 1825–1838.

Cunningham-Burley, S. (1984). 'We Don't Talk About it…': Issues of Gender and Method in the Portrayal of Grandfatherhood. *Sociology, 18*(3), 325–338.

Daguerre, A., & Etherington, D. (2014). *Workfare in 21st Century Britain: The Erosion of Rights to Social Assistance.* Middlesex University.

Daly, K. J. (1996). Spending Time with the Kids: Meanings of Family Time for Fathers. *Family Relations, 45*(4), 466–476.

Daly, M. (2018). Towards a Theorization of the Relationship Between Poverty and Family. *Social Policy & Administration, 52*(3), 565–577.

Daly, M., & Kelly, G. (2015). *Families and Poverty: Everyday Life on a Low-Income.* Policy Press.

Davidson, E., Edwards, R., Jamieson, J., & Weller, S. (2018). Big Data, Qualitative Style: A Breadth-and-Depth Method for Working with Large Amounts of Secondary Qualitative Data. *Quality & Quantity, 53*, 363–376.

De Benedictis, S. (2012). Feral Parents: Austerity Parenting Under Neoliberalism. *Studies in the Maternal, 4*(2).

Demey, D., Berrington, A., Evandrou, M., & Falkingham, J. (2013). Pathways into Living Alone in Mid-Life: Diversity and Policy Implications. *Advances in Life Course Research, 18*(3), 161–174.

Dencik, L., Hintz, A., Redden, J., & Trere, E. (2019). Exploring Data Justice: Conceptions, Applications and Directions. *Information, Communication & Society, 22*(7), 873–881.

Dennis, N., & Erdos, G. (1992) *Families without Fatherhood.* The Cromwell Press.

Dermott, E. (2008). *Intimate Fatherhood: A Sociological Analysis* (2nd ed.). Routledge.

Dermott, E. (2012). 'Poverty' versus 'Parenting': An Emergent Dichotomy. *Studies in the Maternal, 4*(2) www.mamsie.bbk.ac.uk

Dermott, E. (2016). Non-resident Fathers in the UK: Living Standards and Social Support. *Journal of Poverty and Social Justice, 24*(2), 113–125.

Dermott, E., & Miller, T. (2015). More Than the Sum of its Parts? Contemporary Fatherhood Policy, Practice and Discourse. *Families, Relationships and Societies, 4*(2), 183–195.

Dermott, E., & Pantazis, C. (2014). Gender and Poverty in Britain: Changes and Continuities Between 1999 and 2012. *Journal of Poverty and Social Justice, 22*(3), 253–269.

Desmond, M. (2012). Disposable Ties and the Urban Poor. *American Journal of Sociology, 117*(5), 1295–1335.

Dobash, R. P., & Dobash, R. E. (2004). Women's Violence to Men in Intimate Relationships: Working on a Puzzle. *The British Journal of Criminology, 44*(3), 324–349. https://doi.org/10.1093/bjc/azh026

Donald, L., Davidson, R., Murphy, S., Hadley, A., Puthussery, S., & Randhawa, G. (2021). How Young, Disadvantaged Fathers Are Affected by Socioeconomic and Relational Barriers: A UK-Based Qualitative Study, *Families, Relationships and Societies* (published online ahead of print 2021). Retrieved July 3, 2022, from https://bristoluniversitypressdigital.com/view/journals/frs/aop/article-10.1332-204674321X16321468785082/article-10.1332-204674321X16321468785082.xml

Dorey, P. (2010). A Poverty of Imagination: Blaming the Poor for Inequality. *The Political Quarterly, 81*(3), 333–343.

Dorling, D. (2020a). The Unprecedented Rise of Mortality Across Poorer Parts of the UK, Guest Blog, Glasgow Centre for Population Health, 13th November. https://www.gcph.co.uk/latest/news/965_the_unprecedented_rise_of_mortality_across_poorer_parts_of_the_uk

Dorling, D. (2020b). *Forward, in Ian Thompson and Gabrielle Ivinson, Poverty in Education Across the UK: A Comparative Approach.* Bristol University Press.

Doucet, A. (2020). Father Involvement, Care and Breadwinning: Genealogies of Concepts and Revisioned Conceptual Narratives. *Genealogy, 4*(1), 14.

Douglas, G., & Ferguson, N. (2003). The Role of Grandparents in Divorced Families. *International Journal of Law, Policy & Family, 41*, 41–67.

Duncan, S. (2012). Using Elderly Data Theoretically: Personal Life in 1949/1950 and Individualisation Theory. *International Journal of Social Research Methodology, 15*(4), 311–319.

Dwyer, P. (Ed.). (2019). *Dealing with Welfare Conditionality: Implementation and Effects.* Policy Press.

Dwyer, P., & Wright, S. (2014). Universal Credit, Ubiquitous Conditionality and its Implications for Social Citizenship. *Journal of Poverty and Social Justice, 22*(1), 27–35.

Dwyer, P., Scullion, L., Jones, K., McNeill, J., & Stewart, A. B. R. (2020). Work, Welfare, and Wellbeing: The Impacts of Welfare Conditionality on People with Mental Health Impairments in the UK. *Social Policy & Administration, 54*(2), 0144–5596. https://doi.org/10.1111/spol.12560

Eckhard. (2018). Does Poverty Increase the Risk of Social Isolation? *Insights Based on Panel Data from Germany, The Sociological Quarterly, 59*(2), 338–359.

Edin, K., & Lein, L. (1997). Work, Welfare, and Single Mothers' Economic Survival Strategies. *American Sociological Review, 62*(2), 253–266.

Edin, K., & Nelson, T. J. (2013). *Doing the Best I Can: Fatherhood in the Inner City*. University of California Press.

Edminston, D. (2021). Plumbing the Depths: The Changing (Socio-Demographic) Profile of UK Poverty. *Journal of Social Policy* [online first].

Edmiston, D., Begum, S., & Kataria, M. (2022). *Falling Faster Amidst a Cost-of-living Crisis: Poverty, Inequality and Ethnicity in the UK*. Runnymede Trust.

Edwards, R. (2022). Unfunded Research: Why Academics do it and its Unvalued Contribution to the Impact Agenda, https://blogs.lse.ac.uk/impactofsocialsciences/2020/08/13/unfunded-research-why-academics-do-it-and-its-unvalued-contribution-to-the-impact-agenda/

Edwards, R., Davidson, E., Jamieson, L., & Weller, S. (2020). Theory and the Breadth-and-Depth Method of Analysing Large Amounts of Qualitative Data. *Quality and Quantity, 55*, 1275–1280.

Edwards, R., & Gillies, V. (2012). Farewell to Family? Notes on an Argument for Retaining the Concept. *Families, Relationships and Societies, 1*(1), 63–69.

Edwards, R., & Irwin, S. (2010). Lived Experience Through Economic Downturn in Britain – Perspectives Across Time and Across the Life-course. *Twenty-First Century Society, 5*(2), 119–124.

Edwards, R., McCarthy, J., & Gillies, V. (2012). The Politics of Concepts: Family and Its (Putative) Replacements. *The British Journal of Sociology, 63*(4), 730–746.

Elder, G. (1994). Time, Human Agency, and Social Change: Perspectives on the Life Course. *Social Psychology Quarterly, 57*(1), 4–15.

Elias, N. (1997). Informalization and the Civilizing Process. In J. Goudsblom & S. Mennell (Eds.), *The Norbert Elias Reader*. Blackwell.

Elliott, K. (2016). Caring Masculinities: Theorizing an Emerging Concept. *Men and Masculinities, 19*(3), 240–259.

Elliott, K. (2020). Bringing in Margin and Centre: 'Open' and 'Closed' as Concepts for Considering Men and Masculinities. *Gender, Place & Culture, 27*(12), 1723–1744. https://doi.org/10.1080/0966369X.2020.1715348

Elliott, S., McKelvy, J. N., & Bowen, S. (2017). Marking Time in Ethnography: Uncovering Temporal Dispositions. *Ethnography, 18*(4), 556–576. https://doi.org/10.1177/1466138116655360

Emmel, N. (2017). Empowerment in the Relational Longitudinal Space of Vulnerability. *Social Policy and Society, 16*(3), 457–467.

Emmel, N., & Hughes, K. (2009). Small-N Access Cases to Refine Theories of Social Exclusion and Access to Socially Excluded Individuals and Groups. In D. Byrne & C. Ragin (Eds.), *The SAGE Handbook of Case-Centered Methods*. SAGE.

Emmel, N., & Hughes, K. (2010). 'Recession, It's All the Same to Us Son': The Longitudinal Experience (1999-2010) of Deprivation. *Twenty-First Century Society, 5*(2), 171–181.

Emmel, N., & Hughes, K. (2014). Vulnerability, Intergenerational Exchange and the Conscience of Generations. In R. Edwards & J. Holland (Eds.), *Understanding Families Over Time: Research and Policy.* Palgrave Macmillan.

Emmel, N., Hughes, K., Greenhalgh, J., & Sales, A. (2007). Accessing Socially Excluded People—Trust and the Gatekeeper in the Researcher-Participant Relationship. *Sociological Research Online, 12*(2), 43–55.

Emmel, N., & Malby, B. (2000). *Meeting Health Needs in Gipton — Regeneration and Health.* East Leeds Primary Care Group.

Erhard, F. (2020). The Struggle to Provide: How Poverty Is Experienced in the Context of Family Care. *Journal of Poverty and Social Justice, 28*(1), 119–134.

Ezzy, D. (2010). Qualitative Interviewing as an Embodied Emotional Performance. *Qualitative Inquiry, 16*(3), 163–170.

Farmer, E., & Moyers, S. (2008). *Kinship Care: Fostering Effective Family and Friends Placements.* Jessica Kingsley.

Farthing, R. (2014). What's Wrong with Being Poor? The Problems of Poverty, as Young People Describe Them. *Children and Society, 30*(2), 107–119.

Featherstone, B. (2009). *Contemporary Fathering: Theory, Policy and Practice.* Policy Press.

Fee, A., McIlfatrick, S., & Ryan, A. (2020). Examining the Support Needs of Older Male Spousal Caregivers of People with a Long-term Condition: A Systematic Review of the Literature. *International Journal of Older People Nursing, 15*, e12318.

Feltwell, T., Vines, J., Salt, K., et al. (2017). Counter-Discourse Activism on Social Media: The Case of Challenging "Poverty Porn" Television. *Computer Supported Coop Work, 26*, 345–385.

Fielding, N. (2004). The Shared Fate of Two Innovations in Qualitative Methodology: The Relationship of Qualitative Software and Secondary Analysis of Archived Qualitative Data. *FORUM: Qualitative Social Research, 1*(3). https://www.qualitative-research.net/index.php/fqs/article/view/1039/2247

Finch, J. (2007). Displaying Families. *Sociology, 14*(1), 65–81.

Fink, J., & Lomax, H. (2016). Sharing Images, Spoiling Meanings? Class, Gender, and Ethics in Visual Research with Girls. *Girlhood Studies: An Interdisciplinary Journal, 3*, 20–36.

Fisher, P., & Buckner, L. (2018). Time for "Resilience": Community Mediators Working with Marginalised Young People Offer a Novel Approach. *International Journal of Sociology and Social Policy, 38*(9/10), 794–808.

Fodor, E. (2006). A Different Type of Gender Gap: How Women and Men Experience Poverty. *East European Politics and Societies, 20*(1), 14–39.

Foucault, M. (1976). *Discipline and Punish*. Allen Lane.

Garthwaite, K. (2016). *Hunger Pains: Life Inside Foodbank Britain*. Policy Press.

Garthwaite, K., Collins, P., & Bambra, C. (2015). Food for Thought: An Ethnographic Study of Negotiating Ill Health and Food Insecurity in a UK Foodbank'. *Social Science and Medicine, 132*, 38–44.

Garthwaite, K., Patrick, R., Power, M., Tarrant, A., & Warnock, R. (2022). *Covid Collaborations: Researching Poverty and Low-Income Family Life During the Pandemic*. Policy Press.

Gatrell, C. J., Burnett, S. B., Cooper, C. L. & Sparrow, P. (2015). The Price of Love: The Prioritisation of Childcare and Income Earning among UK Fathers. *Families, Relationships and Societies, 4*(2), 225–238.

Gillies, V. (2006). Working Class Mothers and School Life: Exploring the Role of Emotional Capital. *Gender and Education, 18*(3), 281–293.

Gillies, V., & Edwards, R. (2005). Secondary Analysis in Exploring Family and Social Change: Addressing the Issue of Context. *FORUM: Qualitative Social Research, 6*(1). https://doi.org/10.17169/fqs-6.1.500

Golin, C. E., Haley, D. F., Wang, J., Hughes, J. P., Kuo, I., Justman, J., Adimona, A. A., Soto-Torres, L., O'Leary, A., & Hodder, S. (2016). Post-traumatic Stress Disorder Symptoms and Mental Health over Time Among Low-Income Women Are Increased Risk of HIV in the US. *Journal of Health Care Poor Underserved, 27*(2), 891–910.

Gooch, K. (2019). Kidulthood': Ethnography, Juvenile Prison Violence and the Transition from 'Boys' to 'Men. *Criminology and Criminal Justice, 19*(1), 80–97.

Granovetter, M. S. (1973). The Strength of Weak Ties. *American Journal of Sociology, 78*(6), 1360–1380.

Gray, J., Geraghty, R., & Ralph, D. (2016). *Family Rhythms: The Changing Textures of Family Life in Ireland*. Manchester University Press.

Gupta, A., & Featherstone, B. (2016). What About My Dad? Black Fathers and the Child Protection System. *Critical and Radical Social Work, 4*(1), 77–91.

Gupta, A., & Featherstone, B. (2020). On Hope, Loss, Anger, and the Spaces in Between: Reflections on Living with/in Adoption and the Role of the Social Worker. *Child & Family Social Work, 25*, 165–172. https://doi.org/10.1111/cfs.12674

Hagedoorn, P., & Helbich, M. (2021). Longitudinal Exposure Assessments of Neighbourhood Effects in Health Research: What Can be Learned from People's Residential Histories? *Health & Place, 68*, 1–7.

Hall, S. M. (2019). *Everyday Life in Austerity: Family, Friends and Intimate Relations*. Palgrave Macmillan.

Halpern, A., Perez-Vaisvidovsky, N., & Mizrahi, R. (2021). Involving Fathers in Family Social Services in Israel: In the Shadow of a Conflicted Policy. *Families, Relationships and Societies*. https://bristoluniversitypressdigital.com/view/journals/frs/aop/article-10.1332-204674321X16297306778771/article-10.1332-204674321X16297306778771.xml

Hamer, J. (2001). *What it Means to Be Daddy: Fatherhood for Black Men Living Away from Their Children*. Columbia University Press.

Hammersley, M. (2010). Can We Re-Use Qualitative Data via Secondary Analysis? Notes on Some Terminological and Substantive Issues. *Sociological Research Online, 15*(1), 5.

Harding, D. J. (2009). Violence, Older Peers, and the Socialization of Adolescent Boys in Disadvantaged Neighborhoods. *American Sociological Review, 1, 74, 3,* 445–464. https://doi.org/10.1177/000312240907400306. PMID: 20161350; PMCID: PMC2776742.

Harman, D. (2001). Aging: Overview. *Annals of the New York Academy of Science, 928*(1), 1–21.

Hartman, Y., & Darab, S. (2012). A Call for Slow Scholarship: A Case Study on the Intensification of Academic Life and Its Implications for Pedagogy. *Review of Education, Pedagogy, and Cultural Studies, 34*(1–2), 49–60.

Haywood, C., & Johansson, T. (2017). *Marginalized Masculinities: Contexts, Continuities and Change*. Routledge.

Hearn, J. (2004). From Hegemonic Masculinity to the Hegemony of Men. *Feminist Theory, 5*(1), 49–72.

Henderson, S., Holland, J., McGrellis, S., Sharpe, S., & Thomson, R. (2006). *Inventing Adulthoods: A Biographical Approach to Youth Transitions*. Sage.

Henwood, K., & Proctor, J. (2003). The 'Good Father': Reading Men's Accounts of Paternal Involvement During the Transition to First-Time Fatherhood. *British Journal of Social Psychology, 42*(3), 337–355.

Henwood, et al. (2012). 'Why aren't you at work?' Negotiating Economic Models of Fathering Identity. *Fathering, 10*(3), 274–290.

Hofferth, S. L., Pleck, J. H., & Vesley, C. K. (2012). The Transmission of Parenting from Fathers to Sons. *Parenting, Science and Practice, 12*(4), 282–305.

Holland, J., Thomson, R., & Henderson, S. (2006). *Qualitative Longitudinal Research: A Discussion Paper*. London Southbank University. Retrieved May 20, 2019, from www.researchgate.net/publication/242763174_Qualitative_Longitudinal_Research_A_Discussion_Paper

Houborg, E., Kronbæk, M., Kappel, N., Relsted Fahnøe, K., Mørch Pedersen S., & Schepelern Johansen, K. (2022). Marginaliserede stofbrugeres hverdagsliv i København – stofmiljøer og velfærdstilbud. https://www.researchgate.net/publication/362932106_Marginaliserede_stofbrugeres_hverdagsliv_i_Kobenhavn_-stofmiljoer_og_velfaerdstilbud

Hubbard, G., Backett-Milburn, K., & Kemmer, D. (2001). Working with Emotion: Issues for the Researcher in Fieldwork and Teamwork. *International Journal of Social Research Methodology, 4*(2), 119–137.

Hübgen, S. (2018). Only a Husband Away from Poverty'? Lone Mothers' Poverty Risks in a European Comparison. In L. Bernardi & D. Mortelmans (Eds.), *Lone Parenthood in the Life Course*. Springer Link.

Hughes, K. (2007). Migrating Identities: The Relational Constitution of Drug Use and Addiction. *Sociology of Health & Illness, 29,* 673–691. https://doi.org/10.1111/j.1467-9566.2007.01018.x

Hughes, K., & Emmel, N. (2012). *Analysing Time: Times and Timing in the Lives of Low-Income Grandparents.* Timescapes Methods Guides Series 2012 Guide No. 9. https://timescapes-archive.leeds.ac.uk/wp-content/uploads/sites/47/2020/07/timescapes-emmel-analysing-time.pdf

Hughes, K., Goodwin, J., & Hughes, J. (2016). Documenti e reperti umani come figurazioni. *Cambio. Rivista Sulle Trasformazioni Sociali, 6*(11), 123–138. https://doi.org/10.13128/cambio-18788

Hughes, J., Hughes, K., Sykes, G., & Wright, K. (2020a). Beyond Performative Talk: Critical Observations on the Radical Critique of Reading Interview Data. *International Journal of Social Research Methodology, 23*(5), 547–563. https://doi.org/10.1080/13645579.2020.1766757

Hughes, K., Hughes, J., & Tarrant, A. (2020b). Re-approaching Interview Data Through Qualitative Secondary Analysis: Interviews with Internet Gamblers. *International Journal of Social Research Methodology, 23*(5), 565–579.

Hughes, K., Hughes, J., & Tarrant, A. (2022). Working at a Remove: Continuous, Collective, and Configurative Approaches to Qualitative Secondary Analysis. *Quality & Quantity, 56,* 375–394.

Hughes, K., & Tarrant, A. (2020). *Qualitative Secondary Analysis.* Sage.

Hunt, J. (2018). Grandparents as Substitute Parents in the UK. *Contemporary Social Science, 13*(2), 175–186.

Hunt, J., Waterhouse, S., & Lutman, E. (2008). *Keeping Them in the Family: Outcomes for Abused and Neglected Children Placed with Family or Friends Carers Through Care Proceedings.* BAAF.

Irwin, S. (2013). Qualitative Secondary Data Analysis: Ethics, Epistemology and Context. *Progress in Development Studies, 13*(4), 295–306.

Irwin, S., Bornat, J., & Winterton, M. (2012). Timescapes Secondary Analysis: Comparison, Context and Working Across Data Sets. *Qualitative Research, 12*(1), 66–80.

Irwin, S., & Winterton, M. (2011a). *Debates in Qualitative Secondary Analysis: Critical Reflections.* Timescapes Working Paper No. 4. http://www.timescapes.leeds.ac.uk/assets/files/WP4-March-2011.pdf

Irwin, S., & Winterton, M. (2011b). *Qualitative Secondary Analysis: A Guide to Practice.* Timescapes Working Paper, Guide 19. chrome-extension://efaidnbmnnnibpcajpcglclefindmkaj/https://timescapes-archive.leeds.ac.uk/wp-content/uploads/sites/47/2020/07/timescapes-irwin-secondary-analysis.pdf

Jamieson, L. (1999). Intimacy Transformed? A Critical Look at the 'Pure Relationship'. *Sociology, 33*(3), 477–494.

Jamieson, L. (2011). Intimacy as a Concept: Explaining Social Change in the Context of Globalisation or Another Form of Ethnocentrism? *Sociological Research Online, 16*(4), 151–163.

Jamieson, L., & Lewthwaite, S. (2019). *Big Qual – Why We Should Be Thinking Big About Qualitative Data for Research, Teaching and Policy*. https://blogs.lse.ac.uk/impactofsocialsciences/2019/03/04/big-qual-why-we-should-be-thinking-big-about-qualitative-data-for-research-teaching-and-policy/

Jamieson, L., Ribe, E., & Warner, P. (2018). Outdated Assumptions About Maternal Grandmothers? Gender and Lineage in Grandparent–Grandchild Relationships. *Contemporary Social Science, 13*(2), 261–274.

Jensen, T. (2014). Welfare Commonsense, Poverty Porn and Doxosophy. *Sociological Research Online, 19*(3), 277–283.

Jensen, T. (2018). *Parenting the Crisis: The Cultural Politics of Parent-Blame*. Policy Press.

Jensen, T., & Tyler, I. (2012). Austerity Parenting: New Economies of Parent-Citizenship. *Studies in the Maternal, 4*(2), 1.

Jones, T., & Pratt, T. (2008). The Prevalence of Sexual Violence in Prison: The State of the Knowledge Base and Implications for Evidence-Based Correctional Policy Making. *International Journal of Therapy and Comparative Criminology, 52*(3), 280–295.

Joseph Rowntree Foundation. (2022). Poverty Report. https://www.jrf.org.uk/report/uk-poverty-2022

Kahneman, D., & Deaton, A. (2010). High Income Improves Evaluation of Life but Not Emotional Wellbeing. *Proceedings of the National Academy of Sciences, 107*(38), 16489–16493.

Karnieli-Miller, O., Strier, R., & Pessach, L. (2009). Power Relations in Qualitative Research. *Qualitative Health Research, 19*(2), 279–289.

Kearns, A., Keanrs, O., & Lawson, L. (2013). Notorious Places: Image, Reputation, Stigma. The Role of Newspapers in Area Reputations for Social Housing Estates. *Housing Studies, 28*(4), 579–598.

Kerr, W. C., Kaplan, M. S., Huguet, N., Caetano, R., Giesbrecht, N., & McFarland, B. H. (2017). Economic Recession, Alcohol, and Suicide Rates: Comparative Effects of Poverty. Foreclosure, and Job Loss. *American Journal of Preventative Medicine, 52*(4), 469–475. https://doi.org/10.1016/j.amepre.2016.09.021

Kilkey, M., & Clarke, H. (2010). Disabled Men and Fathering: Opportunities and Constraints. *Community, Work and Family, 13*(2), 127–146.

King, L. (2015). *Family Men: Fatherhood and Masculinity in Britain, C. 1914–1960*. Oxford University Press.

Kinship, (2017). State of the Nation 2017 Survey Report. https://kinship.org.uk/report/state-of-the-nation-2017-survey-report/

Klein, R. (2012). Collusion with Perpetrators. In *Responding to Intimate Violence Against Women: The Role of Informal Networks* (Advances in Personal Relationships) (pp. 100–114). Cambridge University Press. 10.1017/CBO978113910.1016/j.016483.006

Ladlow, L. (2021). *Housing Young Parents: A Micro-dynamic Study of the Housing Experiences and Support Needs of Young Mothers and Fathers*. PhD thesis, University of Leeds.

Lambert, M. (2017). *"Problem Families" and the Post-war Welfare State in the North West of England, 1943–74*. PhD Thesis, Lancaster University.

LaPlaca, V., & Corlyon, J. (2015). Unpacking the Relationship between Parenting and Poverty: Theory, Evidence and Policy. *Social Policy and Society, 15*(1), 11–28.

Layte, R., & Whelan, C. T. (2003). Moving in and out of Poverty. *European Society, 5*, 167–191.

Leisering, L., & Walker, R. (1998). *The Dynamics of Modern Society: Poverty, Policy and Welfare*. Policy Press.

Lichtenwalter, S. (2005). Gender Poverty Disparity in US Cities: Evidence Exonerating Female-Headed Families. *Journal of Sociology and Social Welfare, 32*(2), 75–96.

Liebow, E. (1967). *Tally's Corner: A Study of Negro Streetcorner Men*. Rowman & Littlefield.

Lister, R. (2005). *Poverty*. Polity Press.

Livingstone, I., & Macmillan, R. (2015). More Than a Provider: The Voluntary Sector, Commissioning and Stewardship for a Diverse Market in Criminal Justice. *Voluntary Sector Review, 6*(2), 221–230.

Lohan, M., Brennan-Wilson, A., Hunter, R., Gabrio, A., McDaid, L., Young, H., French, R., Aventin, A., Clarke, M., McDowell, C., Logan, D., Toase, S., O'Hare, L., Bonell, C., Gillespie, K., Gough, A., Lagdon, S., Warren, E., Buckley, K., et al. (2022). Effects of Gender-Transformative Relationships and Sexuality Education to Reduce Adolescent Pregnancy (the JACK Trial): A Cluster-Randomised Trial. *The Lancet Public Health, 7*(7), 626–637.

Lupton, R. (2003). *Poverty Street: The Dynamics of Neighbourhood Decline and Renewal*. Policy Press.

Lupton, R., & Tunstall, R. (2008). Neighbourhood Regeneration Through Mixed Communities: A 'Social Justice Dilemma'? *Journal of Education Policy, 23*(2), 105–117.

MacDonald, R. (1997). *Youth, the 'Underclass' and Social Exclusion*. Routledge.

MacDonald, M., Hayes, D., & Houston, S. (2016a). Families First Informal Kinship Care: A Review of the Research, In *Families First* Health and Social Care Board (N.I.).

MacDonald, M., Hayes, D., & Houston, S. (2016b). Understanding Informal Kinship Care: A Critical Narrative Review of Theory and Research. *Families, Relationships and Societies, 7*(1), 71–87.

MacDonald, M., Hayes, D., & Houston, S. (2018). 'Understanding Informal Kinship Care: A Critical Narrative Review of Theory and Research'. *Families, Relationships and Societies, 7*(1), 71–87.

MacDonald, R., Shildrick, T., & Furlong, A. (2020). 'Cycles of Disadvantage' Revisited: Young People, Families and Poverty Across Generations. *Journal of Youth Studies, 23*(1), 12–27.

MacDonald, R., Shildrick, T., Webster, C., & Simpson, D. (2005). Growing Up in Poor Neighbourhoods. *Sociology, 39*(5), 873–891.

Macmillan, R., & Ellis Paine, A. (2020). The Third Sector in a Strategically Selective Landscape – The Case of Commissioning Public Services. *Journal of Social Policy, 50*(3), 606–626.

Maguire, D. (2020). *Male, Failed, Jailed: Masculinities and "Revolving-Door" Imprisonment in the UK.* Palgrave Macmillan.

Manhica, H., Straatmann, V. S., Lundin, A., Agardh, E., & Danielsson, A. (2021). Association Between Poverty Exposure During Childhood and Adolescence, and Drug Use Disorders and Drug-Related Crimes Later in Life. *Addiction, 116*(7), 1747–1756.

Mann, R., Tarrant, A., & Leeson, G. (2016). Grandfatherhood: Shifting Masculinities in Later Life. *Sociology, 50*(3), 594–610.

Mare, R. D. (2014). Multigenerational Aspects of Social Stratification: Issues for Further Research. *Researching Social Stratification and Mobility, 1*(35), 121–128. https://doi.org/10.1016/j.rssm.2014.01.004. PMID: 24748709; PMCID: PMC3987910.

Martikainen, P., Adda, J., Ferrie, J., Smith, G. D., & Marmot, M. (2003). Effects of Income and Wealth on GHQ Depression and Poor Self Rated Health in White Collar Women and Men in the Whitehall II Study. *Journal of Epidemiology & Community Health, 57*(9), 718–723.

Mason, J. (2002). *Qualitative Researching.* Sage.

Mason, J. (2007). 'Re-Using' Qualitative Data: On the Merits of an Investigative Epistemology. *Sociological Research Online, 12*(3). https://doi.org/10.5153/sro.1507

Mason, J., May, V., & Clarke, L. (2007). Ambivalence and the Paradoxes of Grandparenting. *The Sociological Review, 55*(4), 687–706.

Mätzke, M., & Ostner, I. (2010). Introduction: Change and Continuity in Recent Family Policies. *Journal of European Social Policy, 20*(5), 387–398.

Mauthner, N. S., Parry, O., & Beckett-Milburn, K. (1998). The Data Are Out There, or Are They?: Implications for Archiving and Revisiting Qualitative Data. *Sociology, 32*(4), 733–745.

May, V., & Lahad, K. (2018). The Involved Observer: A Simmelian Analysis of the Boundary Work of Aunthood. *Sociology, 27*(3), 1–16.

Maycock, P., Sheridan, S., & Parker, S. (2012). Migrant Women and Homelessness: The Role of Gender-based Violence. *European Journal of Homelessness, 6*(1), 59–82.

McAra, L., & McVie, S. (2016). Understanding Youth Violence: The Mediating Effects of Gender, Poverty and Vulnerability. *Journal of Criminal Justice, 45*, 71–77.

McArthur, D., & Reeves, A. (2019). The Rhetoric of Recessions: How British Newspapers Talk about the Poor When Unemployment Rises, 1896–2000. *Sociology, 53*(6), 1005–1025.

McCartan, C., Bunting, L., Bywaters, P., Davidson, G., Elliott, M., & Hooper, J. (2018). A Four-Nation Comparison of Kinship Care in the UK: The Relationship Between Formal Kinship Care and Deprivation. *Social Policy and Society, 17*(4), 619–635.

McCarthy, R. (2012). The Powerful Relational Language of 'Family': Togetherness, Belonging and Personhood. *The Sociological Review, 60*(1), 68–90.

McDowell, L. (2000). The Trouble with Men? Young People, Gender Transformations and the Crisis of Masculinity. *International Journal of Urban and Regional Research, 24*(1), 201–209.

McDowell, L. (2003). Masculine Identities and Low Paid Work: Young Men in Urban Labour Markets. *International Journal of Urban and Regional Research, 27*(4), 828–848.

McDowell, L. (2009). *Working Bodies: Interactive Service Employment and Workplace Identities.* Wiley-Blackwell.

McDowell, L. (2017). Youth, Children and Families in Austere Times: Change, Politics and a New Gender Contract. *Area, 49*(3), 311–316.

McDowell, L., & Bonner-Thompson, C. (2021). Digital Geographies of Austerity: Young Men's Material, Affective and Everyday Relationships with the Digital. *Geoforum, 120,* 113–121.

McKenzie, L. (2015). *Getting By: Estates, Class and Culture in Austerity Britain.* Policy Press.

McLanahan, S. S., & Kelly, E. L. (2006). The Feminization of Poverty. In *Handbook of the Sociology of Gender. Handbooks of Sociology and Social Research.* Springer. 10.1007/0-387-36218-5_7

Meek, K. (2007). Parenting Education for Young Fathers in Prison. *Child & Family Social Work, 12*(3), 239–247.

Mendola, D., Busetta, A., & Milito, A. (2011). Combining the Intensity and Sequencing of the Poverty Experience: A Class of Longitudinal Poverty Indices. *Statistics in Society, 174*(4), 953–973.

Merton, R. K. (1972). Insiders and Outsiders: A Chapter in the Sociology of Knowledge. *American Journal of Sociology, 78*(1), 9–47.

Mervyn-Smith, O. (2018). *Kinship Care: State of the Nation.* Grandparents Plus. https://www.basw.co.uk/system/files/resources/kinship_care_2018.pdf

Milardo, R. M. (2005). Generative Uncle and Nephew Relationships. *Journal of Marriage and Family, 67*(5), 1226–1236.

Milardo, R. M. (2010). *The Forgotten Kin: Aunts and Uncles.* Cambridge University Press.

Millar, J. (2007). The Dynamics of Poverty and Employment: The Contribution of Qualitative Longitudinal Research to Understanding Transitions, Adaptations and Trajectories. *Social Policy and Society, 6*(4), 533–544.

Millar, J. (2019). Self-Responsibility and Activation for Lone Mothers in the United Kingdom. *American Behavioural Science, 63*(1), 85–99.

Millar, J. (2021). Families, Work and Care: Qualitative Longitudinal Research and Policy Engagement. *Social Policy and Society, 20*(4), 629–634. https://doi.org/10.1017/S1474746420000482

Millar, J., & Ridge, T. (2009). Relationships of Care: Working Lone Mothers, Their Children and Employment Sustainability. *Journal of Social Policy, 38*(1), 103–121.

Miller, T. (2010). *Making Sense of Fatherhood: Gender, Caring and Work.* Cambridge University Press.

Milligan, C., & Morbey, H. (2016). Care, Coping and Identity: Older Men's Experiences of Spousal Care-giving. *Journal of Aging Studies, 38*, 105–114.

Mills, C. W. (1959). *The Sociological Imagination.* Oxford University Press.

Mincy, R. B., Jethwani, M., & Klempin, S. (2015). *Failing Our Fathers: Confronting the Crisis of Economically Vulnerable Fathers.* Oxford University Press.

Moore, N. (2007). (Re)-using Qualitative data? *Sociological Research Online, 12*(3), 1–13.

Morgan, D. (1992). *Discovering Men: Sociology and Masculinities.* Routledge.

Morgan, D. (1996). *Family Connections: An Introduction to Family Studies.* Polity.

Morgan, D. (2011). Locating Family Practices. *Sociological Research Online, 16*(4), 14.

Morgan, D. (2020). Family Practices in Time and Space. *Gender, Place and Culture, 27*(5), 733–743.

Morrow, V. (2013). Troubling Transitions? Young People's Experiences of Growing Up in Poverty in Rural Andhra Pradesh, India. *Journal of Youth Studies, 16*(1), 86–100. https://doi.org/10.1080/13676261.2012.704986

Mountz, A., Bonds, A., Mansfield, B., Lloyd, J., Hyndman, J., Walton-Roberts, M., Basu, R., Whitson, R., Hawkins, R., Hamilton, T., & Curran, W. (2015). For Slow Scholarship: A Feminist Politics of Resistance Through Collective Action in the Neoliberal University. *ACME: An International Journal for Critical Geographies, 14*(4), 1235–1259.

Murali, V., & Oyebode, F. (2004). Poverty, Social Inequality and Mental Health. *Advances in Psychiatric Treatment, 10*(3), 216–224.

Nandy, S., & Selwyn, J. (2013). Kinship Care and Poverty: Using Census Data to Examine the Extent and Nature of Kinship Care in the UK. *The British Journal of Social Work, 43*(8), 1649–1666.

Nandy, S., Selwyn, J., Farmer, E., & Vaisey, P. (2013). *Spotlight on Kinship Care: Using Census Microdata to Examine the Extent and Nature of Kinship Care in the UK at the Turn of the Twentieth Century.* University of Bristol Report.

Nayak, A. (2006). Displaced Masculinities: Chavs, Youth and Class in the Post-industrial City. *Sociology, 40*(5), 813–831.

Neale, B. (2000). *Theorising Family, Kinship and Social Change*. Workshop Paper 6 Prepared for Workshop Two: Statistics and Theories for Understanding Social Change. https://www.leeds.ac.uk/cava/papers/wsp6.pdf

Neale, B. (2013). Adding Time into the Mix: Stakeholder Ethics in Qualitative Longitudinal Research. *Methodological Innovations Online, 8*(2), 6–20.

Neale, B. (2015). Time and the Lifecourse: Perspectives from Qualitative Longitudinal Research. In N. Worth & I. Hardill (Eds.), *Researching the Lifecourse*. Policy Press.

Neale, B. (2016). Introduction: Young Fatherhood: Lived Experiences and Policy Challenges. *Social Policy and Society, 15*(1), 75–83.

Neale, B. (2020). *The Craft of Qualitative Longitudinal Research*. Sage.

Neale, B., & Bishop, L. (2012). The Timescapes Archive: A Stakeholder Approach to Archiving Qualitative Longitudinal Data. *Qualitative Research, 12*(1), 53–65.

Neale, B., & Davies, L. (2015). *Hard to Reach? Re-thinking Support for Young Fathers*, Briefing Paper no. 6. https://followingfathers.leeds.ac.uk/wp-content/uploads/sites/79/2015/10/Brieifing-Paper-6-V7.pdf

Neale, B., Henwood, K., & Holland, J. (2012). Researching Lives Through Time: An Introduction to the Timescapes Approach. *Qualitative Research, 12*(1), 4–15.

Neale, B., & Ladlow, L. (2015). *Finding a Place to Parent? Housing Young Fathers*. Briefing Paper no. 7. https://followingfathers.leeds.ac.uk/wp-content/uploads/sites/79/2015/10/Brieifing-Paper-7-V3.pdf

Neale, B., & Lau Clayton, C. (2014). Young Parenthood and Cross Generational Relationships: The Perspectives of Young Fathers. In J. Holland & R. Edwards (Eds.), *Understanding Families Over Time*. Palgrave Macmillan.

Neale, B., & Patrick, R. (2016). *Engaged Young Fathers? Gender Parenthood and the Dynamics of Relationships*. FYF Working Paper Series no. 1. https://followingfathers.leeds.ac.uk/wp-content/uploads/sites/79/2015/10/FYF-Working-Paper-Engaged-young-fathers.pdf

Neale, B., Lau Clayton, C., Davies, L., & Ladlow, L. (2015). *Researching the Lives of Young Fathers: The Following Young Fathers Study and Dataset*. Briefing Paper no. 8. https://followingfathers.leeds.ac.uk/wp-content/uploads/sites/79/2015/10/Researching-the-Lives-of-Young-Fathers-updated-Oct-22.pdf

Neale, B., & Smart, C. (1998). *Family Fragments?* Blackwell.

Nelson, T. J. (2004). Low-Income Fathers. *Annual Review of Sociology, 30*, 427–451. https://doi.org/10.1146/annurev.soc.29.010202.09594

Newman, K. S., & Peeples Massengill, R. (2006). The Texture of Hardship: Qualitative Sociology of Poverty. *Annual Review of Sociology, 32*(1), 423–446.

Newsome, M., & Kelly, S. (2004). Grandparents Raising Grandchildren: A Solution-Focused Brief Therapy Approach in School Settings. *Social Work with Groups, 27*(4), 65–84.

Neysmith, S. M., Reitsma-Street, M., Baker-Collins, S., Porter, E., & Tam, S. (2010). Provisioning Responsibilities: How Relationships Shape the Work That Women Do. *Canadian Review of Sociology, 47*(2), 149–170.

Office for National Statistics. (2018). *Health Inequalities Current Patterns and Trends in Ill Health and Death by Measures of Socio-Economic Status.* https://www.ons.gov.uk/peoplepopulationandcommunity/healthandsocialcare/healthinequalities#:~:text=Male%20healthy%20life%20expectancy%20(HLE,53.3%20and%2070.2%20years%2C%20respectively

O'Laughlin, B. (2008). Missing Men? The debate over rural poverty and women-headed households in Southern Africa. *The Journal of Peasant Studies, 25*(2), 1–48.

Parsons, T. (1952). *The Social System.* Routledge.

Parton, N. (2012). Reflections on 'Governing the Family': The Close Relationship Between Child Protection and Social Work in Advanced Western Societies – The Example of England. *Families, Relationships and Societies, 1*(1), 87–101. Retrieved November 12, 2022, from https://bristoluniversitypressdigital.com/view/journals/frs/1/1/article-p87.xml

Patrick, R. (2018). *For Whose Benefit? The Everyday Realities of Welfare Reform.* Policy Press.

Patrick, R., Treanor, M., & Wenham, A. (2021). Introduction: Qualitative Longitudinal Research for Social Policy – Where Are We Now? *Social Policy and Society, 20*(4), 622–628.

Pearce, D. (1978). The Feminization of Poverty: Women, Work and Welfare. *Urban and Social Change Review, 11*, 28–36.

Philip, G., Youansamouth, L., Bedston, S., Broadhurst, K., Hu, Y., Clifton, J., & Brandon, M. (2020). "I Had No Hope, I Had No Help at All": Insights from a First Study of Fathers and Recurrent Care Proceedings. *Societies, 10*(4), 89–105.

Pilcher, J., Williams, J., & Pole, C. (2003). Rethinking Adulthood: Families, Transitions, and Social Change. *Sociological Research Online, 8*(4), 181–185.

Poole, E., Speight, S., O'Brien, M., Connolly, S, & Aldrich, M. (2016). Who are Non-Resident Fathers?: A British Socio-Demographic Profile. *Journal of Social Policy, 45*(2), 223–250.

Portes, J., & Reed, H. (2018). *The Cumulative Impact of Tax and Welfare Reforms.* Equality and Human Rights Commission. https://www.equalityhumanrights.com/sites/default/files/cumulative-impact-assessment-report.pdf

Public Health England. (2018). A Review of Recent Trends in Mortality in England, PHE Publications Gateway Number: GW-686. https://assets.publishing.service.gov.uk/government/uploads/system/uploads/attachment_data/file/827518/Recent_trends_in_mortality_in_England.pdf

Rauh, V., Landrigan, P. J., & Claudio, L. (2008). Housing and Health: Intersection of Poverty and Environmental Exposures. *Annals of New York Academy of Science, 1136*, 276–288. https://doi.org/10.1196/annals.1425.032

Ray, L. (2018). *Violence and Society* (2nd ed.). SAGE.

Ridge, T. (2009). *Living with Poverty: A Review of the Literature on Children's and Families' Experiences of Poverty*, Department for Work and Pensions Research Report No 594. http://www.bris.ac.uk/poverty/downloads/keyofficialdocuments/Child%20Poverty%20lit%20review%20DWP.pdf

Ridge, T., & Millar, J. (2008). *Work and Wellbeing Over Time: Lone Mothers and Their Children*, Department for Work and Pensions Research Report No 536.

Roberts, S., & Elliott, K. (2020). Challenging Dominant Representations of Marginalised Boys and Men in Critical Studies on Men and Masculinities. *Boyhood Studies, 13*(2), 87–104.

Robinson, M., Templeton, M., Kelly, C., Grant, D., Buston, K., Hunt, K., & Lohan, M. (2022). Addressing Sexual and Reproductive Health and Rights with Men in Prisons: Co-production and Feasibility Testing of a Relationship, Sexuality and Future Fatherhood Education Programme. *International Journal of Prisoner Health*. https://doi.org/10.1108/IJPH-02-2022-0008

Rodríguez-Dorans, E. (2018). Reflexivity and Ethical Research Practice While Interviewing on Sexual Topics. *International Journal of Social Research Methodology, 21*(6), 747–760.

Rojas, Y., & Stenberg, S.-A. (2010). Evictions and Suicide: A Follow-up Study of Almost 22,000 Swedish Households in the Wake of the Global Financial Crisis. *Journal of Epidemiological Community Health, 70*(4), 409–413.

Rose, W., & McAuley, C. (2019). Poverty and its Impact on Parenting in the UK: Re-defining the Critical Nature of the Relationship Through Examining Lived Experiences in Times of Austerity. *Children and Youth Services Review, 97*, 134–141.

Rowntree, B. S. (1902). *Poverty: A Study of Town Life*. Macmillan.

Roy, K. (2006). Father Stories: A Life Course Examination of Paternal Identity Among Low-income African American Men. *Journal of Family Issues, 27*(1), 31–54.

Roy, K. (2014). Fathering from the Long View: Framing Personal and Social Change Through Life Course Theory. *Journal of Family Theory and Review, 6*, 319–335.

Roy, K., & Jones, N. (2014). *Pathways to Adulthood for Disconnected Young Men in Low-Income Communities*. Wiley.

Roy, K., Messina, L., Smith, J., & Waters, D. (2014). Growing Up as "Man of the House": Adultification and Transition into Adulthood for Young Men in Economically Disadvantaged Families. In K. Roy & N. Jones (Eds.), *Pathways to Adulthood for Disconnected Young Men in Low-Income Communities. New Directions in Child and Adolescent Development*, (pp. 55–72), Jossey-Bass.

Roy, K., Palkovitz, R., & Waters, D. (2015). Low-income Fathers as Resilient Care-givers. In J. A. Arditti (Ed.), *Family Problems: Stress, Risk, and Resilience* (pp. 83–98). Wiley Blackwell.

Russell, R. (2007). The Work of Elderly Men Caregivers: From Public Careers to an Unseen World. *Men and Masculinities, 9*(3), 298–314. https://doi.org/10.1177/1097184X05277712

Ruxton, S. (2002). *Men, Masculinities and Poverty in the UK.* Oxfam.

Savage, M., Devine, F., Cunningham, N., Taylor, M., Li, Y., Hjellbrekke, J., Le Roux, B., Friedman, S., & Miles, A. (2013). A New Model of Social Class? Findings from the BBC's Great British Class Survey Experiment. *Sociology, 47*(2), 219–250.

Scourfield, J. (2006). The Challenge of Engaging Fathers in the Child Protection Process. *Critical Social Policy, 26*(2), 440–449.

Scourfield, J. B., & Lewinson, E. (2016). Engaging Black Fathers in Child Protection Services. In C. Bernard & P. Harris (Eds.), *Safeguarding Black Children: Good Practice in Child Protection* (pp. 165–176). Jessica Kingsley.

Settersten, R. (Ed.). (2003). *Invitation to the Life Course: Towards New Understandings of Later Life.* Baywood Publishing.

Shefer, T., & Hearn, J. (2022). *Knowledge, Power and Young Sexualities: A Transnational Feminist Engagement.* Routledge.

Shildrick, T. (2018). *Poverty Propaganda: Exploring the Myths.* Policy Press.

Shildrick, T., & MacDonald, R. (2013). Poverty Talk: How People Experiencing Poverty Deny Their Poverty and Why They Blame 'The Poor'. *The Sociological Review, 61*(2), 285–303.

Shildrick, T., MacDonald, R., Webster, C., & Garthwaite, K. (2010). *The Low-Pay, No-Pay Cycle: Understanding Recurrent Poverty.* Joseph Rowntree Report: York.

Shildrick, T., MacDonald, R., Webster, C., & Garthwaite, K. (2012). *Poverty and Insecurity: Life in Low Pay, No Pay Britain.* Policy Press.

Shirani, F., Henwood, K., & Coltart, C. (2012). Meeting the Challenges of Intensive Parenting Culture: Gender, Risk Management and the Moral Parent. *Sociology, 46*(1), 25–40.

Skevik, A. (2006). 'Absent Fathers' or 'Reorganized Families'? Variations in Father-child Contact After Parental Break-up in Norway. *The Sociological Review, 54*(1), 114–132.

Skoglund, J., & Thørnblad, R. (2019). Kinship Care or Upbringing by Relatives? The Need for 'New' Understandings in Research. *European Journal of Social Work, 22*(3), 435–445. https://doi.org/10.1080/13691457.2017.1364702

Smart, C. (2007). *Personal Life.* Polity Press.

Smethers, S. (2015). What Are the Issues Affecting Grandparents in Britain Today? *Quality in Ageing and Older Adults, 16*(1), 37–43.

Smith, N., & Middleton, S. (2007). A Review of Poverty Dynamics Research in the UK, Joseph Rowntree Foundation. https://www.jrf.org.uk/sites/default/files/jrf/migrated/files/2040-poverty-dynamics-review.pdf

Sobo-Allen, L (2019). The last resort? Initial findings of a PhD study exploring the circumstances, and motivations, of non- resident fathers taking on the full time care of their children though the involvement of social services. Link to

Leeds Beckett Repository record: https://eprints.leedsbeckett.ac.uk/id/eprint/8141/

Sobo-Allen, L., & Howarth, S. (2020). Social Work with Single and Non-resident Fathers: How Inclusive Is Our Practice and Where Do We Go from Here? In B. Nikku (Ed.), *Global Social Work Cutting Edge Issues and Critical Reflections* (pp. 163–182). IntechOpen.

Soja, E. W. (2000). *Postmetropolis: Critical Studies of Cities and Regions.* Blackwell.

Stack, C. B. (1974). *All Our Kin: Strategies for Survival in a Black Community.* Harper & Row.

Staley, S. (1992). *Drug Policy and the Decline of American Cities.* Transaction Publishers.

Stanko, E. A. (2001). The Day to Count: Reflections on a Methodology to Raise Awareness about the Impact of Domestic Violence in the UK. *Criminal Justice, 1*(2), 215–226. https://doi.org/10.1177/1466802501001002005

Stanley, L. (1993). On Auto/Biography in Sociology. *Sociology, 27*(1), 41–52.

Statista. (2022). Number of People Receiving Three Days' Worth of Emergency Food by Trussell Trust Foodbanks in the United Kingdom from 2008/09 to 2021/22. https://www.statista.com/statistics/382695/uk-foodbank-users/

Stephens, M., & Leishman, C. M. (2017). Housing and Poverty: A Longitudinal Analysis. *Housing Studies, 32*(8), 1039–1061. https://doi.org/10.108 0/02673037.2017.1291913

Stewart, K., Reeves, A., & Patrick, R. (2021). *A Time of Need: Exploring the Changing Poverty Risk Facing Larger Families in the UK.* https://sticerd.lse.ac.uk/CASE/_NEW/PUBLICATIONS/abstract/?index=8275

Strange, J.-M. (2012). Fatherhood, Providing, and attachment in Late Victorian and Edwardian Working-class Families. *The Historical Journal, 55*(4), 1007–1027.

Sudbury, L., & Simcock, P. (2007). Grandparenthood and Cognitive Age: Key Variables for Targeting the Over-50 Market. *Micro and Macro Marketing, 3.* https://papers.ssrn.com/sol3/papers.cfm?abstract_id=2362835

Sullivan, M. L. (1989). *Getting Paid: Youth Crime and Work in the Inner City.* Cornell University Press.

Tarrant, A. (2013). Grandfathering as Spatio-temporal Practice: Conceptualizing Performances of Ageing Masculinities in Contemporary Familial Carescapes. *Social and Cultural Geography, 14*(2), 192–210.

Tarrant, A. (2014). Negotiating Multiple Positionalities in the Interview Setting; Researching Across Gender and Generational Boundaries. *The Professional Geographer, 66*(3), 493–500.

Tarrant, A. (2016). The Spatial and Gendered Politics of Displaying Family: Exploring Material Cultures in Grandfathers' Homes. *Gender, Place and Culture, 23*(7), 969–982.

Tarrant, A. (2017). Getting Out of the Swamp? Methodological Reflections on Using Qualitative Secondary Analysis to Develop Research Design. *International Journal of Social Research Methodology, 20*(6), 599–611.

Tarrant, A. (2018). Care in an Age of Austerity: Men's Care Responsibilities in Low-income. *Families, Ethics and Social Welfare, 12*(1), 34–48.

Tarrant, A. (2021). *Fathering and Poverty: Uncovering Men's Participation in Low-Income Family Life.* Policy Press.

Tarrant, A., Featherstone, B., O'Dell, L., & Fraser, C. (2017). "You Try to Keep a Brave Face on But Inside You Are in Bits": Grandparent Experiences of Engaging with Professionals in Children's Services. *Qualitative Social Work, 16*(3), 351–366.

Tarrant, A., & Hughes, K. (2019a). Qualitative Secondary Analysis: Building Longitudinal Samples to Understand Men's Generational Identities in Low Income Contexts. *Sociology, 53*(3), 538–553.

Tarrant, A., & Hughes, K. (2019b). The Ethics of Technology Choice: Photovoice Methodology with Men Living in Low-Income Contexts. *Sociological Research Online, 25*(2), 289–306. https://doi.org/10.1177/1360780419878714

Tarrant, A., & Hughes, K. (2020). Collective Qualitative Secondary Analysis and Data-Sharing: Strategies, Insights and Challenges. In K. Hughes & A. Tarrant (Eds.), *Qualitative Secondary Analysis* (pp. 101–118). Sage.

Tarrant, A., & Hughes, K. (2021). Qualitative Data Re-use and Secondary Analysis: Researching In and About a Crisis. In H. Kara & S.-M. Khoo (Eds.), *Qualitative and Digital Research in Times of Crisis.* Policy Press.

Tarrant, A., Ladlow, L., & Way, L. (Eds.). (2023). *Men and Welfare.* Routledge.

Tarrant, A., & Neale, B. (forthcoming). *Following Young Fathers: Lived Experiences, Policy Challenges.* Policy Press.

Tarrant, A., Terry, G., Ward, M.R., Ruxton, S., Robb, M., & Featherstone, B. (2015). Are Male Role Models Really the Solution?: Interrogating the 'War on Boys' Through the Lens of the 'Male Role Model' Discourse. *Boyhood Studies, 8*(1), 60–83.

Thapar-Björkert, S., & Henry, M. (2004). Reassessing the Research Relationship: Location, Position and Power in Fieldwork Accounts. *International Journal of Social Research Methodology, 7*(5), 363–381. https://doi.org/10.1080/1364557092000045294

Trammell, R. (2012). *Enforcing the Convict Code: Violence and Prison Culture.* Lynne Rienner Publishers.

Treanor, M. (2020). *Child Poverty: Aspiring to Survive.* Policy Press.

Tucker, S., Hargreaves, C., Cattermull, M., Roberts, A., Walker, T., Shaw, J., & Challis, D. (2021). The Nature and Extent of Prisoners' Social Care Needs: Do Older Prisoners Require a Different Service Response? *Journal of Social Work, 21*(3), 310–328. https://doi.org/10.1177/1468017319890077

Tucker, S., Hargreaves, C., Roberts, A., Anderson, I., Shaw, J., & Challis, D., (2018). Social Care in Prison: Emerging Practice Arrangements Consequent Upon the Introduction of the Care Act 2014. *The British Journal of Social Work, 48*(6), 1627–1644.

Tyler, I. (2013). The Riots of the Underclass?: Stigmatisation, Mediation and the Government of Poverty and Disadvantage in Neoliberal Britain. *Sociological Research Online, 18*(4), 6.

Valentine, G., & Hughes, K. (2010). Ripples in a Pond: The Disclosure to, and Management of, Problem Internet Gambling with/in the Family. *Community, Work & Family, 13*(3), 273–290.

Venkatesh, S. A. (2000). *American Project: The Rise and Fall of a Modern Ghetto.* Harvard University Press.

Wacquant, L. (1995). Pugs at Work: Bodily Capital and Bodily Labour among Professional Boxers. *Body & Society, 1*(1), 65–93.

Wacquant, L. (2004). Decivilizing and Demonizing: The Weakening of the Black American Ghetto. In S. Loyal & S. Quilley (Eds.), *The Sociology of Norbert Elias* (pp. 95–121). Cambridge University Press.

Wajcman, J. (2015). *Pressed for Time: The Acceleration of Life in Digital Capitalism.* Chicago University Press.

Wakeling, K., & Lynch, K. (2020). Exploring Substance Use in Prisons: A Case Study Approach in Five Closed Male English Prisons. *Ministry of Justice Analytical Series.* https://www.drugsandalcohol.ie/33284/1/HMPPS_ Exploring-substance-use-prisons.pdf

Walsh, D., Dundas, R., McCartney, G., Gibson, M., & Seaman, R. (2022). Bearing the Burden of Austerity: How Do Changing Mortality Rates in the UK Compare Between Men and Women? *Journal of Epidemiology and Community Health, 76*(12), 1027–1033.

Walsh, D., Wyper, G. M. A., & McCartney, G. (2022). Trends in Healthy Life Expectancy in the Age of Austerity. *Journal of Epidemiology and Community Health, 76*(8), 743–745.

Waquant, L. (2009). *Urban Outcasts: A Sociology of Advanced Marginality.* Polity Press.

Ward, M. R. M. (2015). *From Labouring to Learning: Working-Class Masculinities, Education and De-Industrialization.* Basingstoke: Palgrave Macmillan.

Ward, M., Tarrant A., Terry, G., Featherstone, B., Robb, M., and Ruxton, S. (2017). Doing Gender Locally: The Importance of 'Place' in Understanding Marginalised Masculinities and Young Men's Transitions to 'Safe' and Successful Futures. *The Sociological Review, 65*(4), 797–815.

Webb, C., Bennett, D., & Bywaters, P. (2022). Austerity, Poverty, and Children's Services Quality in England: Consequences for Child Welfare and Public Services. *Social Policy and Society,* 1–22. https://doi.org/10.1017/ S147474642200001X

Wellard, S., Meakings, S., Farmer, E., & Hunt, J. (2017). *Growing Up in Kinship Care: Experiences as Adolescents and Outcomes in Young Adulthood.* Grandparents Plus Report.

Welshman, J. (2006). The Concept of the Unemployable. *The Economic History Review, 59*(3), 578–606.

Wenham, A. (2016). "I Know I'm a Good Mum - No-one Can Tell me Different": Young Mothers Negotiating a Stigmatized Identity Through Time. *Families, Relationships and Societies, 5*(1), 127–144.

Whelan, C. T., Layte, R., & Maître, B. (2003). Persistent Income Poverty and Deprivation in the European Union. *Journal of Social Policy, 32*, 1–18.

Whelan, C. T., & Maitre, B. (2006). Comparing Poverty and Deprivation Dynamics: Issues of Reliability and Validity. *The Journal of Economic Inequality, 4*, 303–323.

Whitaker, E. M., & Atkinson, P. (2022). *Reflexivity in Social Research.* Springer Link.

Wijedasa, D. (2017). *Children Growing Up in the Care of Relatives in the UK,* Policy Bristol. https://www.bristol.ac.uk/media-library/sites/sps/documents/kinship/policy-bristol-report.pdf

Wikström, P.-O. H., & Treiber, K. (2016). Social Disadvantage and Crime: A Criminological Puzzle. *American Behavioral Scientist, 60*(10), 1232–1259.

Williams, F. (1998). Troubled Masculinities in Social Policy Discourses: Fatherhood. In J. Popay, J. Hearn, & J. Edwards (Eds.), *Men, Gender Divisions and Welfare* (pp. 63–100). Routledge.

Williams, F. (2003). *Rethinking Families.* Calouste Gulbenkian Foundation.

Wilson, W. J. (1985). Cycles of Deprivation and the Underclass Debate. *Social Service Review, 59*(4), 541–559.

Wirth, L. (1938). Urbanism as a Way of Life. *The American Journal of Sociology, 44*(1), 1–24.

Women's Budget Group. (2018). The Female Face of Poverty. https://wbg.org.uk/analysis/the-female-face-of-poverty/

Wright-Mills, C. (1959). *The Sociological Imagination.* Oxford University Press, Oxford.

Wright, S., & Patrick, R. (2020). Welfare Conditionality in Lived Experience: Aggregating Qualitative Longitudinal Research. *Social Policy and Society, 18*(4), 597–613.

Yeandle, S., & Buckner, L. J. (2017). Older Workers and Care-giving in England: The Policy Context for Older Workers' Employment Patterns. *Journal of Cross-Cultural Gerontology, 32*, 303–321.

Yeandle, S., & Cass, B. (2013). Working Carers of Older People: Steps Towards Securing Adequate Support in Australia and England? In T. Kroger & S. Yeandle (Eds.), *Combining Paid Work and Family Care.* Bristol University Press.

Zanoni, L., Warburton, W., Bussey, K., & McMaugh, A. (2013). Fathers as 'Core Business' in Child Welfare Practice and Research'. *Children & Youth Services, 35*, 1055–1070.

INDEX

Printed by Printforce, United Kingdom